D1601688

Chasing Mother

A Memoir
by
Monique Parrish

Azalea Art Press
Sonoma | California

© **Monique Parrish, 2017**
All Rights Reserved.

ISBN:
978-1-943471-19-5

Cover Photo | David D. Parrish
Author Photo | Wendy M. Richardson

Dedication:

For Morgan,
who has always believed in me

Contents

Chasing Mother

Prologue

As a young child I loved fairy tales. The stories I liked best were the ones in which the heroine, typically a young girl, escaped terrible situations alone through sheer moxie that her villain, usually a wicked stepmother, could only dream about. Back then, I didn't know why I identified with these stories or coveted the girls' determined strength. Now, as a grown woman, my childhood passion makes sense. Somewhere in my developing brain I knew that my family didn't work. Fiction gave me hope. It made me feel that that my life could and would get better.

It didn't.

My mother was the skipper on a half-submerged boat. Each time it looked as though my mother had bailed enough water for us to be able to sail, we would spring another leak. My mother's unique cruelty was her extraordinary indifference toward us, sprinkled with confusing moments of warmth and sweetness: the latter always delivered with theatrical charm. If she were not the person I needed for love and nurturing, I would have thought her a fascinating character study. Unlike anyone I have ever met, my mother firmly believed in her life as theater. For her audience—mostly people outside our family, but us too at times—she played beautifully etched theatrical roles with great range. One day she was Mother Extraordinaire, the next Mother Teresa, and then, without skipping a beat, The Ultimate Victim. With every role, she was wholly convincing. Few people ever guessed what went on behind the curtain. Life with my mother was a masquerade.

Since my physician father abandoned my mother and us with a cruelty all his own, it's hard to fathom why they had six children in six years. It's possible their rapid baby making might have been a product of the times. We were all born between 1953 and 1959, prime baby boom years when there was a big national push to have children. It might also have been associated with the Catholic Church's ban on using any "artificial" means of contraception, a powerful admonition for my Catholic parents. Last but certainly not least, having so many children fulfilled a dream for my mother. She constantly boasted about having so many children so close in age, loving all the attention her big brood brought her. She would often say that had my father not left her, she would have had twelve children. It's a thought that still chills me.

Despite our twisted upbringing, my mother could be both attentive and kind at times. It was that elusive mother that I chased for decades. As she dangled affection and the hope of something more in front of me, I was certain that if I tried hard enough she would love me completely. All the while, I ignored the signs that told me otherwise. Down one parent—my father—I wasn't prepared to lose another. It wasn't until I was in my late forties that I suddenly realized that from the earliest moments of my consciousness, I had been chasing a chimera.

The trigger for this epiphany was my work as a clinical social worker in a community health clinic. Over the course of several years at the clinic, I noticed that a number of women referred to me by their doctors for counseling had childhoods similar to mine. I was careful, however, not to let it disrupt our work together. When I was no longer seeing the women, I became curious. Just how much overlap was there between their lives and mine? Free to more fully examine their stories, I acknowledged that we shared a baseline of parental neglect, poverty, despair, and . . . more. All the women had been sexually abused as young girls, and their mothers either blamed them for the abuse or remained indifferent to it. It was a heartbreaking moment when each woman told me how the double betrayal had permanently desecrated her sense of self.

That was not the end of their stories or connection to mine. Scraping the bottom of their brokenness, the women told of one more heartache. In spite of maternal rejection, over the years each had continued to bring offerings of kindness and self-sacrifice to her mother in an effort to win her love. But nothing changed. In a final act of hopefulness, the women had returned home in their forties, fifties, and sixties to care for their elderly mothers, believing this time their mothers would love them at last. The mothers took the help but were unable to give their daughters what they wanted most. Jolted by the awareness that the strange, convoluted twister that had touched down on these women's lives had touched down on my own life as well convinced me: it was time to tell my story.

Writing it, I hoped, would be cathartic, and it has been. But I was also motivated by the hope that I might help others—not because my story is unique—but because suffering is common, particularly the kind that occurs when one human being, intentionally or not, crushes the soul of another. Respecting that there are different degrees of this suffering, many of us who have experienced deep and painful rejection, neglect, and abuse—especially from a mother—come to believe we aren't lovable or worthy. That was my bedrock belief, and I laid a host of other distorted beliefs about myself directly on top of it. I only began to let go of this conviction when after many years I finally faced my thought distortions and discovered that they weren't true.

For readers who have not experienced this kind of suffering, I hope my story allows you to better understand people who have. And for those who have experienced similar trauma, and may still be struggling with it, I hope my story encourages you to connect to the part of you that is worthy and lovable, even though it might be buried under the rubble of pain. Digging out that part of you may be necessary to feel more whole, more deserving. I've learned that sometimes to discover your own happy-ending fairy tale, you must become your own heroine.

In this memoir, I describe most of my childhood by the three houses I lived in: the Ranch House, the Tudor, and the Colonial. The houses provide an external frame for the years of turmoil that characterized my upbringing, with each new house offering the hope of a safe and loving home that never materialized. Additionally, throughout the book I discuss several incidents involving my siblings. I include those experiences to provide context to the turbulence of our lives when we were all young, and to illustrate more clearly how each of us was a victim of our parents and our circumstances. With these few exceptions, however, I chose not to delve deeply into my siblings' experiences and lives. They have a right to their own stories.

Although I am a clinical social worker and could possibly identify mental health diagnoses for both my parents, in telling my story I focus more on describing how their behaviors affected my thoughts and feelings, because the process of connecting meaningfully to my thoughts and emotions is ultimately what changed my life. At the end of the book, I write about my decision to cut all communication with my parents. As of today, both still are living, but I have no contact with either one. It was the hardest decision I have ever made. Continuing any kind of relationship with either of them, I came to realize, was very unhealthy for me.

This memoir represents my memory and my truth. I use my name and the name of my spouse but have changed the names of my siblings and other people in the book, except my parents. I am no longer afraid to admit the truth of them or of my story.

My Mother

Chapter One

The House of Trouble

I am wobbly. I steady myself by curling my toes over the top step of the steep wooden staircase. My right hand grips Beau's fur. Beau is strong, bigger than I am, and warm. His pink tongue licks me. I feel safe with him. Each time I try to find an earlier memory, all I see is Beau, our black-brown German shepherd rhythmically panting with moist brown eyes rimmed in sweetness. And the staircase. It's all I remember of my early life in a brick house on the grounds of a state mental hospital.

My fuller memories begin in our next house, a single-level, three-bedroom Ranch House in Wayne, Pennsylvania, just a few miles away from the mental hospital. We moved there in 1961 when I was three years old and stayed until I was nine. The Ranch House was nestled in a neighborhood of similar uninspired ranch houses, a half-dozen miles east of Philadelphia's wealthy Main Line suburbs. Our new home looked as forgotten as I felt. Its bland interior and exterior walls surrounded us. My father, who had been doing his psychiatric residency at the mental hospital when we lived there, didn't join us. I was too young to know why.

Life in the Ranch House resembled a rubber band stretched tight. With constant tension in our lives, there was frequent snapping—eruptions of chaos, fighting, and despair. It happened after weeks of bare cupboards and chaotic meals, out-of-control parent and sibling fights, and constant kid medical emergencies. Most likely the tension and snapping took a toll on my ability to form memories. My recollections from the Ranch House are disjointed, tenuous, and sometimes anchored only by later memories.

Throughout our six years in the Ranch House, my mother resembled an out-of-control Macy's Thanksgiving Day Balloon, but with no string connecting her to us. She floated above us big and chaotic, bobbing and weaving in and out of our lives, exciting and scary at the same time. With thick, dark hair, tawny skin, deep-set clear blue eyes, and an oval face and full lips, my mother was beautiful and she knew it. Although a Swedish-Irish mix, she emphatically believed her beauty was the result of her father's Black Irish roots. Whatever the dominant genes, growing up she benefited from a collage of features not typically seen in her hometown of Omaha, Nebraska. Added to her striking physical beauty and charm were a quick wit and a keen memory for the smallest details. When my mother focused on me, even for a few moments, I felt happy, complete. For as far back as I can remember, I physically ached for her attention and affection.

2

Although my father didn't divorce my mother until I was eleven, the role he played in our lives was that of a disturbing visitor. While we barely eked out an existence in the Ranch House, he lived away from us in a clean, well-appointed apartment with sculptures, paintings, and classical music playing on the record player.

Tall and slender, my father possessed a geometry to his facial features that spelled attractiveness—warm blue eyes evenly spaced, a perfectly centered masculine but not obtrusive nose, a wide mouth outlined by full lips, and a marked chin. Blond curly hair completed his look, although sometime in his early thirties he lost his hair and forever after wore a toupee. It was not until I was around twelve that I learned his technique for keeping the straw-colored mat on his head. Visiting him at his apartment, I walked into his bedroom and saw him hooking a portion of the toupee to his scalp. After seeing the rows of metal hooks sticking out of his skin, I quickly looked away. Why, I wondered, would he hurt himself like that? Just to have hair?

At a distance, my father looked friendly. When I was small, I sometimes imagined that faraway father, the one who appeared kind to strangers, would scoop me up into his arms delighting in my smell, still new, still fresh. In real life, the closer he got to me, the colder and more distant he became. His iciness scared me. Nobody seemed acceptable to him, least of all his family. Impatient and imperial, my father's presence in our lives promised that screaming and fury were never far behind.

When I was born, my sister Gillian was one, my brother Michael was two-and-a-half, my sister Celeste was almost four, and my brother Alan was five. Within five months of my birth, my mother was pregnant with my younger brother, Patrick. Six kids in six years—each of us a stepping-stone to the next. The older three children were called The Big Kids, the younger three The Little Kids. We were one large clump of want separated into two smaller clumps of need.

Physically, we were one of those families whose genetic link is striking. As siblings, we share similar facial features: slightly broad faces, high cheekbones, and blue eyes. Except for Alan, the oldest sibling, who was brown-haired, we were all blond as children. We weren't identical, but there was no mistaking that we were related. I was a small thin child with a mop of wispy hair that became progressively curlier as I got older. And I had a voice that was so deep for a little girl it made people laugh.

The most prominent feature of life in the Ranch House was fighting between my brothers and sisters. We learned from the experts. Every time my father grudgingly decided it was time to do rounds at our house, my parents' verbal warfare would escalate into thunderous screaming. The angrier my father got, the more he forced his low-pitched voice into a boom that would shake the walls. His goal, it seemed, was to shout louder than my mother until she eventually surrendered out of exhaustion. It was a successful strategy. Part of his anger, I think, was his allergy to us. There was nothing about marriage or family life that interested him. His passions were expensive cars, art, and the beauty of everyday items—silverware, dishes, undershirts, socks, razor blades—made with the finest materials.

In 1953, the year after my parents were married, my father rented a Jaguar Coupe for $30 a month. At the time, he was in medical school and he and my mother were living in subsidized government housing, with a monthly rent of $20. While my father was in class, my mother was home alone, isolated and struggling to care for an infant, with a Jaguar in the garage. Although my father dared not drive it to medical school where it could get dinged, he made it out-of-bounds for my mother to use under any circumstance.

My father's obsession with finery never abated. One cold day when I was in kindergarten, I recall him revving his engine as he drove up for a house inspection—a sporadic but dreaded obligation on his part. Despite the frigid temperature, he slid out of his car in one fluid movement. Underneath his expensive, thick blue peacoat, I could see he was wearing one of his many crisp oxford dress shirts with his initials, DDP for David Dean Parrish, on the pocket. Fine woolen pants completed his outfit. He moved impatiently up our steep driveway, eyes glaring at the house. Calculating risks to his car, he never parked next to the house. His temperamental but engine-enhanced Corvair stayed at the bottom of the driveway, far from my mother's beat-up car at the top, far from a house that had long ago surrendered to the forces of pandemonium, and far from us.

Initially I couldn't read my father's footsteps. I couldn't tell if he was feeling anger or revulsion. As he walked into the house and immediately yelled at my brother Michael to get out of his way, I knew it was both. Within seconds he and my mother began screaming at each other. Peering out from behind the half-closed door to the bedroom I shared with my two sisters, I watched and waited. My parents fought like two angry rams with their horns intertwined snorting mucous-y hot air at each other. Death of one or the other always appeared to be the only path to disentanglement.

This fight, like all the fights before it, began losing steam after an hour of back-and-forth screaming. With the smug look of a victor, my father disengaged himself from my spent mother, and began walking rapidly in and out of each room. Stepping over piles of dirty laundry that resembled skyward-bound termite mounds, he scowled at our unmade beds and the house's two filthy bathrooms, each with rings of dirt in the tubs, sinks, and toilets. When he peered into the kitchen, he grunted. Not an inch of counter space was free of conical piles of empty food containers and dirty dishes. I could feel his hatred of us as he made brief eye contact with me and those of my brothers and sisters who had given up their hiding places. We were extra body parts that slowed him down, parts he would have preferred to amputate. He moved to the front door and pulled it open hard. Stepping across the threshold, he slammed it shut. The door was still vibrating when he reached his Corvair at the bottom of the driveway.

My father never stayed long and didn't come often. I was relieved about that. Although his role in our family was only vaguely defined, in our color alert system, he was red: most dangerous.

In the Ranch House, there were no hugs or kisses or feathery words of encouragement from my father, and almost none from my mother. This bleakness, paired with our inadequate and irregular food supply, squeezed us daily. We never sat down for a meal together. Our usual fare, which we mostly organized ourselves as soon as we were old enough (for me, I think it was around age three or four), consisted of cereal, peanut butter, bologna or SPAM sandwiches, and canned soup. Assuming responsibility for feeding ourselves relieved us of having to beg or cry for my mother to feed us. Since my father gave money to my mother sparingly and infrequently, how we survived day-to-day is still a mystery. There is so much that I didn't understand about my early childhood, and many of my memories from that time are missing, but a handful are still vivid.

Once, Gillian fell to the floor of our worn-out kitchen littered with trash, dirty dishes, and empty cereal boxes. A scream preceded the moment of impact. She and Alan had been arguing right before and then Alan pushed her, hard. Suddenly, Gillian lay on her back not moving, in agony. I was a bystander with a few of my siblings and mother. Terrified, I didn't know what to do or how to help her. My mother didn't either. After what felt like a long time, Gillian was taken away. As the ambulance rocketed down our street and away from our house, its siren confirmed what was no longer a question for our neighbors: *we were the house of trouble.* Weeks later when Gillian came home from the hospital, I found out that when Alan pushed her, she had hit her back on the kitchen doorknob and nearly fractured her spine. She spent months at home on her back so her spine could heal.

Alan was always angry in the Ranch House, although exactly why, I'm not sure. In another dramatic fight sequel with Gillian, I remember his face stretched even tighter than usual and darkened with fury. From across the room, his sucked-in cheeks, narrowed eyes, and lips pulled inward meant one thing: he was ready to inflict punishment. Towering over Gillian and at least double her weight—Gillian was seven or eight, Alan eleven or twelve—he again shoved her, hard. Gillian lost her balance and fell backwards, landing on top of an overstuffed brown paper bag of trash. Perched perilously on top of the garbage was an empty food can. Its lid, connected to the can by just a few steel threads, was sticking straight up. As soon as Gillian hit the bag, the can fell. In seconds, blood was spurting everywhere. The lid nearly sliced Gillian's heel all the way through. Only later did we learn that it had missed a major artery by millimeters. An ambulance was called, and once again Gillian was rushed to the hospital. That day too there was a crowd in the kitchen, including my mother, who stood off to the side, watching.

I imagine to an outsider it might seem as though we took ringside seats near the fights to absorb the energy flowing from such charged conflicts. But the real reason, I think, that we got close to the action was to experience the release that always came at the end. I cried after each big fight and so did most of my brothers and sisters. Crying gave me relief: we were all still alive and the next big fight felt like it was at least a day away. Life in the Ranch House was one long battle with just a few intermissions.

Most of our fighting in the Ranch House was over food. We were left in the care of a mother who did not cook, rarely bought enough food to go around, and disappeared into her room for hours on end. Food in general, and organized meals in particular, were hard to come by. I was hungry, a lot. As soon as I entered Roberts Elementary School in second grade, a public school down the street from our house, I discovered that I could buy lunch (I attended a Montessori school for kindergarten and first grade and had to bring my lunch, a responsibility that was beyond difficult for my mother). I couldn't believe my luck, until I realized thirty-five cents was standing between me and a daily organized meal.

Nabbing a quarter and a dime from my mother's lethargic outstretched hand before school never came without a fully staged morning begging scene. I tried not to ask too often, saving my pleas for the days when there was no food in the house. When I got the coins, I skipped out the door to walk the few blocks to school, beaming. Close to noon on those days, I could barely pay attention to my second-grade teacher. Visions of thick squares of pizza, a juicy slice of meatloaf, or two or three crispy brown fish sticks danced through my head. The minute the lunch bell rang I raced to the cafeteria. Once I had my place in line, I tried to join other girls in my class entertaining each other with silly faces and secret whispers about what the boys did at recess. But there was only one thing on my mind: food.

There is a second reason I think we fought so much. My mother seemed to relish our physical and emotional conflicts, especially when they didn't involve her. Maybe our fighting offered her a scenery change when she felt weighed down and in the wrong movie of her life—a perception that corresponded to her frequent comment, "I never wanted this," *this* meaning her life and us. It's also possible that our fights conveniently diverted any expectation that she parent us. In all the years of our fighting, I don't have a single memory of her interceding to stop a fight or of protecting the younger and more helpless of her dueling children. And last, although my mother was mostly a mute onlooker to the brawls, I always sensed that she had a hand in flaming the fires of our conflicts. As a child, I wasn't sophisticated enough to see how she might have set up our fight scenes or encouraged our ongoing conflicts, but if our adult years were any indication, she was often in the director's chair from the get-go. Behind many of our later sibling conflicts, I discovered my mother surreptitiously whispering lies and half-truths about one of us to the other. As the storms she whipped up burst, she responded with faux shock and disbelief in performances worthy of an Academy Award.

One performance much later (when I was a college student) was notable for its mix of high drama and peculiarity. It was the late 1970s and I was helping put up decorations for a backyard wedding for Gillian, at Celeste and her husband's home. The guest list included my parents, my five siblings, Celeste's husband, and Gillian's fiancé. Moments after I finished hanging streamers on the small white gazebo, my mother stomped across the backyard screaming, "This is ugly! You did it wrong!" With arms scissoring maniacally, she pulled down all the streamers I had just hung, leaving torn nuggets of white and lavender crepe paper trapped under strips of scotch tape—ragged little witnesses to her fury.

I had put up the celebratory streamers thinking they would simultaneously create a sense of normalcy and serve as a talisman—to protect us from ourselves. The streamers failed on both counts, and so did I. My mother accused me of violating Celeste's home and singlehandedly sabotaging Gillian's wedding. Although the episode was far from the only drama that day, my mother conveniently framed my putting up decorations as a targeted transgression against both my sisters. The inevitable family hemorrhage began before Gillian and her new husband exchanged "I Do's." And it lasted a long time afterwards.

My mother's theatrical displays were not restricted to instigating combat between us. Each time Gillian was injured and taken to the hospital, she would swoop into the vigilant role of bedside caretaker. I have no recollection of her being so attentive at home, but in the hospital, she was transformed. She instantly became the deeply-concerned parent, asking doctors and nurses thoughtful questions and calibrating just the right levels of maternal alarm and compassion to impress them. Since she would frequently take all of us with her when she went to see Gillian—five concerned and cowed siblings—I had a front row seat to these performances. I saw how she seamlessly blended self-deprecating humor with obsequious compliments for the medical staff.

"Oh, Dr. Barrett, you have to be joking that I look so put together," she giggled. "That is so sweet of you, really. I wish I did look as good as you say. With six kids, one of course here in the hospital and under your excellent care, I feel like I am on the run every minute of every day. Believe me, the state of my hair tells the real story. When accidents happen with my kids, like they do with Gillian—all too often as you know—I can't tell you how fortunate we are to have you helping us through these difficult times. You and your nurses here make all the difference. Thank you!"

Everyone in the hospital thought my mother was wonderful. So did I. What I could never quite grasp was why she didn't treat me the same way she did the medical staff. I spent hours trying to figure out this conundrum. The only thing I could come up with was that I was doing something wrong. What, I never knew.

Hospitals were monolithic structures of cleanliness and order that fascinated me as a child. During our compulsory visits, I marveled how anyone could keep such

12

enormous buildings so spotless. The hospital staff was equally captivating. The nurses and aides were friendly, caring, and funny, and they seemed to get a kick out of talking to us as we formed a semi-circle around Gillian's bed. And then there were the meals. They magically came three times a day, varied dishes in Technicolor: red wiggly Jell-O, fluffy white mashed potatoes, golden brown chicken-fried steak, and perfect French cut green beans. All just for my sister. The attention she got made me wish that I would get hurt, not badly of course, just enough to get admitted to the hospital.

In retrospect, I can see that my sister's injuries were a metaphor for our home life: severe and on the brink of becoming something worse. Daily life was defined by anarchy and junk, the latter literally. Detritus from seven people's lives littered the hallways, bedrooms, and kitchen of the small three-bedroom Ranch House. In one of those bedrooms, my two sisters and I shared a triple bunk bed; my three brothers shared another bedroom with their own triple bunk. My mother occupied the third bedroom, the one with an adjoining bath. An overflow of newspapers, magazines, clothes, books, and extra furniture decorated her suite. Spying a piece of my mother's bed free from clutter was like finding an island in the middle of the ocean promising a hospitable and safe place to land.

I don't think my mother spent much time looking for islands on her bed. Each time I went into her room in the early morning, I found her asleep on top of dirty clothes, towels, newspapers, magazines, and empty food packages, always with a blanket pulled over her. I felt sad seeing her this way. Somehow things gave her comfort that people couldn't. As though she were assuring herself that her collecting had a purpose, my mother would often tell me that the countless things she collected, mostly from thrift shops, were items she intended to refurbish or that would serve a perfect function in the future: placemats for a dinner party of twenty, and clothes in myriad sizes for people she anticipated meeting. The fact that we rarely could wear what she collected didn't bother her. My mother had absolute faith that her future audiences would congratulate her on her sartorial taste. Oddly, she seemed to cradle this imaginary future in her mind the same way that I cradled her in my heart, both of us believing that once we held the object of our desire we would be fully complete. Most of the time I felt lonely and confused in a house empty of affection but full of things meant for other people.

Turmoil was a constant in the Ranch House. On an afternoon expedition through the woods, a neighborhood boy galloping ahead of a group of us kids swung his stick through the leaves and hit a hornet's nest. In seconds, hundreds of hornets were out and swarming. Gillian, who was running right behind the boy on his heels, ran straight into a black cloud of angry wasps. She was stung over thirty times. By the time we raced home with her to get some help, she had gone into anaphylactic shock. Her entire body was beginning to swell rapidly, beginning with her face. Someone called an ambulance and once again Gillian was rushed to the hospital. During each of Gillian's injuries and everyday life in the Ranch House, my mostly self-exiled father was missing-in-action. Despite my parents' strained relationship, toxic for both, and my father's palpable contempt for my mother and us, my mother ached for him, a longing I truly did not understand.

This ache was on display late one night when I was unable to sleep. Hearing noise from the kitchen, I got up to see what was going on.

"What are you doing?" I asked my mother, who was standing at the stove intently monitoring six Gerber baby food jars, lids off, sitting in an inch or two of boiling water in a pot on the stove. Patrick and I, the youngest in the family, had long outgrown baby food, so I was confused.

"I'm making your father dinner," she said solemnly.

"Why are you making him baby food?" I asked.

She looked at me, exasperated. "Your dad has a sensitive stomach; he has to eat baby food." She moved the jars around the pot in a circle, creating a small tidal wave. Water sloshed up against the sides of the saucepan, threatening to jump into the glass openings of the jars. The liquid commotion didn't seem to bother my mother. She calmly dipped a spoon into each jar and stirred its contents. I was captivated. Her concentration and commitment to my father's meal, to baby food, was nothing I had ever seen.

Preparing my father's baby-food dinner is the only memory from my early childhood that I have of my mother cooking. It may have seared its way into my brain because

I was intrigued that she was cooking or because I was incredulous that she wanted to feed my father, who by then I regarded as the enemy, the person whose touchdowns and takeoffs in our lives always felt violent. I don't remember whether my father came home that night and ate the pureed carrots, peas, chicken or banana, but I do remember that he ate baby food for a long time. Visiting him in his various apartments over the years I would see those same jars of Gerber baby food, frequently lined up next to bottles and bottles of pills on the kitchen countertops. I was never quite sure what to make of the baby food—or of the pills.

Comparing early and later memories of how my mother and my father typically interacted with people, I was surprised to notice their patterns didn't change much. To the outside world, my mother exuded abundant charm, while shrewdly hiding virtually everything about herself, including how intensely she struggled to function in everyday life. My father's way was different. Unfamiliar with the basics of balanced interpersonal exchange ("you say something, I listen, I respond; and then I say something, you listen, you respond"), he customarily spoke to others like he was driving unimpeded on the wrong side of the road. Ignoring oncoming traffic, he barreled ahead, indifferent to what anyone said, or felt, or did. His peculiar verbal style was made even more eccentric by his habit of selectively forcing his voice into a lower octave when he was trying to impress or intimidate. This gravelly *basso profundo*, which he periodically adopted and never failed to use when introducing himself as *Dr. Parrish*, terrified me as a child.

I was always wary of my father. Since my guardedness toward him didn't change over time, when my mother made the unilateral decision when I was in kindergarten that each of us would have to go on occasional one-on-one play dates with him, I balked. To sell the play dates, my mother built them up as sweet and as high as an ice cream sundae. She said they were critical opportunities for us to spend time with our father, to get to know him. This justification was topped off with a cherry: because she considered herself an expert in child development, spending time with our father, she declared, was essential to our emotional development.

It didn't seem to matter to my mother that she never spent meaningful one-on-one time with any of us that I can remember or examined how we spent time with our father—none of my forced play dates with him ever involved play, for me anyway. Neither was addressed in her persuasive speech. It's most likely that she engineered the excursions to punish my father for living away from her, for abandoning her. Since he generally didn't want to take us, and we didn't want to go, everyone suffered, except my mother. That was the first time that I noticed how exuberantly happy she became knowing that someone who had rejected or hurt her was miserable. Later, I learned there is a word for this: Schadenfreude.

I dreaded play dates with my father. Most involved me trailing after him as he checked items off his to-do list.

But there were two outings that didn't follow this pattern and I've never forgotten them. The first was the time he took me to a late-afternoon matinee. I thought we were going to a cartoon or family adventure film, but the movie we saw was not for kids. The absence of a long ticket line in front of the movie theater, the kind filled with moms and dads trying to keep their happy giggling kids in tow, was the first clue.

My father marched straight up to the ticket taker, with me behind a few paces because I could not match his long strides, and bought his ticket. He never said a word to me. I don't remember the full title of the movie, but it had the name Bluebeard in it. Once we settled into the plush red theater chairs I could only see the heads of a few men in the theater, no kids, no women. As the movie started I waited for the animation that typically dances across the screen in children's features, but there were no cartoons. Grownups soon came into view speaking the language of adults. Within seconds, I knew the movie was not meant for me.

The film hadn't been playing long before the male lead—a man called Bluebeard—had a physical interaction with a woman that I didn't quite understand. I remember both were naked. Confused and uncomfortable with the scene, I wasn't sure what to think when in the next frame Bluebeard savagely killed the woman. Then he repeated the pattern with another woman. After watching a third paramour murdered via the same sequence, I covered my eyes and waited, hoping the movie would end fast. I wanted to leave but dared not say a word to my father.

The other unforgettable play date happened one sunny summer afternoon. At the time my father was honing his high-art photography skills and decided that I would be the subject of a shoot. He picked me up at the Ranch House in his shining clean Corvair that smelled of leather. I climbed into the big front passenger seat and tried to make myself even smaller than I was. I inched over to the passenger door as far away from him as I could. I didn't know what would come next with my father and dared not ask, "Where are we going?" "Why?" "How long will we be there?" My father didn't say much either. He drove quickly, efficiently shifting gears while alternately looking at the road and the dashboard, firmly gripping the steering wheel with hands sheathed in dark brown leather driving gloves. He drove fast like he was the lead car in a road race and winning was paramount.

Leaving our lower-middle-class neighborhood behind, my father drove to a wealthier town about ten miles away, full of large, expensive homes and estates. As we penetrated this dome of affluence, he began taking left and right turns down sleepy roads. His quest: the perfect shooting location that would make him famous. In this part of town, the wood and stone mansions were all set back from the road to protect the owners' privacy and exclusive membership among the Main Line elite. Seeing a thick canopy of trees next to a small stream, he parked the car, told me to put on the dress, shoes, and socks he had brought, and then ordered me out of the car. The large white rambling private house sitting less than a hundred yards away from the stream didn't faze him one bit.

"Climb over. It's just on the other side," he barked, his voice authoritative and firm.

The *No Trespassing* sign stood tall and foreboding. It was planted firmly on a patch of tufted grass between the split rail fence outlining the property and the road where we had parked. Since I could read the *No* in *No Trespassing* and guessed the intent of the rest, I must have been around six. I told my father, "Dad, I don't think we can go in there," and pointed to the sign. My father ignored the sign and me. "Climb over!" he demanded. Frightened, I obeyed. In a matter of seconds both of us had scaled the fence and trespassed into someone's lush, overgrown backyard.

The fact that it was someone's property never bothered my father. Positioning me in various poses of childhood sweetness next to a stream, my father clicked his camera away, intent on capturing an innocence I had never experienced. The entire shoot all I could think about was that we should not have been there. I wanted to go home. As we were finally walking off the property, a small but surprising thought surfaced beneath my anxiety. I knew something my father didn't—*a wrong didn't magically become a right just because you thought it so.*

The six years we spent in the Ranch House were a mixture of daily dullness and unexplained party-popper-like explosions. Christmas fit more in the category of a party popper, but not the first one that I remember. I couldn't have been more than four and was putting myself to bed on Christmas Eve when I heard the tinkle of sleigh bells in the distance. Convinced something wonderful was about to happen, I ran to my bedroom window and put my hands on the ice-cold pane that framed the darkness outside. Moments later a sleigh came into view. It was on our street and moving slowly toward our house, pulled by a large live horse, much prettier than any doll horse I had ever seen. Right away I knew it was Santa. I had no experience sitting on Santa's lap at the store but I knew what he looked like, and there he was in a red suit, big and round with a flowing white beard, sitting on the sleigh bench. It didn't matter to me that he wasn't flying; he was real. With snow on the ground and Santa coming to my house, it was a perfect night for hope.

As Santa approached our distressed house, I held my breath. But he didn't stop. Just beyond us, on the opposite side of the street, he turned into the Russo's steep driveway and made his way up to the only graceful house in the neighborhood. The Russo dad was a dentist, the mom a homemaker. The Russo kids were nice but didn't fraternize with the hoi polloi—us. With four of them, lots of toys, and a huge backyard swing set, they preferred to stay to themselves. I followed the sleigh piled high with wrapped presents until it disappeared around a bank of tall trees next to the house. Satisfied that I had discovered Christmas the way it was supposed to be, I steamed up the glass with my breath. I wanted to wait until the exact moment Santa came to our driveway before running to bed. I didn't want to ruin all the surprise. After what seemed an interminable time, the empty sleigh inched down our neighbor's driveway. But instead of making its way up ours, it drifted past our house before disappearing in the dark. That's when I learned that Christmas sometimes happens . . . across the street.

Christmas in the Ranch House was not the stuff of fairytales. The year after I saw Santa at the neighbors' house, my mother abruptly left our house on Christmas Eve in the dark. The moment she closed the door, I panicked. Where was she going? Would she ever come back? We were a disparate band of six, so there was plenty to fear inside as well as outside the house. Although we were leaderless when my mother was home, her departure made me feel more frightened than usual. If a crisis happened, as they regularly did, would we be able to manage it? Would we call the police? Who would help us? I waited, anxiety mounting.

Close to midnight my mother burst through the door full of excitement, her face flush with the color of on-the-edge living. Her look said it all: she had conquered Christmas. In her arms were several large black plastic garbage bags filled to the brim. Spilling the bags' contents on the floor, she proudly showed us the Christmas Eve super-sale toys, clothes, and other items she had bought at the nearby mall. With a barely-there budget from my father, she presented our Christmas presents, a manic and indiscriminate jumble of toys and clothes regurgitated for us. Nothing was wrapped. Nothing had my name on it. Nothing was what I wanted.

For several years my mother repeated her Christmas hunting expeditions. As darkness descended Christmas Eve night, she would run out of the house in pursuit of things. It's hard to know what propelled her. I suspect it was a combination of procrastination, a compulsion to collect, a lack of feeling for what Christmas means to children, a need to pull off a heist of sorts, and a belief in her life as theater, that is, her dynamic role of single mother who rescues Christmas for her half-orphaned brood of six. Once we got a little older we joined her on a few of her Christmas Eve rummages. We would arrive at the mall an hour or two before closing, infected with her enthusiasm for shopping and collecting. Running into the store with a few dollars each, we all had the same goal: get something on sale for each family member. Whether it was wanted or needed was immaterial. It was fun to run unrestrained under department store fluorescent lights, crisscrossing the aisles in one store before running out and repeating it in another. Still, each year walking out of the mall at close to midnight, a strange feeling would overcome me. I sensed that the only reason we could participate in our madcap shopping spree was because someone looking over us felt sorry for us. Someone, I believed, had granted us a last-minute reprieve—to experience Christmas.

In contrast to the haphazard, unwrapped, and unwanted Christmas presents my mother indicated might be mine, I loved the large boxes full of presents that my paternal grandmother and great-grandmother sent from Omaha. From each grandmother, I received a prettily wrapped present with my name on it; inside was usually a brand-new colorful outfit that fit me perfectly. Although both grandmothers were far away, I secretly treasured the fact that I had two relatives who differentiated me from my siblings and made me feel a little special.

Several times while growing up my mother would pile us into the car and drive from Pennsylvania to Omaha to visit relatives who, I suspect, paid for the trips. Once there, we usually spent a week alternately staying with our cousins and our paternal grandmother. On one of those trips, I met my paternal great-grandmother, an immigrant from Bohemia. Standing less than five feet tall and dressed all in black, my great-grandmother spoke a halting English that was both melodic and charmingly incomprehensible. I only recall meeting her once, but could not forget that she was nothing like my mother or my paternal grandmother. For starters, she burst into joyful tears at the sight of us. A wisp of a woman, she would grab and hold whichever great-grandchild was within her vicinity. The lock-down hug lasted until the child in her embrace signaled it was time for air.

In contrast to my great-grandmother, my father's mother was tall and thin, with short hair colored a honey blonde that elevated around her head in a perfect coiffure. Despite dressing in the latest bold color fashions with perfectly accented costume jewelry, she was deadly serious. Hugs were relegated to the first-entrance hello and final-exit goodbye, and her laughter was a Cracker Jack surprise. You had to dig for it.

With quiet restraint, my grandmother asked lots of questions of us when we visited but shared little about herself. Even though my father was the elephant in the room—and a very big one considering that he was never with us on our family visits—she never mentioned him. But she took good care of us. Every visit included eggs and toast for breakfast, thick meat sandwiches for lunch, and dinners that came with two vegetables (one of them always green beans), potatoes, and a chicken or beef dish. Because she had a palsy that made her hands shake, I don't know how she cooked and kept her small two-bedroom house immaculate, but she did. She and my grandfather (my father's stepfather) slept in one bedroom with twin beds with matching bedspreads in rich brocade; the other was a guest bedroom with a full bed. Since we were often an overflow crowd, several of us would sleep downstairs in her storm cellar, on foldaway beds propped next to the wood-paneled pantry that held an emergency supply of food—canned meats, beans, soups—in the event of a tornado, and a few board games for us.

Our car trips to Omaha were wild events. The exact moment of departure came without warning. One minute my mother was throwing bundles and bundles of dirty laundry into the back of the car and the next we were driving away, most of us with our heads turned to watch our house shrink into invisibility. My mother brought the laundry because she confidently imagined that between visiting and staying with relatives in Omaha, there would be plenty of time to wash, dry, and fold loads and loads and loads at a Laundromat or one of our relatives' houses. "Vacation," she told us, "is the perfect time to catch up on laundry." That this intent might be complicated by expectations from relatives that she parent us while on vacation apparently didn't occur to her.

The best part of our trips to Omaha was frolicking with my cousins—my mother's brother's children—all eight of them. Even better, my maternal uncle and his wife had lots of love to spare. Whenever I got to stay at their house, I was ecstatic. At night, I would bunk down with my girl cousins closest in age to me, whispering when we should have been asleep, happy that the next day there would be enough cereal and milk for everyone, a big hug from my aunt, and another full day of kid-fun with my aunt and uncle in charge. Imagining that my mother needed a break, my aunt and uncle took over parenting us, unaware that my mother's detachment from us and her inability to jump in to help with cooking or cleanup, unless given detailed instructions and help at each sequential step, were her baseline. In response, my mother concentrated on playing the role of witty, charming, overwrought mother. She was terrific. My aunt and uncle loved her.

As I ambled into my cousins' kitchen one morning, I found my mother chatting with my aunt and uncle, a cup of coffee in her hand. Eyeing the rectangular wooden kitchen table loaded with cereal boxes and gallons of milk and orange juice, I quickly slid into a spot on the wooden bench next to one of my cousins and tentatively looked at my aunt for permission before grabbing a big box of cereal and a plastic bowl. My aunt looked back at me with a smile, and I reached for the cereal closest to me.

"David does come by to take the kids out one at a time," I heard my mother tell my aunt and uncle, who were both eager to know how things were going at our house. Then, as though to normalize my father's glaring absence in her life and ours, she added, "But you know, David has a busy practice, and the kids *are* a handful. I have the gray hairs to prove it. Coming here was tough, driving and refereeing backseat arguments and fighting. And you both know with your big brood, just feeding the kids on the road is exhausting. But I firmly believe they need to see their relatives. That's what is important." She nodded in my direction. I kept my head down, grateful for the cereal.

Of course, my mother never did laundry during our visits with family. It came home untouched after every trip in the same place it had originally been thrown: the trunk or back of the car. Since it served no purpose other than to crowd the six of us even more on road trips, I'd like to believe that had we had a rear-end collision, our unique load would have at least offered some protection. Luckily, we didn't have to live through that test. We made the 2,400-mile round-trips without any accidents, but definitely looked odder than most caravanning families. Anyone whizzing by who happened to glance at the interior of our car might have thought the tangle of limbs, the helter-skelter messy front and back row seats, and the slivers of dirty laundry peeking out from wherever they had previously been pounded down, were sure signs that we were nomads, people likely to skip out on a hotel bill, or both.

Despite my mother's grandiose laundry ideas and fuzzy travel itinerary, it was courageous of her to drive us by herself halfway across the country and back. Each trip was a major accomplishment. And the road trips had moments of fun. In addition to the respite they offered from our chaotic life in the Ranch House, we had spells of laughing, tickling each other in the back seat, and playing *I Spy a Cheap Motel*. The moment someone read a billboard on the freeway advertising a discount motel rate, he or she would yell out to my mother. Generally, we stayed in one room together with seven of us spread across two queen beds and two cots. Holiday Inns displaying *Kids Stay Free* signs probably regretted that offer the next morning as we pulled out of the parking lot. Chaos was Velcroed to us. It went where we went.

As unexpectedly as mirth appeared on our trips, it disappeared. Spasms of uncontrolled laughing were quickly replaced by near-death experiences. As one of the little kids, I became somewhat adept at modified dodge ball, the ball being any hand, elbow, foot, or knee that might be thrown intentionally or unintentionally in my direction.

Another danger zone for me on our road trips was when my mother drove at night. Sometimes she drove after dark because we hadn't found a motel we could afford; sometimes she just wanted to go a little farther before stopping. Regardless of the reason, on any nocturnal drive I soon found I was incapable of joining my slumbering siblings in the back. I worried my mother would fall asleep at the wheel. Just imagining what would happen kept me wide awake. Not wanting to die, I designated myself watchman and climbed into the front seat next to her. I talked about anything I could think of to make sure she didn't succumb to sleep, all the while keeping my eyes on the road. For years, I made myself the nighttime lookout. Right or wrong, I calculated the odds: without a sentry, our risk of experiencing danger at night was high and the probability of surviving that danger low. In my child brain, feeling groggy the next day seemed an insignificant price to pay for being alive.

Thinking about my watchman habit, I wonder if it had roots that went way back, before all the knock-down-drag-out fighting and lawlessness inside our home. On some level, I must have begun paying attention to what was happening, *and not happening,* around me when I was just days old. With so many children so close in age, and a mother who struggled every day to keep herself clean and fed, let alone us, I can imagine my early cries were not responded to with any urgency—a likely experience that probably heightened my sense that I was pretty much on my own.

In the summer of 1964, my mother's absentee parenting was suddenly on display for anyone curious or willing enough to look behind the curtain. It was the summer that Colonial Village, a swimming pool not far from our house, became our babysitter. The catalyst for the new arrangement was my mother's acceptance into Villanova University's graduate theater program. Her program started later that summer. Beginning in high school and continuing all throughout college, my mother dreamt of becoming an actress. One step closer to this dream, suddenly she needed a plan for us, even though we had been on our own through previous summers and when we weren't in school, whether she was home or not.

Colonial Village was an enormous expanse of green black water fed by local springs that doubled as a very large pond. It was home to snapping turtles, frogs, and snakes, and served as a swimming pool for families without the money to buy a membership to Martin's Dam, the elite swim club with a chlorinated pool just next door. My father surprised us all by paying the pool membership dues that summer. Looking back, I suspect a big reason he decided to fork over the money was that once he had agreed to support my mother's dreams of Broadway, most likely a deft maneuver to get her to stop calling him and complaining about their fractured relationship and us, they both needed an acceptable caretaking arrangement for their offspring. After all, someone, another parent, theater colleague, or distant relative was sure to ask.

Like most young children, I didn't focus too much on making sense of my environment or my parents. I adapted. Still, I was not without the power of observation. I didn't miss how my mother managed to slip into nearly every conversation she had with adults—both before and after her divorce from my father—that she was the single caretaker-parent of six children in six years. And I never missed the response: eyes widened, mouths fell open, admiration flowed, "Wow, that is incredible! You really had six children in six years?" and "That must be so tough! You have to be a saint!" If her audience already knew this number, my mother fluidly switched to complaining about the burden of us. This too provided her with attention, only in the form of sympathy and condolences. Seeing how my mother consistently used *us* as a major way to get attention from people, I could imagine that once she bragged or alternately bemoaned her fate as our mother to her theater colleagues, they would naturally ask, "Who on earth did you find to take care of six children while you are in school?" Colonial Village was the perfect response. And it had the added benefit of fitting nicely into her worldview that it takes a village to raise *her* children. The pool had a dozen or more swim coaches, lifeguards, and pool staff and, although it never occurred to my mother, a cadre of parents who felt sorry for us. After she dropped us off in the morning, she routinely did not come back until sundown.

Every day at Colonial Village started out pretty much the same. I tumbled out of our dinged-up, growling Chevy Bel Air hungry, a feeling I knew well. Making things worse, I never had a towel and my hand-me-down blue Dolfin tank suit permanently pooled around my bottom in waves of extra fabric. Barely glancing back at us, my mother gunned it out of the unpaved parking lot, dirt flying off her tires. With the dulled tiredness that comes from too little sleep and food, my siblings and I could do no more than watch her car until it fully disappeared.

Since we were deposited early in the morning, between seven and eight o'clock, once we could no longer see my mother's car we trudged over to the pool gate like a slow-moving rain cloud, the kind that threatens to unleash a downpour at any moment. Most of the time, none of us said anything. With three hours to wait until my swim practice, my first stop was usually the large wooden lost-and-found bin to look for a towel. My goal was to dig under the heap of rainbow colored beach towels to find one that didn't feel as wet as the others and didn't smell too mildewy. Despite the humidity and heat of East Coast summer weather, there were plenty of cool mornings. I used people's forgotten towels to keep myself warm.

Once I found a towel, I wrapped it around me and ambled back toward the pool looking for a spot on the mossy bank where I could sit. To pass the time until the pool swarmed with kids my age, I watched. My focus was anything moving—ants in the grass, mothers securing the best patches of grass to camp out on with their offspring for the day, teenagers as they sluggishly filed in for practice. Coach Louie and the fifteen-to-eighteen-year-old boys were a particularly fun group to watch. Standing on the long narrow cement jetty in the middle of the enormous pool wearing a floppy bucket hat, Coach Louie would scream at the boys to get in the water. The jetty was a cement wall that jutted out into the water halfway across the pond, opposite the bank of starting blocks. Swimmers touched or did flip turns on the jetty wall to mark twenty-five yards. "Get in NOW!" was part of Coach Louie's daily refrain to the boys. Like magic, they quickly organized their adolescent limbs, so long and loose they seemed unattached to their bodies, into cannonballs and quirky jackknives, competing to see who made the biggest splash or the goofiest dive into the water. It was my favorite morning show.

Getting into the pool was hard for me too. The dark water fascinated and terrified me. It was big and cold and I couldn't see the bottom. I never, ever just jumped in. I descended slowly: toes, then ankles, knees, thighs, waist, shoulders—up to the point where I could stand. Only then would I plunge into the cold, cold water. I was not much of a swimmer, so I avoided competition in that arena, but I did experience something of an internal competition often enough at the pool: whether to stay at my morning observation site or respond in some way to pangs of hunger. The hunger usually won when my stomach rumblings coalesced into one big, "You can't ignore me now." That was when I abandoned my post to search for dropped pennies. Occasionally Gillian and I hunted for money together, pooling what we found and sharing the tall pretzel sticks they bought from the snack bar. But most of the time we hunted alone, each girl for herself.

The best hunting grounds for dropped coins were the pool's outdoor changing stalls. The stalls were a long line of shoulder-height wood enclosures sitting on a hill overlooking the pool. I would typically slip into the first stall, close the door, and drop to my knees. Since there was a 10-inch gap between the cement floor and the wooden divider between each stall, down on my hands and knees I could look the entire length of the stalls for pocket change that slipped out of swim bags and pants pockets, unnoticed by their owners. Not always, but frequently enough, I would find a few pennies, nickels, and dimes scattered on the floor. When I did, I would inch over to them doing a stomach crawl. One penny for each pretzel stick. On bonanza days when I found two nickels or a dime, I would buy ten pretzel sticks at the snack bar, waiting impatiently for it to open at 10 a.m. before running down to the pool for practice. Those were good days.

I loved Colonial Village for the two summers we were members. I folded myself into a structure that was comfortingly regular with swim practice every morning, same time, same place. After practice, I played tag or hide-and-seek with kids in my age group on the swim team. I had a great list of hiding places where I could squeeze my small body so that it disappeared, out of sight. One was between the stacks of wooden chaise longues; another was underneath a row of brambly low-rise bushes. The bushes were an especially good hiding place. Nobody wanted to look in there because even looking left you all scratched. The scratches didn't bother me; I liked not being found. There were several other perks to going to the pool. Occasionally swim friends' parents would give me extra bologna sandwiches wrapped in waxed paper at lunchtime, or discreetly give me a few coins and then gently push me into the stampede of kids running to the snack bar for an ice cream cone. Once I got my cone, I savored it, licking it slowly, enjoying the drips on my hand in equal parts to the ice cream on the cone.

My favorite day each summer at Colonial Village was the end-of-the-season party. On the day of the party, swim coaches strung multicolored streamers to trees and lampposts flanking the pool. To add mood lighting for when the sun went down, they placed brown paper lunch bags filled with sand and votive candles in a long line on the pool sidewalk. At five p.m. sharp the party was kicked off by a host of Silly Swim Races. Each race had a different challenge. Inner tube races had one teammate sitting in an inner tube and the other in the water pushing. Raft races had both teammates on top of a blow-up raft paddling the length of the pool as fast as they could. Any falls into the water were grounds for immediate disqualification.

Everyone who was not in the water was cheering from the sidelines. During the party swim races, I would run barefoot back and forth on the sidewalk watching the teams and feeling happy. Music blaring out of speakers on the pavement around the pool added to the exhilaration that I felt. From the beginning to the end of the fiesta, I was free of the low-grade buzz of worry that normally vibrated throughout my body. After the races, I would run to the snack bar for as many free hot dogs, cokes, and pretzel sticks as I could eat. Knowing our family's feast-or-famine cycle by heart, my limit was two hot dogs, two glass bottles of Coke, and four pretzel sticks. That amount gave me a stomachache, but one I could manage. My extended abdomen felt good.

A big sadness, however, came with the end-of-the-season party. All the swimmers' parents came except mine. I remember one year watching Pam, my swim friend, team up with her dad for the parent-child raft race. With his thick strong shoulders and large biceps, Pam's dad paddled their raft furiously across the water while Pam held onto the edges of the thick green raft shrieking with laughter. Her mouth was open so wide that even from the sidewalk I could see the gap where her left front baby tooth had been just days before. She looked so pretty in her new pink racing suit that shimmered in the late afternoon sun. I desperately wanted to be Pam and giggle freely like that. I wanted a mother who would put Coppertone skin lotion on my back before practice and tuck my flyaway curls neatly under a swim cap. I wanted a dad who would pluck me out of the water with a strong arm before catapulting me a half dozen feet away, just to watch me fly and hear me laugh. Most of all, I wanted to have so much food that I could generously give friends extra sandwiches and treats.

When my mother picked us up from the parties it was always dark. Before she got there, lots of adults streaming out to their cars would veer toward the six of us standing in the parking lot to ask, "Hey, are you guys OK? Is someone coming to get you?" One of my brothers or sisters always murmured back, "Yeah, our mom's coming." Coach Louie didn't follow that pattern. As one of the last to leave, he would approach us more directly. Still wearing his bucket hat, he would say, "Really, do you guys need a ride home?" Only Michael had the courage to meet his gaze and mumble back, "Thanks, but my mom will be here any minute." Usually an hour after everyone had left my mom would drive up, gushing that she was late because something had come up or she had just started rehearsals for a new play. Her excuses didn't mar my once-a-year ball. It was the one day all summer at the pool I didn't feel cold. Driving away, I wished the night would happen again, tomorrow.

I have other cherished memories from the pool. Because I was neither a good nor strong swimmer, I spent a lot of time out of the pool, sitting on the sides. A big chunk of that time was spent practicing whistling. The technique I mastered involves placing the index and middle finger from both hands into my mouth above my curled-back tongue and blowing. To this day I can hail a cab across a busy intersection and congratulate a birthday boy or girl with a strong, sharp whistle. My other main activity was chattering to the lifeguards. Whenever I could, I would sit on the pool deck next to the lifeguard stand. The job I gave myself was giving the guard on duty a blow-by-blow of who was doing what in the water. It was a rewarding occupation. The lifeguards would tell me I was funny and cute, and sometimes would sweep me up in a lunch run to Burger King, treating me to a burger and fries. In an unguarded moment one day, one of the male lifeguards hoisted me onto his broad muscled shoulders. Being carried by someone strong who didn't want to harm or take advantage of me felt good. It also felt strange. It was the first time I remember feeling like a child; it is my only memory of being carried.

Before that summer when my mother told us she was going to school, all I understood was that she was going to be in plays. Although I didn't grasp fully what she was doing, her decision seemed to make sense. It helped, too, that the moment she entered the program she changed; she was animated and happy. For the next four years she spent a lot of time away from home. Back in school and acting in plays, as she had done in college, she seemed to come alive. Little, however, changed in our everyday lives; we continued to raise ourselves with little supervision from either parent. When we were not at the pool or in school ourselves, I spent a lot of time roaming around the neighborhood with other bands of kids. It wasn't an unusual activity. It was a time when kids across the country were let loose by their parents to explore, hang out, or just be gone. There was, however, one major difference between most kids and us: our mother didn't call us home at dusk for dinner. She didn't call us home, ever.

My self-sufficiency, though, had limits. In the Ranch House, I learned I couldn't always be on the lookout. One night when I was six or seven years old and deeply asleep, I felt something heavy on top of me. I was not very big and remember the weight almost smothered me. Half asleep, I tried to make sense of the physical intrusion and wiggled to release it. It didn't budge. Along with the dead weight bearing down on me, my brain registered pressure. I remember feeling like I should wake up to pee. Then there was a second feeling, strange and unfamiliar. It was a rubbing feeling that felt a little good. Both sensations quickly morphed into a feeling of danger. Letting go of the gauzy world between sleep and consciousness, I woke up and screamed.

My brother Alan, then ten or eleven, with no underwear, was lying on top of me. He had pulled my panties down and was doing something bad to me, something terrible—he was pushing his penis against the part of my body that I only knew was for going to the bathroom. "Get off me, get off me!" I yelled. Not saying a word, he scrambled down the triple bunk bed I shared with my sleeping sisters and left the room.

Fully awake, I tried to piece together what had just happened. I didn't know the name for what Alan had done to me or why, but I felt angry and couldn't go back to sleep. I lay awake until morning and then, fueled by my anger, marched into the kitchen before my siblings were up and told my mother what happened. When I finished, she didn't say anything. I wanted her to hold me and rock me to make all the hurt I felt go away for a little while, but she didn't touch me. She stood directly in front of me, silent, with no expression on her face.

Sometime later, it could have been weeks or months, my brother sexually molested me again, the same way he had the first time. Waiting for sleep to do the drugging, he once more took advantage of my helplessness. The difference was that whatever REM state I was in that second time, my brain knew the signals of violation and roused me from deep sleep with an urgent wakeup call. I came to consciousness feeling violent. With an authority that came from somewhere, I loudly ordered him, "Stop it, get off me, and get out of our room!" He did. The following morning, I presented myself to my mother again, clear-eyed and determined, and repeated my appeal for her help. "He did it again," I firmly told her. Then I gave her the details of the second abuse. When I was finished, I did something I had not done the first time: I demanded she act. "Make him stop!" I emphatically said. My mother stared straight ahead in a trance, as though I wasn't even there.

For a long time, I was afraid to go to bed at night. I knew my brother could hurt me again when I was asleep, when I couldn't push him away to protect myself. I constantly worried about the next time. When would it happen? What would I do? I had mostly perfected the art of scanning my environment when I was awake to sidestep danger, but asleep, I knew there was nothing I could do. What may have enabled me to cope a little with the trauma of my abuse was my anger. With it, I asserted to myself, my brother, and my mother that a small part of me did matter.

The big, horrible, gaping wound of my sexual assault didn't close for years. When it finally did, it joined a collection of childhood scars I could barely acknowledge. How could I know that one day I would not only look at all my scars, but I would proudly own them as powerful reminders of what I had survived.

Chapter Two

Promise of a Do-Over
Gone Wrong

When I was ten years old, our stay in the Ranch House abruptly ended. One day we saw an enormous stone Tudor house and the next, it seemed, we moved in. The move made no sense. My father continued reluctantly doling out a penny at a time for our day-to-day needs, and my mother had no job. She was still in her graduate program when we moved. Making things even more confusing, my parents maintained their separate living arrangements and corrosive communications. To this day I have no idea how or why they orchestrated the impulsive housing upgrade. But they did and I was overjoyed.

In front of us was a new beginning in a big beautiful house. Receding in the distance were my first years, the years I learned reading, writing, multiplication, deprivation, and paying attention to what was going on around me. The latter to keep myself safe—my own brand of hyper-vigilance. I was giddy with the promise of a do-over in which life would be filled with order and beauty, my parents together and in charge, and the feeling that we belonged in the community. Elegant Louis XIV-style furniture strategically placed in the foyer, dining room, and living room established a French theme to our new home, promising that our shanty-like past was gone forever.

In the spirit of my parents' head-to-toe house makeover, even the triple bunk beds that defined the boys' and girls' rooms in the Ranch House were thrown out. All six of us were given brand-new individual beds, and most of us our own bedroom. On the second floor, down the hall from my mother's master bedroom, my brother Alan had his own room, and next to him my brothers Michael and Patrick shared a room. My sisters and I were relocated to the third floor. Each of us had our own room wallpapered in the same toile French countryside design, but in three different colors. Like refugees who had miraculously made it to land in a leaking dinghy, we felt euphoric and settled into the promise of a new and better life.

Remarkably, my parents, who didn't agree on anything that I could remember, planned and coordinated our move to the Tudor in a leafy town on the Main Line, a wealthy suburb of Philadelphia. The day we moved in I was amazed that my mother could have played any part in such a dramatic feat. Despite so much that she perpetually left undone, it was the first time I noticed that she had an uncanny ability to complete tasks that brought her closer to the opening nights of her life. Our move was one of those nights. It was as though the new town and the new house gave her what she imagined from the moment she said, "I do": an opulent but understated interior-designed home; a devoted physician husband whom she believed would give up his private apartment and separate life of so many years to reunite with her; and an affluent well-educated community of peers in which to socialize and be admired. Our role stayed the same. We were backdrop to her story, rolled onto a scene whenever children were required.

Shortly after we moved, my brothers and sisters and I were enrolled in new schools. I entered fourth grade at the public elementary school closest to our house. From the expensive clothes worn by kids at my school to the enormous estates dotting our new neighborhood, I wasn't sure I would fit in, but I was hopeful and concentrated hard on the possibility of future belonging. As I settled in, trusting the contours of my life would be less misshapen, my mother suddenly announced that she had taken a position as associate producer of a children's show at a local CBS television station.

Although it wasn't part of the news, we all knew the reason why she had to go to work: my father, who had never moved into the Tudor, was not giving her enough money to support us. Pre-Tudor, he had never freely shared his money with us, but I thought that would change with the do-over. For months, I dreamed that a nicer, more approachable version of my father would become part of our family. I thought he would want to financially support us, and I believed that the tension between my parents would disappear. My mother's work announcement punctured those dreams. In the gloom of disappointment that followed, I couldn't help feeling perplexed that together my parents had bought and decorated a house that my father would not pay for or live in.

Confounding me further was that just as we were getting situated in the Tudor, I briefly visited my father in his new luxury apartment in the coveted high-rent, historic Rittenhouse Square section of downtown Philadelphia. It was my turn for a compulsory visit and I approached it with the usual dread. Bigger than his previous apartments, it was sparsely but expensively decorated. Mixed in with first seeing that apartment is a memory of meeting his beautiful dark-haired young girlfriend, Alicia. Alicia was sitting on the couch in a sophisticated white pantsuit reading a magazine when my father and I walked in. My father said hi to her but didn't introduce us. Instead he walked briskly to a back office and closed the door. Alicia scowled at his back, apparently offended that she had been left alone with a rugrat. After several minutes she asked me, "When are you going home?"

Despite feeling puzzled by my parents' relationship to each other, I spread out in the Tudor. The house was big and dignified, with space for dreaming. It had twelve rooms, including a breakfast room and a sunroom. The entire third floor where my sisters and I lived had once been the maid's quarters. A narrow, well-worn servants' back stairway coiled its way from our floor all the way down to the kitchen. My bedroom, a small separate alcove off my sister Gillian's room, had an exterior wall shorter than the other walls and a ceiling that met that wall in a downward slope, matching the pitch of the roof. The odd configuration gave my room an unbalanced but cozy look. I reveled in its uniqueness and the fact that it was mine. Daydreaming, I imagined someone long before me delighting in the off-kilter space, finding it an out-of-the-way quiet retreat, as I did.

I began to play in the new house. For hours I pretended to be a housemaid traipsing up and down the tightly tapered back stairs, carrying food and linens to the master and mistress of the house. After making friends with two girls from school who were wealthy, Jewish, and had doting mothers, I created a new fantasy. I pretended that I was Jewish and rich and had a mother who thought I was perfect. Like my friends' real mothers, my make-believe mother made dinner every night and had beautiful dresses, shirts, and pants from a swanky department store brought to our gorgeous home for me to try on. Soon I begged my sister Gillian to join my fantasy game. Revising the story, I made her my twin sister, Suden. I took the name Susan, a popular name at the time and the opposite of my then unusual first name, Monique, and nickname, Nikki. Gillian indulged me but quickly tired of the game Not me: I loved my make-believe world and continued to play in it by myself.

In time, I relied less and less on my inner imaginary world, replacing pretend friends with real friends. With few restrictions in my life, I was out of the house as much as possible playing at friends' houses or running around the neighborhood with other kids. During all the time I spent eating and sleeping at other people's homes, my mother never once suggested or even mentioned reciprocating in any way. Victim that she was, her load, as she would often say, was heavy with the burden of us. It was a belief that breezily freed her from any obligation to return parenting favors or participate in village life.

In contrast to my mother, I did think about having friends over. It was an idea that never lived for very long. Our fancy digs couldn't hide an unpredictable home life. I was afraid if I had a friend over I wouldn't be able to control what might happen in the event of a sibling blowup. Besides, it's tough to entertain kids without snacks, and we didn't have any I could give a playmate. Sadly, the food part of our life never changed when we moved. And I had to contend with one other significant barrier: our house was a mess. The jetsam of things abandoned and discarded had begun to build up again, and there was no way to camouflage or explain so many things to a friend. I felt bad that I couldn't reciprocate play dates and sleepovers, but I had no choice. I carried on socializing, far from our house.

Sometime during the first year in the Tudor, the lid came off and the fighting resumed. Little explosions erupted, sometimes followed by big ones. Most of the fights were between a sibling bursting with frustration or anger and an unlucky sibling who may or may not have been the provocateur. In the Ranch House, watching the fighting fireworks had been cathartic; but in the Tudor, most of us understood that if you were not directly involved in the argument, it was better to keep your distance and skip the grand finale. Most fights still disproportionately took place in the kitchen, hunger and food scarcity being the most common kindling. When my mother did get to the supermarket, erratically, she came home with bags of groceries that we eagerly unloaded from the car, grateful for another airdropped supply of food. Within hours, days at most, everything she bought was gone. That was always a frightening moment because the next drop was always in doubt. In the frenzied moments of plenty we ate frozen TV dinners, casseroles, and chicken potpies. When those were gone, we ate our standard fare: peanut butter sandwiches.

Between our first and second year in the Tudor, a little help came in the form of Ella, the first real adult in our house that I remember. Ella was hired by my mother to help put our house right-side up. A middle-aged African-American woman with quiet superpowers, Ella did that and more. She achieved the impossible. Twice a week she arrived at our house early in the morning after taking several buses from downtown Philadelphia. Undaunted by the twisters we let loose between her comings, she methodically set about cleaning and repairing our lives from the moment she crossed our threshold. She scrubbed, vacuumed, mopped, changed bedding, and did laundry. Then before going home, she made us a home-cooked dinner. She even brought the ingredients with her, on the bus, to make our dinners. The fried chicken, spaghetti with enormous meatballs, meatloaf, and rich beef stews she left for us on the stove smelled of so many good things: onions, garlic, savory spices—and mercy. Overnight she became our mooring, and for the short time she was with us, we held on tight to her.

On the days I knew Ella was scheduled to work I skipped home from school. Ordinarily I would get off the school bus, touch home plate, stopping only long enough to finish my homework, and then race off to be elsewhere. Once Ella became a presence in our house, I lingered. My favorite sensation was cracking open the back door and waiting for the smell of Pine Sol to greet me. That smell meant good things. It meant Ella was home, the house was clean, and we would have dinner that night. I would scurry into the kitchen to talk to her while she put the finishing touches on whatever dish she was making. Initially our conversations were light, but as I got to know and trust her, I talked more about my feelings. My brother remembers overhearing me tell her one afternoon about a girl bullying me at school. With just the right blend of comfort and humor, Ella gave me a squeeze and said, "Baby, I am going to that school of yours and I am going to make that girl a one-eyed Susan." Ella was a grownup willing and wanting to come to my defense.

As quickly as she arrived at our house, Ella had to leave. My mother couldn't afford to pay her. I was heartbroken. Selfishly, I wanted Ella to stay forever and take care of me. She was warm, strong, capable, and dependable. I wished she were my mother. I wonder then and wonder still what Ella thought about our family.

Despite her short tenure, she knew our innards—our craziness, our sadness. When she left, I hope she felt we were kind to her, appreciative, too. Our sanity and functionality were always circling the drain, but when she was with us, she kept them from flowing down to the sewer. We didn't fight as much, we were nicer to each other, and we laughed just a little bit more. Two days a week we were kids with less worry. I hope she knew that.

Following Ella's departure, the facade of our renovated life crumbled. One sunny afternoon I got off the school bus and was walking up the driveway when I saw some of my brothers and sisters standing outside, in front of our house. They were talking and gesturing excitedly. As soon as I reached them, I asked what was going on. They told me that while we were at school and my mother was at work, someone had robbed our house. The thief had taken nearly all our furniture. The only items left were our beds and a few other non-showroom pieces. I was dumbfounded. Who would be so heartless as to steal the chairs we sat on, the dressers we put our clothes in, and the upholstered living room sofas and settees that gave us a touch of class?

Although our house was at the end of a long driveway obscured by a handful of tall mature trees, I was sure someone in the neighborhood had seen a moving-sized truck going in or out of our driveway in the middle of the day. But the police weren't at the house, or out interviewing neighbors to ask if they had seen a truck or suspicious people lurking about. As it turned out, my mother came home from work and told us the thief was our father. In a matter of hours, he coldly and calculatedly emptied our house. No empathy for us, no guilt for him. The theft immediately extinguished the frayed delusional belief we all held that next week, next month, or next year, life in the Tudor would get better.

Not long afterwards—I was still processing my father's burglary of our home—while we were all asleep, my mother's Greenbrier van was stolen. Again, my mother informed us the culprit was my father. Rules of engagement were clearly obsolete to my father. To win the war he was waging against my mother he operated with a take-no-prisoners approach; to him, his children were simply collateral damage. Burned twice, I began to feel sizzling rage toward him but was afraid to express it. I boiled inside with 'whys' that were never answered. Why had my father stolen from us? Why had he taken the one car that seven people, his family, depended on even though he had several expensive cars? Why didn't he act or feel like other people?

Many years later my brother Michael told me the reason that our furniture had been removed: my parents could not pay the decorator, so it had been repossessed. Apparently, the decorator's services cost nearly as much as the house, but my father never explained this or his exact role in the furniture removal to us. Not one to reflect on his behavior or how he might have contributed to the problem, he was comfortable acting as though everything that happened to us was my mother's fault. To my recollection, none of his apartment furniture or cars were ever repossessed. There was, however, one silver lining: he did give us back our van.

Money had always been a problem in my family, but after my father's home invasion it became a much bigger problem. My father didn't share it and my mother couldn't manage it, a noxious mix for children. When my mother did have money, she couldn't create or follow a budget of any kind. This was just the tip of the iceberg. Several layers below were two more serious money-management handicaps. First, she was unable to organize activities that didn't interest her, and paying bills didn't interest her. Second, she only opened personal letters: bills, work checks, and other important correspondence were routinely left untouched. Years later I understood that my mother's inability to cash checks or open and respond to bills was linked to her fear of divulging personal information to banks, companies, and the government. Doing so, she believed, would result in grave harm toward her.

With no organized bill-paying structure in place, all mail except personal letters was tossed unopened into paper and plastic bags randomly strewn around the house. That meant my mother relied on her default system to pay bills: companies had to track *her* down. Since that arrangement didn't work too well, the lights and phone were regularly disconnected. Often enough I would come home from school, flick on the light switch, and find myself in a darkened room. While I took great pains to hide our regular blackouts from friends, I got used to the dark. I knew the lights would eventually come back on. Fortunately, back in the '70s when the electricity was off, the phone still worked. If we discovered the power outage after school, we could still call our mother at work and beg her to pay the bill. Discerning patterns of everyday life, like the need for food and paying bills, was difficult for my mother. Each time we lost our lights or phone service, she seemed genuinely surprised. When her astonishment wore off days later, she would contact the company responsible and sweetly pledge to pay the bill right away.

Similar to how she approached bills, my mother regarded all school forms and announcements as suspicious and another responsibility to ignore. To get what I needed for school, I would approach her early in the morning. In the stretch between her first eye flutters and her agitated runs out the door to get to work, I would plead with her to read and sign my report card or find the dollar or two I needed for a field trip. Years later when my college scholarship and financial aid package required her signature each fall, I became that little girl again imploring her to sign my paperwork. Like clockwork, I would repeatedly call her from my dorm room or apartment before classes started, and beg her to sign the financial documents so I could matriculate. The process took weeks, sometimes months. In the end, she always signed the forms but I never felt victorious. Instead, every year I felt like I was forced to jump into the washing machine of her mind, and only through some stroke of good luck managed to avoid getting completely crushed by her agitator.

Adapting to life with my mother became second nature, down to my clothes. In the Ranch House I wore hand-me-downs and thrift-shop clothes. In the Tudor, nearly all my clothes were from thrift shops. That was the time in my life when my mother took thrift shopping to new heights. Several times each year she would pile us all into the car for Saturday thrift-store shopping sprees. Most of the time she went by herself. When we accompanied her, we followed her around for hours as she combed through racks and baskets of clothes and dejected furniture in second-hand stores owned by local hospital foundations and women's charity leagues. The moment we stepped into the shops, my mother would happily drift off to another world like a reader who plunges deep into a story and can't come up for air until the end. Invariably, we were the only remaining customers politely told, "Fifteen minutes to closing." After checkout, we lugged our loot to the car: brown paper grocery bags of clothes and knick-knacks, stray chairs, lamps, and tables. On the way home, we engaged in a familiar struggle. Things and us duking it out for space.

By late elementary school I had mixed feelings about thrift shops and second-hand clothes. I genuinely liked the opportunity to choose a few items that I wanted to wear, and most of the time could find at least one shirt or skirt reasonably in fashion that didn't advertise its origins. But as good as I would feel wearing something new to me to school, I was mortified that we were poor. All around me, the upscale community where we lived communicated subtly and not so subtly that we were outsiders. From majestic houses whose internal organs had not been removed by the family patriarch, to old-money private schools and country clubs whose membership criteria we would never meet, we were undeniably the riff-raff the Main Line wanted to keep out.

As soon as my father denuded my mother's dream and her home, she began aggressively filling up the house. She had a collecting problem in the Ranch House but back then relegated most of her oversize collection to her bedroom. Not so in the Tudor. Her thrift-shop finds soon populated the two bookends of the house, the breakfast room and the sunroom. Initially my mother organized her discarded items and second-hand furniture in the two rooms neatly, thinking each possession would eventually be used, thrown away, or assigned a more permanent location. But that never happened. Soon her abandoned things had company. More and more items were recklessly thrown into the two rooms. As the piles grew higher the rooms became unusable. Nobody went in or out. I began averting my eyes whenever I walked by either room. Towers of discarded junk, I learned firsthand, are oppressive.

Once the breakfast room and sunroom were full, my mother started filling up the basement. To her, every item she owned had a purpose and a meaning. Letting go of anything was impossible. As children, we didn't understand her hoarding. We only knew that we were slowly being swallowed up from the inside out. Clothes, furniture, books, old toys, paper, mail, newspapers, almost anything

54

you can think of made its way down to the basement. Just as in the bookend rooms, my mother started out with a few tidy piles. She even used water pipes that crisscrossed the basement ceiling to hang dozens of shirts, pants, dresses, and coats. Entropy took over. In no time, the basement took on the colors and dimensions of a landfill, except for the properly-hung clothes on the water pipes. They seemed a visible reminder to my mother that despite everything, she had class and a few organizational skills.

In a bizarre development that took her hoarding to a new level, my mother added a live animal to the below ground repository of things. Sammy, a miniature Doberman pinscher that someone had given us, had aggressively bitten a policeman while a neighborhood kid had taken him out for a stroll, sans leash. The police subsequently issued my mother a stern warning to contain the dog or it would be forcibly removed from our home. Unable to care for us, let alone an animal, my mother inexplicably kept Sammy. Her solution: warehousing him in the basement. To while away the endless hours of boredom and loneliness, Sammy shredded and urinated and defecated on as much of my mother's hoarding collection as he could reach. Months later, when Sammy was given to another family, I was overwhelmed with relief.

From fables to real life, I began feeling kinship with children I perceived were like me. One of these children was a slight girl who showed up one day at our school bus stop. Her name was May. Because she dressed like me, I assumed she too was poor. Maybe it was her clothes or because she was African-American in a largely white community, but within seconds of her arrival a group of white boys at the bus stop started taunting her. "Shut up and leave her alone," I yelled at them. Stunned for a moment, the boys backed off but soon regained their courage and began jeering at her again, wanting a fight. Up until then I had always kept to myself at the bus stop, but something clicked in my head. I physically inserted myself between the boys and May and dared them to take the fight any further. They slunk off. Realistically I'm not sure what I would have done if they had taken me on. I was only nine or ten years old and a skinny kid. But I was tired of bullies.

The boys never picked on May again. That was the first time I recall standing up for another person. Several years later I felt a similar overpowering tug to defend and protect, but this time it was for a fictional character. I stumbled on the book *Manchild in the Promised Land* in a pile of my older brother Alan's books lying around the house. It was summertime and I was bored. The second half of the title, *Promised Land*, intrigued me, although I didn't know what *Manchild* meant. I was only twelve years old. So I started reading and within the first few pages was spellbound. The book chronicles the childhood of the author, Claude Brown. Claude, called Sonny in the book, is an African American boy growing up in Harlem in the 1950s who describes his journey through juvenile hall, boys' schools, a Harlem throbbing with drugs, gangs, and violence, and a larger society that disregards him and his African American peers. Before the book ends, Sonny

56

discovers that Harlem is a big part of him, part of his soul, but to matter to himself and stay alive he decides to physically leave Harlem.

That I was a preteen girl, white, and living in a community so unlike Harlem made no difference to me. I identified with Sonny and could feel each of his heartaches and each of his fears. Throughout the book I was by his side when things were bad and cheered him on when he began to hope for something better. Even the temptations he wrestled with and ultimately rejected—drugs, crime, and fast money—made sense to me. My neighborhood, too, had kids who drank and did drugs. Intuitively, I knew that if I joined them I would be rewarded with belonging to a group that accepted me. Yet somehow, I understood that doing that would require giving up the little control I had over my life. I couldn't do it. I already felt way too vulnerable.

I never talked with my brothers and sisters about these choices. I wish I had. I felt so alone. Our years of warfare, deftly encouraged by my mother, had led us to be cautious of each other. Growing up we didn't rely much on one another or take care of each other as most siblings might. Without a father, we all chose fealty to our mother. If given the chance to remake that decision, I would make a different choice. I would choose my siblings. Banding together, we might have realized our mother was unfit to raise us. We could have helped each other more to survive, inside and outside our craziness. Sadly, in our family Venn diagram, there was a distant mother circle, a far distant father circle, and six little sibling circles, but none of our circles overlapped.

As I gained greater independence in late elementary school at the Tudor, my little circle began overlapping with life outside of my family. In the fall of fifth grade, I was walking alone on a street near my house with no destination in mind when I experienced something entirely new. Within the outline of this memory, I can still smell leafy autumn in the air and see the last thread of summer sunlight dance its way down through a canopy of gigantic trees and touch the ground in front of me. With random thoughts bouncing around in my head that day, I remember nonchalantly looking up at the sky and stopping. The sky and trees were suddenly new to me and beautiful. I was awestruck. In that moment, I had a brand-new realization: I was part of a bigger world. About six months later, I had another similar experience. I was riding my bike home from school one afternoon. Gliding along the two-mile stretch from school to my house I remember feeling strong and peaceful, and then something else I seldom felt: happy. Both experiences subtly shifted my interior monologue. The world I had largely perceived up until that time as small and prison-like was big, bigger than I had ever imagined.

At the Tudor I continued watching and listening, just like I had at the Ranch House. But other experiences outside my family were stretching and challenging me. The most difficult was my relationship with Mrs. Harry, my fourth-grade teacher, whose class I entered just after we moved to the Tudor. Despite the excitement of our new beginning and a house bedecked in finery, I struggled with the transition to a new school and new teacher. The cause may have been that I didn't feel like I fit in, or that my home life continued to be precarious. It's also possible that the moment I met Mrs. Harry I didn't trust or like her. For all those reasons and others, I often came to school unprepared. Mrs. Harry knew this and delighted in asking me for assignments. When I responded with a blank or crimson-tinged face, she would drily remark, "Of course. Naturally you haven't done the assignments." Mrs. Harry's dislike of me evenly matched my dislike of her.

In the spring of fourth grade, Mrs. Harry and I really banged heads. Shortly after Christmas vacation she announced to our class that the entire fourth grade would present *Alice in Wonderland*. She would be the director. As soon as tryouts were scheduled, I decided to audition for the role of Alice. I'm not sure why. Maybe on some unconscious level I wanted to redeem myself with Mrs. Harry, who by then seemed convinced I wasn't capable of much of anything. Mixed in there too must have been my hope that if I got the lead role in the play, my mother would be proud of me; I would be doing something that she would appreciate. Last, and probably buried further down, I was convinced that if I played Alice, I would be more like her—spunky, outspoken and bursting with fearlessness.

Fearing ridicule at home, I didn't tell my mother or any of my brothers or sisters about the play or my desire to play Alice. I practiced my lines in secret. On the day of tryouts, I thought my audition went well, but the next day when the parts were posted on the school wall, my name was not next to Alice, or the understudy role. I thought a long time about why I didn't get the part. Initially I thought it was because of my mother. She wasn't like other moms. She rarely came to school, didn't go to PTA meetings, and barely responded to the letters and forms Mrs. Harry routinely sent home with me requiring a parental signature. Maybe to safeguard a smidgeon of dignity, I eventually concluded that the reason I didn't get the part was because I didn't look like Alice. With my messy, knotted hair and street urchin clothes, I looked more like Little Orphan Annie than Alice in Wonderland.

Weeks after the lead roles were settled, Mrs. Harry reluctantly assigned me the role of a playing card with no lines. I was only in a few scenes. Wearing a sandwich board with the six of hearts on each side, I was instructed to stand at the far back of the stage with other playing cards. I felt deflated. Meantime, the part of Alice went to a beautiful, slender girl with perfectly straight blonde hair who fit the storybook illustrations of the adventurous protagonist: dainty with exquisitely coiffed tresses. As rehearsals got underway, though, I started noticing that Alice had difficulty remembering her lines and saying them with any feeling. Indignant, I couldn't help wondering how she would bring the audience with her through the looking glass. Convinced I could do better, I hoped that somehow I might still get to play Alice. With each successive rehearsal that hope dimmed before flaming out entirely.

Feeling the jilted thespian, I was desperate to prove that I wasn't a loser. One day I got my opportunity. Since my part was so minimal, I spent a great deal of time in rehearsals watching the other actors and tracking the logistics of the production. In one of the last dress rehearsals, I saw Mrs. Harry ordering some of the actors to do something that I knew wouldn't work—I don't remember what. To prevent disaster from happening, I immediately went up to her and earnestly told her that the change she was implementing was doomed. "Mrs. Harry, you are asking Bobby to do this," I said. "But I have been watching everything, and it won't work."

Rather than ask me why, she ordered me off stage and into an auditorium seat to sit out the rest of the rehearsal. I was humiliated. Several days later during the actual performance in front of the school, I noticed Mrs. Harry's change did fail. Feeling good that I had not challenged her for nothing and wasn't stupid, I went up to her after the play and said, "I was right when I told you the change you made Bobby do wouldn't work." Seconds later I was in the principal's office sitting on a hard-wooden bench trying to explain my insolent behavior.

Fourth grade was the worst academic year of my life. I was convinced two things drove my exceedingly poor school performance: the first was my strained relationship with Mrs. Harry, who treated me like an unwanted and undomesticated animal that she had to tolerate for a year. I was right about that. The second was my belief that I wasn't very smart. I was wrong about that. I didn't fully challenge this thought for decades, but the following academic year, my fifth-grade teacher, Mrs. Taylor, allowed me to punch a few holes into it.

Walking into Mrs. Taylor's classroom, I felt as though I had entered the safety of a hospital during wartime. She was warm, smart, and funny. Even more surprising, she liked me. I let the disappointment of fourth grade sink into the past and focused on thriving with a teacher who didn't treat me like I was intellectually disabled. I soaked up everything she taught, particularly her section on Mesopotamia. For months, I was determined to become an archeologist when I grew up. Digging for pottery and remnants of past lives struck me as a fascinating and essential occupation. Something about validating ancient peoples appealed to me. They existed; they meant something . . . to someone.

While my fifth-grade class was busy doing a reading comprehension exercise one afternoon, Mrs. Taylor called me up to her desk. I was doing well in her class. I had completed all the assignments, actively participated in class discussions, and had no run-ins with her, but I was still worried. I was sure I must have done something wrong. So I was surprised when Mrs. Taylor spoke to me in a soft and gentle voice. She began by telling me that I was doing very well in her class and that she was extremely proud of me and of how hard I was working. I beamed. Then she asked, "I'm wondering if you can tell me what happened last year in fourth grade in Mrs. Harry's class? I was looking at your report card from last year and your grades were all Ds and

Cs, but this year you have mostly As. Can you tell me about fourth grade?"

The bottle of carbonated water that was me, the me that had been shaken and shaken by both my parents and Mrs. Harry, finally exploded. In a rush of tangled words and aggrieved feelings, I told Mrs. Taylor that I hadn't liked Mrs. Harry. I told her that she was mean and picked on me. Then, exposing my most secret hurt, I told her that Mrs. Harry made me feel like I was dumb. What I didn't say, because I didn't know how, was that Mrs. Harry was another adult in my life who didn't give me much thought. From the minute I stepped into her fourth-grade classroom, she was convinced I was destined to fail, and for an entire year I dutifully met that expectation. After I finished, Mrs. Taylor was quiet and then in a firm whisper said, "I want you to continue doing well here. You are very bright and deserve to be at the top of the class." Her words were a perfect kiss on my forehead.

While I was busy experiencing life outside my family, much of it positive, I received a jolting reminder that one of my early childhood traumas was still with me, albeit in a half-dormant state. It happened when I was out riding bikes with two girlfriends in my neighborhood. Two large Doberman pinschers that had gotten out of their fenced enclosures saw us in their scope and charged. Paralyzed by their speed and bared teeth, I panicked and stopped pedaling; my girlfriends kept going. I thought if I weren't moving the dogs would assume I was non-threatening and would run right past me. I was wrong. The larger of the two dogs made a big circle around me gnashing his teeth and barking maniacally. A small mound of white spittle foamed at the bottom of its mouth. Distracted by his herding action and teeth, I missed the other dog leaping straight at me.

Before I knew it, I was bitten multiple times on my thigh just below my shorts. Terrified, I kicked at the attacking dog's head, forcing a temporary retreat. Tears mixed with mucus covered my face, and then I started shaking. Alone with two vicious snarling dogs that were highly motivated to finish their job, I knew I had no choice but to get back on my bike. Jamming the right pedal forward, I pushed off with a great heave and headed straight for home. The dogs ran after me for a short while, then gave up and just stopped. All the way home I could hear them barking at me, the intruder. My thigh bore witness to their indignation—bleeding bite wounds and an imprint of the attack dog's canine teeth.

Reaching my house, I ran to the back door breathless and crying. No one was home except my brother Alan. Through streaming tears, I told him that two Dobermans belonging to a neighbor were out running loose on the street and had attacked me. Still shaking, I looked down and saw blood gushing down my leg from the deep bites on my thigh. Speaking authoritatively but gently, Alan told me to go upstairs and run a bath. He would come up soon to help me clean the wounds. Trembling from shock I moved to do what he told me, but on the way up the stairs, I remembered and froze; I would be naked in front of the brother who had molested me in the Ranch

House. I panicked. I had never told anyone about the sexual abuse except my mother when it happened, and since then I tried never to think about it. Suddenly exposing myself to my brother felt more dangerous than a circling pack of dogs eager to maul me.

Several minutes later Alan came up to the third floor and leaned over the tub. Taking great care with my physical injuries, he pressed a towel against the cuts to stanch the bleeding, then found a broken piece of soap to disinfect them—we had no doctor to call for a tetanus shot. Minutes after he started, I told him I was fine, he could leave. As he walked away, I felt raw and jagged. Sitting in the tub of blood-tinged water, I emotionally re-experienced his abuse. I felt angry, upset, and scared, feelings that catapulted me into an emotional tailspin that lasted for days.

Life in the Tudor didn't have the same number of cliffhangers as life in the Ranch House, but it was far from uninteresting. Sometime during our second year there, my mother came up with a plan to enforce better behavior in all of us. Possibly sensing that my father was slipping away from her, she arranged for him to come to our house every few weeks to spank us, one after the other. The arrangement continued for months. It was a surreal form of punishment: we were never told what it was that we had done wrong, and the absence of any reasonable temporal relationship between an infraction that we may or may not have committed and the spanking consequence was truly bizarre.

Of course, the crazy crime-and-punishment formula intended to motivate us to change our behavior was colossally unsuccessful. What it did achieve, to all our surprise, was the creation of a brief underground solidarity movement. Since my parents had requested we all line up in an adjacent room to wait our turn to be beaten, we quickly created a book-sharing system. Somehow each sibling up to be whacked managed to stuff a paperback book in his or her pants to minimize the sting (hard books would have been too obvious). Through unpracticed comical sleights of hand, I would take the book from Gillian as she rounded the corner after getting her thwacking, and stuff it quickly between my underwear and my pants. After my beating, I would pass closely by Patrick, who was next up, and slip him the book. I'm sure my father had to have felt the book in our pants, but he never let on. We all played our parts in his and my mother's theater of the absurd.

That same year, my father announced with his signature disdain, "I am divorcing your mother." Within weeks, my mother became very ill. Several of us had had the flu, and then my mother came down with it. But her trajectory was different. One day she was home and the next she was in the hospital. No adult ever explained to me why she had to go to the hospital. The little kids—Gillian, my brother Patrick, and I—were trundled off to stay with two different women, both aspiring friends of my mother. I don't remember where my older siblings went.

For the first week or so of my mother's hospitalization, we stayed with the Larsons, a family my mother initially met through my father—the Larson dad was also a psychiatrist. Although we had attended one or two Christmas parties at the Larsons' house and spent a couple of days with them in their rustic family cabin in Maine one summer, they felt more like relatives you see only on special occasions, not close family friends you move in with during a crisis.

With the benefit of hindsight, I have an inkling why the Larsons volunteered to help my mother out: they were dazzled by her. She was the sparkler at every gathering. Mrs. Larson and my mother's conversations ran the gamut from everyday pedestrian events to literary works and back. "I have always been so curious about Shakespeare. Haven't you, Gloria?" my mother trilled to Mrs. Larson, during our Maine visit. "What a mind he has. Can you imagine writing dramas like *Hamlet*, *King Lear*, and *Macbeth* and hysterically funny plays like *A Midsummer Night's Dream*, *Twelfth Night*, and *The Merry Wives of Windsor*? What I would do to play any of his female leads, especially in London at the Royal Shakespeare Theatre!" My mother said dreamily.

Mrs. Larson uttered a deep throaty laugh. "Maria, you could play any Shakespeare character, male or female!" Inspired by her audience's free-flowing admiration, my mother moved from disclosing her true theater ambitions to telling Mrs. Larson how difficult we all were. "Sometimes I feel like I can't go on. The kids take so much out of me, always fighting. David hasn't been around much to help, he's so busy with work. That's why he lives in an apartment near the hospital. But I am sure he will be back soon," my mother said with over-the-top pathos. In response, Mrs. Larson's somber face and watery eyes communicated complete compassion for my mother. Seeing that she was still hooked, my mother changed subjects again, this time to another injustice du jour, our most recent electricity cutoff. "When they shut off the electricity without a notice, I couldn't believe it. I know I had paid the bill. So, I got on the phone right away and . . ."

As a child, I thought my mother's acquaintances must have wondered if my father existed. There didn't seem to be any proof. He was completely absent from our everyday lives. He never took us to dinner, spent any holidays with us, celebrated anyone's birthday, or attended any school events. Because he was more a stick figure drawing than a flesh-and-blood member of our family, I was surprised that when the divorce was announced the Larsons seemed stunned. I assumed anyone who had any familiarity with our family was aware of my father's hate for my mother and us. It seemed impossible to miss. But I had also seen how my mother consistently watered down my father's infidelities and cruelties, and her own behavior in our lives. She seemed to dangle dangerously between the world she lived in and the world she imagined she lived in.

Regardless of what they thought or felt about the divorce, the Larsons and just one other woman who worked hard for a while at being my mother's friend generously agreed to care for us during my mother's hospitalization. By day Mrs. Larson was a piano teacher, by night a mom. Friendly and enthusiastic, she treated us the same way I imagine she treated all her piano students. She believed we could do it—unfortunately the *it* was never quite clear. By contrast, her cerebral, carefully spoken husband appeared remote and stern; both parents, however, were emotionally connected to their musically talented and exceptionally bright children. It was a family that worked. At dinner Dr. Larson would ask his kids, similar ages to Gillian, Patrick, and me, to tell him how school was and what they had done that day. Each kid would share highlights from her or his school day, saving nuggets of new learning for the end of the presentation. As they chattered away, Dr. Larson asked them to share their opinions about what they were learning: *What did you think about what the teacher said? Is what you learned related to any other issues you're discussing?* I'd never seen anything like it before: tabletop respect and civilized discussion.

It was tough not to feel like an interloper at the Larsons. Their home was so different from mine it could have been in another galaxy. No rooms were openly or even slyly obstructed by stuff. Family members didn't use high-pitched echolocating or screaming when they had something to say to one another. The house was clean and meals were delicious and served at normal mealtime hours. Most remarkable of all was that despite what appeared to me to be a family gene of stiffness, they deeply loved one another. Once all that goodness began to register, staying with them felt increasingly stressful. It might have been more order than I could manage at the time, or that I was preoccupied with the fear that my mother might die. Probably both.

My mother's illness made everything feel shaky. It was a different feeling from all the times she exploded in anger telling us she easily could have or should have shipped us off to other relatives, foster care, or, more frighteningly, parts unknown. Those blowups had a rhythm and a script: my mother would begin by haranguing us for being ungrateful and lacking. Then, she would drive her talk upwards with intensity before reaching her final melodramatic point, which always began with, "You know, I could have sent you all off to live with your cousins, although I am not sure they would have taken you in. Or, I could have sent you off to live with total strangers. But I didn't. Why? Because of my commitment to keeping us all together as a family. I am keeping that commitment even though your father doesn't help with anything!"

Once she got started, my mother could continue for a long time. "Taking care of all of you is horrible—I can't stand it! This house is a mess. You're all rude and disrespectful. I'm working myself to the bone trying to keep you together, and this is what I get?" I hated it when my mother started talking this way, even though I increasingly felt skeptical about her passion for our togetherness. Fortunately, I eventually became inured to her monologues and stopped worrying that she would actually terminate her parental rights. Her tirades were what she did when she boiled over with anger and frustration. But her hospitalization changed everything. There was no pattern to follow, and I didn't know what would happen next.

To manage my anxiety and keep a low profile at the Larsons, I tried to make myself invisible. I tamped down my natural tendency to question and tried to mimic their children's manners and comportment. I was worried that they might have to correct me, and I didn't want them to think I didn't know manners. I knew some but not many. Their children, however, seemed to know all the rules, what was acceptable behavior, what was not, and most important, what their parents expected of them. If my mother had any expectations of us, other than the generic "be better kids," they were a well-guarded secret. Since I didn't know what the Larsons expected of me, I avoided asking for anything.

One morning at the Larsons', I woke up and realized it was picture day at my school. Not wanting to bother Mrs. Larson and feeling too ashamed to ask her to help me find something nice to wear, especially since I didn't have many clothes and the ones I did bring were more than worn looking, I decided not to tell her. Rifling through the brown paper bag of clothes I had brought with me, I found a thrift store outfit I liked, a red corduroy skirt with suspenders and red cotton turtleneck. Smoothing them out, I thought they looked OK. To appear to the school as though my mother had helped me get ready for the photo, I put my hair in a high ponytail and found a white ribbon to tie around it.

Before leaving for school that day I remember feeling sad, lost, and lonely for my family. They were missing so many necessary parts, but I had made a little burrow in the mess and pain and called it home.

After staying the week with the Larsons, we were driven over to another woman's house. Alma was a divorced single parent and wannabe friend of my mother who was as welcoming as the Larsons but more relaxed. Because she had only one son who wasn't around too much, I exhaled, confident there were no real or imagined contests for best all-around kid. Possibly to celebrate that I was out of a pressure cooker of sorts or to release some of the emotional stress that had been building up from all the unknowns regarding my mother, I got a sudden and unexplainable urge to smoke a cigarette. I had never smoked a cigarette before or even thought about trying one. But something toggled in my brain and the urge was overwhelming. I had to do it.

Moments after Alma, a smoker, stepped out to run an errand I looked around the house for a pack of cigarettes. No luck. Then I saw one of her handbags lying on top of a newish white washing machine in the laundry room. Certain she would have an extra pack somewhere in her bag I stuck my hand in. Just as my fingers curled around the cellophane covering of a soft pack of cigarettes, a ladies' brand, the back door opened and Alma walked in. Not sure what she was seeing, her initial look of surprise rapidly disintegrated into a tense and disapproving stare. With her voice shaking slightly, she asked what I was doing. Just as startled as she was, I answered, "I'm just looking for my ball." It was a ridiculous answer, but it was the first thing that popped into my head. I had been caught red-handed and was terrified. I knew she knew I was lying. But letting her think I was trying to steal from her seemed much better than telling her I wanted to smoke one of her cigarettes, to make the tension eating at me go away for just a little while.

After a few weeks in the hospital my mother came home. That's when she told us how sick she had been. Like all her stories, though, her flu saga was perforated with plenty of holes. When she got sick, how she got to the hospital, and how she came home were presented as unwrapped and incomplete parts of a larger whole. As she lay in the middle of her bed half-buried by her friends—clothes, magazines, candy wrappers, blankets—and surrounded by us, she decided to discuss one event in the hospital in more detail. She began her story.

"I knew that I was sick and getting sicker. Only my flu, not any of yours, had turned into pneumonia. I felt so weak and couldn't breathe. I knew that was it, it was the end. There was nothing else I could do. I was going to die. Then a miracle happened, kids. I heard a comment." Solemnly, and using suspense like elite chefs use saffron—selectively and just the right amount—she dramatically led us to the comment.

"I was lying in my hospital bed feeling foggy when I heard my doctor say to a nurse, right outside my door, 'She isn't going to make it.' It was that comment that inspired me to fight for my life. I remember thinking, I can't let that happen! I have to live! I have children!" My mother looked at all of us triumphantly. Her conviction, she said, the one where she decided to live for us, is what enabled her to get better. Riveted, I didn't flinch. I was terrified that if I moved or said anything, I would be the one to make her sick again, and then she really would die.

Not only did I completely believe my mother's story, from that moment on I was convinced that for her to stay alive, I would have to squash my needs or wants. I would have to be perfect.

Not long after my mother's near-fatal illness and return home, my father roared into our house one weekend morning accompanied by Alicia, who by then was his constant companion. He and my mother, who was still weak from pneumonia and resting on her bed, immediately began yelling at each other, something about their divorce. Their screaming ripped open the day.

Cowering in a corner of the room, several of my siblings and I watched as my father towered over my mother, who was up and standing, yelling profanities at her. Suddenly, the glass safety dome that I imagined physically protected my mother shattered with one aggressive push from my father. As my mother attempted to gain her balance, my brother Michael rushed in to defend her. Infuriated, my father turned his wrath on him, chasing Michael out of the master bedroom and into the bedroom he shared with Patrick. Then he threw him into an empty glass aquarium in the corner. The terror and fear of that moment lives on as a four-inch scar across my brother's back.

Throughout the high-decibel exchange between my parents, and my father's angry pursuit of Michael, my father's girlfriend stood off to the side, body slack, in a pose of indifference. Alicia was beautiful, like my mother, with similar tawny coloring and dark hair. But Alicia had brown eyes, not blue, and the elongated neck and lithe body of a ballet dancer, not the body of a woman who had birthed six children. In a still, she looked like a Modigliani painting. But she was a beauty with a hard expression. Throughout she showed no compassion for my mother or us. Aligned with my father and his belief that my mother was the *problem*, she happily gloated over my mother's annihilation. She was the new chosen one.

Not long after this epic fight, my mother told us that our father was moving to Boulder, Colorado, to set up a new psychiatric practice and was taking Alicia with him. With the divorce proceedings underway and irreversible, and the news that my father was moving, life in the Tudor fell apart even more precipitously. My mother's carefully-constructed fantasy life of marriage to a successful physician disintegrated. Things got grim. My mother continued to go to work each day, but for months had little energy for other activities. She dully went to the store to buy food, but only when our complaints or fights over the bare remains of it became intolerable. On the weekends, she mostly stayed in her master bedroom sleeping or reading magazines, concealed under blankets and surrounded, as always, by heaps of things that made her feel less alone and less empty, things she believed would one day prove their usefulness.

By then, my mother's master bedroom was a dispirited place that never recovered from my father's physical raid. Vestiges of the once tastefully-decorated room that promised marital renewal now broadcast the dissolution of my parents' contract. Junk was everywhere and the once plush off-white carpet contained several large irregularly shaped dark brown coffee stains. The floor-length brocaded curtains with their tassel ties stood alone, no longer accenting high-end furniture and gracefully placed works of art. My father had removed those pieces. Apparently, the curtains could not be returned for cash. It was in this room that my mother hid herself and tried to reconcile her heartbreaking loss. She was inconsolable. I remember climbing on to her bed and chattering away to her, emphasizing all that was positive in her life, including our love and need for her. I thought I could make her happy. Nothing I said changed how she felt. My father had disgraced and betrayed her. She seemed to have lost the compass points that gave her direction. I felt so sad for her, and helpless. I couldn't make her better.

Although my mother was in great emotional pain over my father, I welcomed the announcement that he was relocating to Colorado. It meant no more hittings, freedom from his dripping vitriol toward my mother, and termination of my forced one-on-one outings with him.

Widely spaced, they had continu
early childhood and were sti'
signature expensive driving gl
me up from our den of desp
scheduled. Each time I opene
world of luxury sports cars
music, and not a single child·

typically ate din
not somethi
would re
refrige
bar

The rhythm and focus of our ꙅꙫꙭꙭ
together remained constant: an endless series of stops. First
the dry cleaners to pick up his tailored suits and shirts, then
a swing by the European car store to get a rare part he
wanted for one of his sports cars, and finally hours in art
galleries or museums so he could study the paintings and
sculptures that he found interesting. Making the outings
even more unbearable was my father's habit of lapsing into
baby talk with me, while patting the top of my head as he
drove. He started doing this when I wasn't much out of
babyhood myself, and continued doing it on every play date
until he left for Colorado, by which time I was in sixth
grade. I hated his habit. When his two-year-old personality
emerged, I froze. Deeply uncomfortable, I never
responded.

Since my father typically picked me up in the late
afternoon and didn't finish his last very important task until
dark, occasionally the required afternoons stretched into
inescapable sleepovers. On those days, we would arrive
back at his apartment in downtown Philadelphia around
nine o'clock at night. By then I was tired, bored, and very
hungry. Since my father didn't eat much during the day and

her around ten at night, feeding a child was ng he thought about. Once in the door, he ignedly look through his kitchen cabinets and rator for something to give me. They were always , except for the usual: jars of baby food and bottles and ottles of pills. Sometimes there was a surprise box of crackers. His looking never got too far. In seconds, he was distracted and went off to make a call or attend to something else. When he turned his attention back to me, he would announce he was leaving to find something for us to eat from a neighborhood store with late-night hours. I stayed in the apartment and waited for him to return.

Once my father left Pennsylvania for Colorado, I thought my mother would recover and life would harmonize. That didn't happen. Her mood swings continued. Somehow she consistently made it to work, but at home she went predominantly internal. The impact of this shift on our everyday lives was even fewer meals with any structure, greater laundry buildup than usual, and more fighting between us. For two years, her animated stage face was replaced by a hollow look. Despite her ghostly detachment, she still managed to erupt at us with surprising frequency.

Before and after the divorce, holidays were a major catalyst for many of my mother's upsets. Somehow the responsibility of meeting holiday expectations seemed to put her over the edge. One minute things were fine and the next she was raging. Hands down, Thanksgiving was the holiday with the most blow-ups. The first bad turkey day I remember started before the divorce, when the same two women who housed us during my mother's pneumonia, Mrs. Larson and Alma, decided each would help my mother by inviting us to Thanksgiving dinner. Not wanting to disappoint either host, my mother accepted both invitations, scheduling the first dinner for early afternoon and the second right afterwards. Our instructions were not to tell either host family that we were attending two dinners. Free food and holiday cheer would seem a winning combination, but the duplicity of our act and my mother's directive to eat slowly and not too much at the first house so we didn't offend the next hostess was stressful. So too was her added expectation that we be witty and charming at each meal. Repeating the same stories that we had told hours earlier to a second audience with a staged freshness felt fraudulent.

When Thanksgiving rolled around the next year and my mother accepted the same two dinner invitations, we rebelled. None of us wanted to participate in the deception again. My mother responded with an all-out offensive of her own. In a crushing verbal assault complete with neck veins popping, she screamed, "I go to work every day and for what? To come home to you ungrateful, self-absorbed brats?" Not surprisingly she prevailed. We repeated the charade for another year. It never mattered to my mother that we didn't want to be her traveling sideshow; she reveled in a full day of attention from two different crowds.

For reasons unclear to me, we stopped double-dipping on turkey with the Larsons and Alma. I wonder if it had anything to do with their finally giving up the chase. Like so many other women and men before them, they had doggedly pursued my mother, excited to be near a charismatic person whom they described as "brilliant," "worldly," and "artistically astute." Eventually, though, all my mother's devotees stopped running after her, surrendering, I imagine, to both exhaustion and defeat.

With no one to take on the responsibility of preparing a turkey for us, my mother gave it a try herself, with disastrous results. Organizationally challenged with little interest in cooking, my mother automatically felt overwhelmed and burdened by the day. Things would start off fine in the morning, but a short while later a half-baked turkey was lying on its side at the bottom of the kitchen trashcan. I don't recall any specific precipitating event; no doubt it was something one of us said or did that set her off. The first time she dramatically and aggressively yanked the turkey from the oven and tossed it into the garbage, I felt sick to my stomach. It was clear to me that my family didn't work, and I was powerless to do anything about it. The second time she completed the sequence so seamlessly it seemed a natural part of our holiday preparations. Her annual turkey toss reminded us that we were bad kids and that she suffered from us. After a requisite penalty period, intended for us to reflect on our wrongdoings, my mother would dramatically pull the turkey out of the garbage and we would sit down to eat whatever could be salvaged. Even if merriment stole its way back into our conversation, it was never enough to cover our emotional bruises already turning a deep purple.

Despite the penumbra of darkness in our lives, my brothers and sisters and I were successful in getting ourselves to and from school. And, we occasionally entertained each other with our own offbeat brand of humor. Michael would reenact the ridiculousness of our parent's pact to hit us monthly, first mimicking my mother's strained complaints to my father about how miserable we made her life, and then pantomiming my father hurting his hand from hitting a book instead of a bottom. I would double over from laughing so hard. Comic relief gave us a way to laugh through what chronically made no sense in our lives—our parents' bizarre behaviors, the spankings, our father's theft of our house and car, the Thanksgiving dinner charades. Tinged with uneasiness, our laughter told our story—for anyone listening.

Once my father was gone busy reinventing himself out west, our post-apocalyptic world in the Tudor didn't last long. We had to move. What did endure from that stretch in our life, however, was the beginning of a decades-long twisted dynamic between my parents, in which each made negative claims about the other that contained, perhaps, more than a kernel of truth.

For years, my father could not speak about my mother without unrestrained contempt beginning with, "Your mother is crazy." This opener was always followed by a detailed list of her crimes, each one dressed up and defended by an explanation: she's a hoarder—"I couldn't live with your mother and all her junk"; she can't manage money—"I gave your mother plenty of child support but she can't pay bills or keep anything organized" (my mother did have significant money-management problems, but my father's erratic and far below-poverty-level child support was the greater culprit); and, she is unpredictable—"Your mother is so unstable, you can't talk to her because she goes off the deep end in blazing anger and hysteria."

In turn, my mother would describe how my father emotionally tortured her: "On our wedding night and during our honeymoon, your father prevented me from eating, so I would be stick thin: I nearly passed out from hunger," and how he was severely psychiatrically compromised. "When your father was in his residency program, he had to undergo analysis as part of his psychiatric training. It was really helping him: he began to act more human. But in the middle of his treatment his analyst died, then he regressed." My mother never shied away from implying that she was the sane one and that it was my father who had plummeted free-fall back into madness with no hope of recovery.

My parents' aggressive messaging campaigns were profoundly distressing. Each was determined to assert psychological well-being while condemning the other to a purgatory for the insane, a holding tank for people requiring a mental health overhaul. Throughout all the back-and-forth nastiness, my father never once said he wanted to reunite with my mother. To my amazement, however, my mother routinely suspended her negative profiling of my father to discuss how wonderful he was, and how much she wished she were still married to him. In those pauses she repeatedly described the moment she met him: "The first time I saw your father I was smitten. He looked like a Greek god." From there, she would launch into detailed descriptions of his loving phone calls to her early in their marriage: "Your father could be so kind over the phone, so caring and gentle. He would ask me how I was, how my day went." When she exited these dreamy states, her head hung down. Against her will, she reentered an existence she perceived as deeply defective.

Even more perplexing than my mother's idyllic musings about my father was her scheduled depression every year on their wedding anniversary. On that day as well as the few days that preceded and followed it, she would become withdrawn, sullen, and barely able to function. When I learned the reason for her despair—she was grieving her divorce—I was incredulous. How she could feel *any* positive emotion for the man who had treated her and his own children so cruelly was beyond my comprehension.

Chapter Three

Surviving

Like a tire that begins to wobble jerkily on the freeway before it blows out, life in the Tudor became increasingly unstable. My mother could no longer pay the bills and we needed to get out quickly. After three years of drama, confusion, and unrelenting sadness, we packed up the house. Our load was figuratively and literally heavy. In addition to transporting the used furniture we had collected since my father's repossession of the originals, along with our clothes and kitchenware, we moved many of my mother's hoarded items. She threw some things away but happily relocated a sizeable portion of her collection to the new house, a large rental three miles away in a neighboring town. To hide her habit and feign a fresh start, she had us move her vast ensemble of transitional objects directly into the basement. Everything stayed exactly where we put it for four years, until we moved again.

Our new home, a Colonial three-story rental, was in the same school district as the Tudor. Since I was just beginning seventh grade, I started at the junior high near our new house. Like me, the rest of my brothers and sisters moved on to the next grade at various public schools in the district, except Alan, who continued at the same Quaker school he had been enrolled in at the Tudor. Alan's enrollment in a private school represented another unexplained occurrence in our life. Fortunately, the Quaker school seemed a good fit for him, notwithstanding the fact that he was the go-between for the school administration and my parents regarding tuition payments. Extracting payment from either parent had to be a tedious and exasperating process for Alan and the school. More maddening for the school, I imagine, was that by the time one payment was made the next tuition payment was due.

The rental was nearly as large as the Tudor. It had five bedrooms and five baths. Built in 1900, the house was not constructed with the same aristocratic gracefulness as the Tudor, nor had it been kept up in the same manner, but it was still dignified. Soaring ceilings on both the first and second floors accentuated the hardwood floors beautifully blemished with age. A grand and wide wooden staircase in the center of the first floor met the front door in a sweep of great importance, a nod to the aspirations of previous inhabitants. Possibly because of what it implied, we never used the front staircase. We all used the back stairs: narrow, dark, and to the point. As with the Tudor, there were lots of bedrooms. Again, the girls were placed on the third floor, my brothers and mother on the second. Because of our move, there was no denying it: the do-over in the Tudor had failed. This transition was an act of desperation, a forced migration, and we knew it. Even if we secretly hoped that life would improve, we could no longer ignore that for as long as we lived together as a family unit with my mother at the helm, dystopia would be a permanent roommate. Hope had mostly been replaced by a weary, unsteady focus on survival.

For four years in the Colonial, we all pretty much did our own thing. Inside the house, we usually interacted only when we had to; outside, we were individual acts, participating in separate interests and activities that offered definition and membership status in clubs that wanted us. A few of my siblings played sports and worked jobs; others became involved in activities that provided different opportunities to belong, to feel alive. In the smoldering ruins of an emotionally bombed-out family, home predominantly became a drive-through way station. There was, however, one bright side to our family disbandment: there was much less fighting, even over food.

Food continued to be a scarce resource in the Colonial but we didn't battle over it like we had when we were younger, probably because by then we had all figured out how to supplement our diets outside the house. Whenever I had 50 cents, mostly from mother's helper jobs in the neighborhood, I skipped down the street to Hymie's Delicatessen. Still, hunger was an issue. When I arrived home from school in the evening, finding any semblance of an organized meal was like winning the lottery. Although some of my older siblings occasionally stepped in to buy groceries to complement my mother's hit-or-miss shopping, it wasn't enough to stabilize the food supply.

And even during the moments when we did have food, it was impossible to escape the atmospheric emptiness and desperateness of our home. But neither our environment nor six kids going in six directions seemed to bother my mother. She went to work and came home, spacey and disengaged, except for scheduled emotional breakdowns, when she decided it was time to scream at us.

As soon as I started junior high school, I discovered that unlike in elementary school I was now in a world that provided structured opportunities to stay away from home every day until the last minute possible. Beginning in seventh grade I signed up for a sports team every season: field hockey in the fall, gymnastics in the winter, and lacrosse in the spring. Athletically I was never a standout or even particularly skillful. That's not why I played sports. I played because they gave me an opportunity to physically move—I was a fidgety kid with a lot of energy—and be part of a functioning group, a family of sorts. Those are the reasons I chased balls and tumbled on mats. And there was one more perk: every team had a coach, an adult in charge.

What I didn't understand and wasn't too bothered by in junior high, or later in high school where I continued my afterschool sports career, was how bad I was at sports. Only now can I see how my anxiety and the roots of it may have factored into my consistent second-string status. In field hockey and lacrosse, I shied away from balls thrown in my direction at speeds greater than a gentle lob; in gymnastics, I was afraid of going backwards—a truly career-ending affliction for anyone in the sport. Both fears, I believe, sprouted up in the thorny world of my childhood.

Projectile objects thrown my way may have unconsciously resembled an instrument of our early childhood warfare. Instead of seizing the ball and scoring, I followed my instinct and got out of the way. My fear of going backwards in gymnastics was even simpler to understand: I didn't know what was behind me. Throwing myself into a void seemed like a bad idea. What had kept me mostly safe in my family was maintaining a 360-degree view of activity around me. Logically, albeit unconsciously, I must have decided that giving that up while still vulnerable at home wasn't an option. Naturally, I didn't advance much in gymnastics.

Beyond sports, my new junior high offered me something else I needed, a role model. Without knowing that I was looking for one, I found a fill-in parent in my seventh-grade gym teacher, Mr. Russo, a young, newly-certified physical education instructor. Like my fifth-grade teacher Mrs. Taylor, Mr. Russo was caring and seemed to get a kick out of me. And he was funny too, with a ready set of one-liners and a can-do attitude that was infectious. I tried to be around him as much as possible. Somehow sensing that I needed a bit of extra attention, he spent a few minutes each gym class talking to me, asking how I was doing. That little bit of attention went a long way. His tracking just a few of the details of my life made me feel good. I even enjoyed it when he teased me. One day I was trying to slip through the gym doors undetected, because I was late to gym class, when I heard Mr. Russo bellow from the back of the gym, "Nikki Parrish! You're late! Get all 68 pounds of you over here immediately!" His gentle reprimand made me feel special. I blushed, apologized, and ran to take my place tingling with the feeling that I mattered to someone.

Mr. Russo's belief in me gave me hope that maybe I would amount to something. I can still remember him yelling words of encouragement as I struggled to ascend the twenty-foot rope hanging from the gym ceiling one day in gym class. "Keep going, you can make it! Climb by putting hand over hand but keep the rope between your feet to help you—squeeze it with your feet as you pull yourself up. Come on, Nikki, you're doing great! Remember, there is no such word as can't!" Those words were support enough for me to ignore the rope burn on my thighs, the screaming muscles in my arms, and the embarrassment of my required girl's gym uniform, a one-piece outfit with metal snaps up the chest and billowing bloomer shorts that left my thighs exposed to the itchy rope. On the requisite rope climbs, I nearly always touched the thick heavy metal crossbeam that anchored the rope at the ceiling, and beamed with satisfaction each time I did.

Because Mr. Russo was my gym teacher from seventh through ninth grade, my sex education teacher in eighth grade, and the girls' gymnastics team coach, the imprint he left on me was the most positive of any adult in my young life. After two fun confidence-building years as Mr. Russo's self-appointed sidekick in seventh and eighth grade, without warning I stepped into ninth grade with a changing body. A whole set of sex hormones suddenly announced themselves, and Mr. Russo abruptly changed from father figure to hybrid father-figure/love-interest. Natural as this was, when combined with my Swiss-cheese self-esteem the outcome was destined to be calamitous. And it was. At gymnastics team practice one afternoon I was waiting for Mr. Russo to spot me on part of my floor exercise routine. Seconds before my turn, he announced that he had to leave to attend a school meeting. Upset that he was not available to help me, I muttered something under my breath. Mr. Russo couldn't hear what I said but knew from my tone and facial expression that I had said something disrespectful.

Looking directly at me, his jaw set and unflinching, he asked me to tell him what I had said. I didn't say a word. He asked me again. Head down, I avoided his eyes, scared I would get in trouble. Sensing I would not yield, he told me my behavior was rude; then he said, "Nikki, I don't know what you said, but I want you to know I am very disappointed in you." His admonishment, entirely appropriate, was more than I could bear. Devastated, I turned and ran out of the gym, tears flowing fast. Pounding my way through the empty school hallways, I was sure my life was over. Ironically, I remember enjoying the echo of my footsteps reverberating off the tile walls as I ran. It seemed the perfect background music for my humiliation and drama—a pure teenager moment. Minutes later I hid myself in the girls' locker room.

The heartache I felt that day was a double helix: I felt rejected by the one adult person who had shown concern for me for longer than an academic school year, and I was depressed that Mr. Russo would never be my future husband. Our interaction had cleared up any confusion about that. I had to grow up a lot more before I understood that Mr. Russo had not failed me. By giving me both attention and boundaries, he was modeling something I desperately needed and wanted. It helped too that he sent the girls' basketball coach into the girls' locker room that fateful afternoon to make sure I was OK.

During my adolescent unfolding, a few experiences further confirmed that I was on my own. The most significant was a babysitting incident that happened when I was twelve. As soon as we moved to the Colonial, I realized that I was old enough to be a mother's helper and could earn money to pay for things I needed and wanted, including food. After getting to know some of the kids in our new neighborhood, I found out which families had young children and promptly introduced myself to the mothers. Soon I was getting lots of babysitting jobs; most involved my watching kids in the early evenings or during the day on Saturday or Sunday, parents not far away.

In the Colonial, my mother continued to be only vaguely aware of our whereabouts and what we were doing, so I was surprised when a woman named Claudia called at the house one day asking to speak to me. She had a two-year-old toddler and wanted to know if I could babysit her. She explained that she had met my mother through an event at the television station and my mother had given her my name, assuring her that I was an experienced babysitter. Setting aside my shock that my mother even knew how I was spending my time, I told her I was available. I didn't realize, though, that I would soon be solely responsible for a two-year-old for twelve-hour periods in an inner-city Philadelphia neighborhood I didn't know.

With no training or shadowing period, I began babysitting for Claudia on the weekends. She would pick me up at my house on the outskirts of Philadelphia Saturday morning and drive back to her apartment in the city. The apartment was tiny. It had a small kitchen, living room, and bathroom, and two small bedrooms, one for Claudia and one for her daughter, Lily. As soon as we got back to the apartment I took charge of Lily. Claudia would either run errands, meet with friends, or sleep before going to work. Claudia was a nightclub jazz singer and didn't leave for work until six or seven in the evening, so I always spent the night. The next day around noon, after she woke up, she would pack Lily in her car and drive me back to my house. The arrangement didn't feel right, from the start.

By contrast, the tot in my care was delightfully right. Lily was a bubbly, inquisitive, very happy two-year-old. Flyaway red curls framed her delicate face, which included Cupid's-bow lips and large sparkling blue eyes that immediately invited you to play. Her joy for play was so contagious that as soon as she and I were alone, I dropped to the floor and into her universe. We chased each other, built forts with sheets and kitchen chairs, and scurried around in dress-up clothes—Claudia's old clothes and shoes. And we read, lots and lots of books. I adored Lily and our play.

One evening after I had played a robust round of games with Lily, fed her, and put her to bed, I received a phone call. It was after nine in the evening and I was already in my pajamas: a pair of panties and one of my brother Michael's long tee shirts. The man on the other end of the line asked for Claudia. I told him that she wasn't home. Casually and with implied intimacy, he told me, "Claudia is going to meet me back at the apartment after her current jazz set, but she forgot to give me the address. Can you give it to me?" His friendly tone made me think they were good friends and that Claudia had arranged to meet him. Foolishly, I gave him the address.

Twenty minutes later there was a knock at the door. I opened it and a large mustached man with slicked-back brown hair in his thirties, dressed in a button-down shirt and jeans, pushed his way into the apartment. In an urgent raspy voice, he asked for Claudia. When I told him that she wasn't home yet, he became agitated and began nervously scanning the little apartment. Before I could say another word, he grabbed and pushed me against the front door. For just a moment I was angry with myself for letting the man in before Claudia got home. That thought didn't linger. The man pinned both my arms above my head with one hand. With the other he began pulling at my tee shirt, trying to rip it. Seconds later with his full weight pressed against me he smashed his mouth onto mine and started kissing me. I fought back. I kicked him with my legs and violently thrashed back and forth trying to release my pinned arms and mouth. Every chance I got my mouth free, I screamed, "Get out! Get out!" After several minutes of fighting, the man let go of me. Shoving me off to the side he yanked open the door and ran out, worried, I think, that someone in the apartment building had heard me screaming and would call the police.

As soon as he left I quickly locked the door. Trembling, I ran to Lily's room to check on her. In the dark room accented by a faint yellow light coming from a street lamp outside her window, I saw that she slept peacefully, blissfully uncontaminated by disturbed people and the terrible things they do. Relief held me momentarily in large forgiving arms. I thought about calling the police myself, but my twelve-year-old brain believed I would be severely punished for opening the door. Calling my mother did not feel like an option either. I decided I would tell her only after Claudia and I had discussed the incident. Since I was certain Claudia had arranged to meet her horrible friend, I thought she would be home any moment. I slid to the floor next to the front door and waited to hear Claudia's key turning in the lock. I started my vigil around ten in the evening. At two in the morning I crawled into Claudia's bed where I usually slept, still waiting, my body still shaking.

An hour later, Claudia came into the bedroom. Wide awake I urgently confessed that I had let her friend in before she got home. Bookended by sobs and tears I told her the whole story: her friend had pinned my arms and

94

tried to tear off my shirt while he kissed me, but I fought back and screamed, and he had left. Lily, I assured her, had slept through the attack. At the end with no more details to share, I said I was sorry for letting her friend in. Demonstrating little interest in the incident, she told me the man I let in was not a friend. He was an infatuated fan from the nightclub who wanted to date her. She said nothing else. Just before falling deeply asleep, she wondered aloud, "How did he get my phone number?"

When morning came, Claudia didn't mention the previous evening and neither did I, but I had lain awake all night shaking so I wouldn't wake Claudia. Just as my body bore the signs of the previous evening, so did my mind. I felt ashamed that I had been so gullible and naïve, and I berated myself for letting a stranger into the house, endangering Lily and me. As I staggered around that morning I felt like there was a blimp carrying the sign "it's your fault" circling round and round my head, making sure to physically bump me every other loop.

When Claudia dropped me off at my house later that day I went looking for my mother, dreading telling her what had happened. I hoped she would hold me and love me through my mistakes. After listening to the events of the previous evening she responded with her signature vacancy and few words. Her reaction seemed just like Claudia's: no reprimand but no tenderness either. Twelve years old and ashamed, I retreated inward, just as I had done after Alan molested me. I stopped babysitting for Lily.

In time, I let the babysitting catastrophe, and my shame, fall into the cavernous cracks between consciousness and unconsciousness. I continued taking care of children but only in my neighborhood, and only when I felt the jobs were reasonable and safe for me. Babysitting continued to give me something to do on the weekends, and it gave me money, which in turn expanded my independence. In addition to buying food, I began going to movies with friends, and adding to my collection of brightly colored plastic trinkets manufactured by companies with an uncanny sense for what girls age ten to fourteen can't live without. Occasionally I bought clothes with my babysitting money, but only when I had saved up enough. Like most kids I wanted the latest fashions but couldn't afford them. Frustrated, I wanted to be like the popular girls in junior high who came to school wearing trendy shirts and hip bellbottom pants in a rainbow of colors, coy ensembles that announced to the boys that their bodies were still under construction but would be finished soon. Ignoring my superego, and what I knew was right from wrong, I made a bold and stupid decision at thirteen to try to be one of those girls.

My plan to steal clothes from a local department store lacked both creativity and stealth. I walked directly into the department store and over to a pair of bellbottoms and a shirt I had seen on a previous swing through the store. The items were folded and arranged in piles of like clothes on the round wooden tables department stores use to present their goods in a swirl of enticement and good taste. Clumsily, I grabbed the pants and shirt and stuffed them into a thin brown crinkly paper bag with the store's name printed on it—a used one from a previous purchase. As they slid to the bottom of the bag I panicked. Nothing felt good about what I had done. I walked quickly to the door. Once through, I ran. My heist lasted less than two minutes.

When I got home, instead of feeling thrilled that I had not been caught and had gotten away with something for nothing, I felt suffocated by guilt. The only relief I could think of was to return the stolen items. Later the same day I went back to the store and when the saleswomen were looking the other way, I put the jeans and shirt back on their respective tables and sprinted for the door, ending my career as a thief as awkwardly as I had begun it.

I could easily cite the superficial reasons why I stole the clothes. We were poor. I wanted some nice clothes and didn't want to wait until I had the money to buy them—a shortcut way of saying to myself that I didn't want to do all the babysitting necessary to afford a complete outfit. And I wanted to fit in with the popular kids. Wearing trendy clothes, I fantasized, would make that happen.

Soon, I began to wonder if I was like my father. Had I modeled myself after a man who for as long as I could remember treated most people and laws with contempt? That this might be the case, or even worse that I might be genetically programmed to disregard the basic rules and rights of others, was deeply disturbing. Ultimately I concluded the evidence wasn't there to support either conclusion. One stealing bout with a prompt return of the stolen items and no other examples of similar behavior just didn't add up or even come close to resembling my father's pattern of behavior.

But I wasn't completely off the hook. Next I thought about my mother. Had her behavior influenced my impulsive decision to steal? She consistently skirted responsibility, lied, and, like my father, didn't seem to connect to or care much for anyone else. But, as far as I knew, she didn't steal. Closely comparing my mother's behavior with mine, I was relieved to conclude that we were also not alike. When I did something I knew I was wrong, I felt overwhelming guilt. Not my mother. With that cleared up, I moved toward the most logical reason for my behavior: I wanted pretty clothes to fit in, and for a brief minute was willing to do anything to make that happen. Only as an adult was I able to understand that a major factor reinforcing my adolescent desire to fit in was a home life that resembled a chaotic orphanage, one with an uncaring, incompetent director on extended break.

A few months after my thirteenth birthday, my mother announced that she could no longer "stand all the fighting" and the "ungrateful, selfish behavior of her children." Feeling modern and noting her superior understanding of the benefits of therapy, a nod to her former marriage to my psychiatrist father and her own dalliance with psychoanalysis when we were babies and toddlers, she decided we would go to family therapy. We went several times following her habit of nonlinear attendance: attend one week, skip three weeks, attend the fourth week, etc. Since we were nearly all teens at the time, family therapy seemed to her an appropriate intervention, noble even. During the sessions, the therapist, a good looking sandy-haired young man in his early thirties, dressed casually in a sports jacket and button-down shirt, with no tie, would ask us to report, as if in confession, our darkest sins. Unbeknown to me or to my siblings, he had a head start on our horrible acts. His knowing responses to our disclosures revealed that my mother had already shared with him, in detail, each of our peccadilloes.

In the family counseling sessions, my mother sat at one end of a large rectangular table in a sleek dress that managed to simultaneously communicate demureness and irresistibility. Her genius chameleon look had the added effect of plumping up whichever emotion she was championing in the moment, beleaguered, beatific, triumphant. She never spoke about her true role in our lives, her profound neglect, the chaos, our desperation. She largely stuck to the same mantra I'd heard all my life, delivered in the voice of a stage actress, using sharp consonants and syllables stretched with emphasis: "I am a single parent of six [read ungrateful] children with no financial or emotional support from my ex-husband, who is a doctor."

This oft-repeated phrase told her story. As young children we were the burden, but as teens we surpassed our father to take top billing as the bad guys in her victim narrative. The therapist agreed. He defended our mother, showering her with sympathy and words of support. His penance for us was to be better kids and shore up our long-suffering materfamilias by doing the chores she gave us, including cleaning the house. It was a strange admonition. By that time in our life, my mother's longstanding problem with hoarding had grown worse. Parts of our house were impassable due to the mountains of things she collected.

During one of our counseling sessions, I decided I would try to get the attention of the therapist. Unconsciously, I think, I was desperate to have a male adult think I was appealing. Looking directly at the therapist with all the grace of an awkward, bumbling teen, I stretched my arms above my head, cocked my head to one side, and smiled openly and warmly at him. He looked back at me, confused. Without warning his face clouded over and he exclaimed loudly, "You are trying to seduce me!" Fear and confusion surged through my body. My face reddened. Devastated, my thirteen-year-old brain launched a rapid rewind. I quickly tried to understand his assertion as well as the motivation behind my behavior. Was I trying to seduce him? Why would he think that? What was I doing? Why would he say something so horrible about me in front of my mother and brothers and sisters?

While I was trying to figure out how to respond, I looked over at my mother. Repelling my silent appeal for help, she turned to the therapist and gave him a finely tuned look of exasperation that communicated two thoughts perfectly: *Now, you can see what I have to deal with* and *I have no idea what would provoke my daughter to so pathetically try to win your affection.* After the session, although my mother never said a word to me about the incident, she clearly conveyed that I should feel ashamed of myself. I did. I felt like a pariah in my own family of outcasts.

After just a few counseling sessions, we returned home to our asylum deflated, nothing inside or outside our lives having changed. No one, it seemed, besides us, would ever know our plight. But the therapy had altered something in my mind. It had nudged aside the feeling that I was merely undesirable to make even more room for the feeling that had always nagged me. The one fueled by my thought that if I were a better kid, or perfect, I would be worthy of my mother's love. Therapy had worked. For my mother. When it was over, I was one hundred percent convinced that she was a victim of me.

Despite believing that I was an albatross around my mother's neck, I thrived in junior high with a degree of heartiness I hadn't known in my earlier years. More capable due to age, I could legitimately stay away from home for longer and longer periods of time. No one would ever question my daily leave of absence to play afterschool sports or babysit neighborhood kids on Saturdays and Sundays. And in seventh grade I found another reason not to go home. I made a best friend. From first grade on I had always had a small circle of neighborhood and school friends, but never a best friend. Angela was the first. Angela was smart, fun, and game for any zany romping athletic adventure that spelled excitement. Petite and olive-skinned with dark eyes and curly hair, she looked like a modern, more beautiful Mona Lisa. I spent as much time as I could with Angela, much of it at her house where family disagreements occasionally happened, but to my astonishment were always quickly resolved.

Angela's Italian-American family orbited around three main priorities—family, education, and authentic Italian cuisine. Like my dad, her dad was a physician. The similarities stopped there. Angela's father was a quietly commanding patriarch deeply committed to his children and their future lives. Angela's mom was equally taciturn but with a different job description. Chicly attired in the sophisticated suits and dresses of the Main Line women's afternoon bridge club, she efficiently and confidently executed her housewifely duties with few words. She kept the house immaculate and the living room elegantly dressed in Old World antiques, paintings, and vintage vases. Everything in the house seemed to speak melodious Italian. On top of the house's upkeep, Angela's mother made sure Angela and her two brothers were well dressed and well fed. Whenever I skipped into the house, I knew I would find a pot of homemade tomato sauce with handmade Italian sausages happily bubbling in time to Frank Sinatra: his gravelly crooning was a constant in their house. Angela's close-knit family was proud of their heritage and their Italian-American identity.

One warm afternoon Angela, another girlfriend, and I were unleashed from school early and had no afterschool activity. Excited for a round on the monkey bars, we headed to the elementary school playground next door to our junior high school. As soon as we arrived, Angela began executing a series of daring trapeze challenges on the bars. Standing on one bar about three feet off the ground she would jump across a space of about two to three feet and grab cross bars positioned at various distances and vertical heights. Each leaping effort was successful as Angela easily clasped her hands around the bar she named she would reach before jumping. Assuming we had exhausted the thrill of the workout, I jumped off the bars ready to go. Angela didn't move. She had identified one last bar she wanted to conquer, the Mount Everest of monkey bar leaps. The bar she coveted was more than four feet away and close to six feet high. Angela asked me and our other friend if we thought she could make it. Risk-averse, I emphatically told her, "No!" I explained, "The distance is too far and the height is too high. Angela, if you miss, you can really hurt herself." Angela shifted her gaze from the bar back to me. I could see she was electrified by the challenge. Then she jumped.

In an impressive show of fierce determination and athletic prowess, Angela missed the bar by only one inch. As she fell downward, she put her hand out to break the fall. In my memory, her descent was slow but her scream entered my ears instantly and at a sharp, loud angle. As my head connected the two I ran over. Angela was curled on her side, one hand holding her wrist, not crying probably due to shock but moaning in pain. Gently, I asked Angela if I could see her wrist. The second she let go, I clamped my right hand over my mouth. The part of the wrist Angela was holding hung down cleanly separated from the radius and the ulna. Her arm was a straight line on both sides of the break interrupted by a descended section that resembled a lower platform. Telling the other girl to stay with Angela, I ran to the nearest house to call Angela's parents. Angela was in a cast for a long time.

I didn't see Angela for several weeks after the accident. One afternoon when we finally caught up with each other she told me why. Her father was furious with me. He believed that I was the one who had told her to make the dangerous jump, and worse, that I was a bad influence on her. She was forbidden to play with me. Angela could not persuade her father otherwise; he was not a man easily corrected. Devastated, I didn't know what to do. Angela's parents knew I was a kid with absentee parents from a family and home that didn't function very well, but they had welcomed me into their lives. With Angela's injury, suddenly I had become someone they were wary of, someone who couldn't be trusted. I felt angry. But I knew there was nothing I could do. Angela's father would never see the person I really was: cautious, studious, and, aside from the department store mistake, generally honest. He would never know that unlike my parents, I didn't feel comfortable lying or manipulating other people. If anything, I tried hard not to be like them. Equally important, he would never know that Angela's decision to jump was hers alone. I was the one who had tried to keep her safe.

Being misunderstood by Angela's father was a stark contrast to a mother who frequently seemed surprised to find me, an afterthought, in her life. So, I was startled when one day I accidentally discovered how to extract a smidgeon of affection from her. I remember I needed to ask her something for school. Tiptoeing up to the couch in the living room where she lay sleeping—things had taken possession of her bedroom—I gently rubbed her shoulder and tentatively whispered my question. Lying on her side, she groggily murmured something incomprehensible. Since I didn't hear her I bent down to ask again. She listlessly swung her arm around my neck and pulled me down closer. My mother had never touched me that affectionately before. Trying to prolong my near embrace, I nestled closer to her, lining up my body alongside hers the length of the couch.

Snuggling with my mother felt so good that I quickly made it a regular before-school activity. Every day for months I would steal into the living room to lie next to her on the couch for a few minutes before dashing off to school. Cocooned in her arms without sibling competition, I felt special. It never occurred to me that to receive this affection, I had to make all the arrangements. One day the snuggling routine stopped. I don't recall why. Years later when I affectionately reminded my mother of the months we spent cuddling and chatting in the morning before I went to school and she went to work, she drew a blank. She didn't remember any of it. I was devastated. I had tattooed the memory on my heart: it was the one time in my life that I felt nurtured by her.

As I got older I was increasingly stunned by my mother's amnesia for any event involving her that elicited deep feeling. The more emotional the event, good or bad, in which she was a principal player, the less likely she remembered it. Her memory lapses were baffling. I couldn't understand how someone who was a walking dictionary-cum-encyclopedia of contemporary and arcane facts and figures, with an equal talent for re-creating, in near-perfect detail, the lives and emotions of people she read or heard about, could forget, as she regularly did, emotional events involving her and her children. But she did, and with alarming consistency. While I was struggling to understand her targeted memory loss, I was perplexed by her tendency to make up memories. What my mother lost in the feeling area, she made up for in fabrication.

After we all left home, my mother began describing our bottom-of-the-barrel childhood to strangers, friends of mine, and relatives she saw infrequently as a classic fairy tale starring her, of course, as our rescuer. Overnight she became the resilient divorcee who, once abandoned by her wealthy physician husband, worked tirelessly to keep her brood of six financially and emotionally afloat. That part of her story never changed, but her characterization of us fluctuated with her mood and audience. We ranged from mentally unbalanced and self-absorbed to moderately successful—the latter implied but never called out directly due to feigned modesty. Left out of these soliloquies,

106

naturally, was any mention of her depressions that lingered for weeks, the unpaid bills, phone and power outages, and her primal neglect of us. Her stories were also scrubbed clean of any details about her hoarding and the claustrophobia we felt from a home eating itself from the inside out.

"It is so hard raising these kids alone," I overheard her tell a colleague at the television station. I was there one afternoon in her office waiting for her. My mother was standing just outside the partially-closed office door, so some of their conversation floated to me. "Between cooking, shopping, doing laundry, driving them all over creation, and working full time, I am exhausted. On top of all that, I have to deal with nonstop fighting at home. I scheduled weekly family meetings just to establish some order. But they talk back and do nothing around the house. Thank God for work. Coming here is like a vacation from home." There was pride in my mother's voice. A *life is hard but I am managing* kind of pride. I couldn't hear her coworker's actual response but could feel her soft soothing words of compassion. I was embarrassed that I was part of my mother's stress, but I was also proud of her for hanging in there, for not giving us away.

In fairness to my mother, being a single parent of any number of children is beyond difficult. Imagining the physical and emotional needs of a half dozen is sobering. But when my mother boasted to others that she successfully raised us using equal parts assembly line and one-on-one attention, I drew the line. One comment, in particular, floored me. "Well, because it was so difficult to get everybody out of the house and off to school in the morning, I made everybody's lunches the evening before, freezing the sandwiches to keep them fresh," I heard her say. Hearing my mother's tale that she not only had to "get everybody out of the house," but had created a systematized process for feeding and caring for us, was something akin to listening to her give an acceptance speech for *Mother of the Year*. I have no memory of her marshalling anyone out the door. And while it is possible that on one, or even more than one, occasion my mother may have been inspired to freeze our lunches, any implication that this was normal operating procedure was ludicrous.

I do have one memory of my mother making my lunch, of sorts. It was the time she brought a fast-food lunch to my younger brother and me at the Montessori elementary school we attended for two years. When my mother came running into my classroom oozing apologies perfumed with charm, I was mortified. Although the saliva-inducing smell of fast-food French fries and hamburgers made all my classmates' mouths water, I didn't feel special. I knew the school had called my mother because once again Patrick and I had shown up without lunches. Most of the time my mother could not be reached and we were given classroom snacks, usually crackers, and parts of our teachers' lunches. So the fanfare that she brought with the food didn't impress me, or, I imagine, the teachers.

My mother's fanciful tales of our childhood did not stop with school lunches. She told other stories. One that she took exceptional pride in telling me was how she breastfed all six of us. Glowing, she described how she defied the social mores of her time to breastfeed each of us: "Most women were bottle-feeding their babies when you kids were born. That was what mothers were expected to do back in the fifties. But I knew better. I told the hospital nurses and the doctors who insisted I bottle-feed each of you that, 'No! I am going to breastfeed my child!' They were always shocked, but I knew it was the right thing to do. I was determined to breastfeed you and give you the nutrition you needed. I am very proud of that choice." Her emphasis on her own daring and belief in our greater good was clear, but whether she breastfed all of us and for how long was not. It was hard to know. As the second youngest child in the family, with my baby brother only fourteen months behind me, I have no memory of my mother breastfeeding anyone.

That my mother took the moral high ground in the breastfeeding debate was not surprising. She was extremely well read, and by the time we were teens and she was regaling us with her version of our life events, breastfeeding had become more accepted and openly encouraged for both nutritional and mother-child bonding benefits. While my mother's perspective on the merits of breastfeeding was not difficult to accept, conjuring up the image of an emotionally-connected mother happily bonding with her newborns one after the other for six years straight was highly problematic. First, because of my father's extreme egotistical pursuits, my mother was alone during her pregnancies and our births. And with no help from him at home, it is hard to fathom her breastfeeding a newborn with an expanding group of children still in or just out of babyhood.

Second, even if my mother were Houdini-like and could manage the physical demands of breastfeeding a newborn, and possibly other children at the same time, it is nearly impossible to imagine her emotionally committing to the experience for long, because of her intense disorganization and disjointedness. A house strewn with half-completed laundry, food preparation, and cleaning projects bore witness to this reality. It is conceivable that she may have nursed my two oldest siblings, Alan and Celeste, for a few weeks or perhaps longer. But, if she had suckled the rest of us, it had to be for the briefest of time. As she continued polishing the memory, it started sounding to me like, "Hey, I haven't been the best mom, but I did do one thing right. I breastfed each of you."

The older we got the rosier my mother painted our childhood. Along with her habit of altering events, she took to verbally listing the special opportunities she had gone to great pains to give each one of us. The thrust of this narrative was more of the same: humble, victim mother goes without to meet her children's individual needs. On the list of opportunities that she had given me, she always started with my attending a Montessori school when we lived in the Ranch House. Patrick and I both attended the school for the same two-year period, preschool and kindergarten for him, kindergarten and first grade for me. My favorite memory from Montessori was learning French. The moment I heard it, its sounds rolled around in my head producing a musicality that was pure sensory pleasure. Unfortunately, that positive memory will always be parked alongside another memory: anxiety.

I was constantly afraid when I was at Montessori that my brother and I would be escorted out of school because my mother didn't do what she was supposed to. When that fear took over, little eddies of worry would pool around me threatening to engulf me. The flooding could happen whether I was sitting in reading circle, finger painting, or chasing a ball on the playground. In reminiscing about the special gift of Montessori that she unduly suffered to give me, my mother never mentioned that she was consistently unable to get us to and from school on time, properly dressed and fed, with lunches in hand. And she conveniently omitted that because she failed to meet the school's required parent work obligations, she dragged my brother and me with her to Saturday work makeup sessions, where she was the only parent backfilling her parent cooperative responsibilities. Reality was not part of her dreamy remembering. Neither, apparently, was my stress.

It was not until I was older that I began to compare what my mother said with what she did. Once I peeked behind the curtain, her behavior became more inexplicable. Despite fluently reciting the Montessori method and its core principles of child development, our home was a desert of learning. There was no corner in any room of our house dedicated to child development activities—no books, no educational toys. Even more peculiar, I have no memory of her reading to me or encouraging any reading at home despite being a voracious reader herself. I'm certain some part of my mother was earnest in wanting to expose my brother and me to the Montessori *learning how to learn* approach, but it's difficult to ignore that her real thrill appeared to be trilling about our attending the school. It seemed to buoy her sense of intellectual superiority by giving her something she coveted—membership in the rarified club of the educational cognoscenti.

Next on my mother's list of itemized things that she had done specifically for me was paying for a cross-country teen tour that I took the summer between eighth and ninth grade, when I was fourteen years old and we were living in the Colonial. Summer was an especially disconnected time for us at the Colonial. Long gone were the days of being dropped at the neighborhood pool to while away the hours when the sun was at its greatest height in the sky. Without school, we were entirely on our own between June and September. Although I spent most of my summers babysitting, at fourteen I was still too young to transition into permanent summer work, so summers were still elastic with enough room for friends.

When I heard some eighth-grade classmates wealthy enough to sniff at the tedium of common summer camp discussing their summer plans to go on a teen tour before ninth grade, I was desperate to go. Getting away, having adventures, and spending a summer with new friends sounded intoxicating. Headstrong, I began lobbying my mother to let me go. I increased my babysitting that spring and insisted that my earnings would help defray some of the costs of the trip, still certain of course that my chances of going were nil. Before school let out for summer, my mother unexpectedly announced that she would pay for the tour. So used to losing, it took a while before it sunk in that I had actually won a prize.

For six weeks, I crisscrossed the United States on a bus with a coed group of teens. The tour was wonderful aside from a few moments of discomfort, like when I didn't have money to buy souvenir trinkets and extra snacks like other kids, or the time when my father and his second wife Alicia came to see me when the tour spent a few days in a national park in the Colorado Rocky Mountains. It was a memorable visit.

I was waiting next to the teen tour's empty buses in the parking lot—everyone else from the tour was on a hike—when I spotted my father. He had just gotten out of his BMW and was striding impatiently toward me, dressed in expensive pants and a dress shirt. Alicia followed. After stiffly greeting me and mumbling something about a growing gas shortage problem, and that he didn't want to wait in line for gas, he turned and walked rapidly back to his car. He opened his trunk and took out a medium-sized gas can and narrow rubber hose about three feet long. A moment later, those objects in hand, he began weaving in

113

and out of the rows of parked cars with Alicia and me trying to keep up. Then he stopped at a car partly obscured by trees. In what appeared to be a very practiced motion, he opened the car's gas cap cover, removed the gas cap, and inserted one end of the hose into the tank and the other into his mouth. He sucked on the tube for a few seconds before quickly dropping that end into the gas can on the ground. Gas started flowing. I was mortified.

Stunned by his behavior, I asked him why he was taking gas from someone else's car. He tersely responded it was only a few gallons. In a condescending tone, he added that the owner would never know he was missing any gas. I felt my skin crawl. After filling the can up halfway, he casually walked back to his car and nonchalantly poured the gas into his tank. Minutes later we drove out of the parking lot in search of a cup of coffee for him.

The incident filled me with shame but thankfully didn't mar my overall teen tour experience: I had six weeks of positive attention from the tour counselors and a regular schedule of meals. And because I knew what to expect each day—the counselors distributed a daily itinerary—I let go of worrying that around every corner was a sinkhole waiting to swallow me up. That summer I breathed in a world that was big and ripe with possibilities. Of all the places we visited, I liked San Francisco the best. It felt open and vulnerable, curious, and determined. A little like me.

The intersection of the teen tour and my adolescence was magical. Each year after that summer I thought about my mother and her decision to send me with great affection. She had given me a bite-sized chunk of time to be a kid without turmoil, and I was grateful. The six-week respite allowed me to camp in the Yellowstone National Park, swim in the Pacific Ocean, see the Grand Canyon and Mount Rushmore, and ride horseback in Colorado. Freed from the turbulence of my home life, I learned how to get along with other kids and make friends.

Sometime in my twenties, my positive memory of that remarkable experience unfortunately changed, forever. I was chatting with my mother about our upbringing and the topic of the teen tour came up. What rose instantly to the top of my mother's memory chain about the decision to send me was the extraordinary financial sacrifices she had made, so I could spend six weeks cavorting with wealthy kids on a bus touring the United States. The comment was dripping with antipathy for me, but was delivered as usual with her complicated charm, "Nikki, sending you on that trip was a huge financial sacrifice; we did not have the money. But I was determined to do something for each of you." With the surface and subtext of the remark laid bare, I experienced the only emotion I could: shame. How could I have been so selfish to beg for something I didn't deserve? Overnight the fizz of that happy time hardened and became petrified. The outside still looked like the memory but the inside had turned to stone.

Deconstructing my mother's version of reality became an important process, not to prove her wrong but to thread my way through to sanity. Years after the teen tour, I dedicated some time to thinking about what was going on in our lives at the time of the tour. I was surprised to recall some events that my mother excluded in her retelling of her good deed. The first was that my grandfather, my mother's father, had died just after I started eighth grade and had left my mother some money. When that came back into focus, I distinctly recalled my mother telling me right before the tour that the only reason she could afford to send me was because her father had left her some money. I have never doubted that my going on the tour created financial hardship for my family, but my remembering that small inheritance opened the portal of truth just a little bit wider.

A second memory also emerged that I suspect might have played into her decision. Sometime after her father died, my mother announced to all of us that she had married a man she had been dating for a very short period of time (despite searching, I've never found a record of their marriage). With very little notice, her new husband, George, moved into our home. None of us liked him. George was alcoholic, ill tempered, and unable to feign even the slightest interest in any of us. When he was drunk, which was often, he didn't seem to like my mother much either. One morning I met her on the back staircase leading to the kitchen and noticed her swollen nose and black eye. I asked her what happened. Initially she said, "Oh, nothing. I fell." But I persisted, "Mom, really, what happened?" In a quiet baby voice, she answered, "George pushed me down the stairs last night." "Mom, you have to get him out of here!" I urged. She moved slowly past me up the stairs. Each step careful and deliberate. The conversation was over. I wanted to believe this battery was the first, but I didn't. I wanted George out of our lives.

Something else about George made me very uncomfortable. Although he never made any advances toward me, I felt sexually unsafe in his presence and intuitively kept my distance. That didn't prevent my subconscious from expressing my fears. At exactly the moment George came into our lives I started having terrible nightmares. They all began and ended the same way. In a half-asleep/half-awake state, I would sense that a grown male had come into my room with the intent of raping me. The only way to save myself was to force myself awake so I could stop the assault, but I couldn't move or speak. For what seemed like hours I would slowly, painfully force myself to full consciousness. It was like moving from the middle of a quicksand pit where I had been buried up to my neck, to the edge of the pit. I'm not sure how but I always managed to unfreeze my body just before something terrible happened, then I would fully wake up.

Vanquishing my nightly enemy came at a great emotional cost. The dreams depleted and confused me. They started when George moved in but continued for another decade at least and were influenced, I am sure, by Alan's sexual abuse of me when I was a small child. I never told my mother about the dreams, but I wonder if her decision to send me on the teen tour, uncharacteristic of her and definitely out of the blue, had something to do with

George. I would like to think that if his entry into our lives was a factor in her decision to finance the trip, it was because she sensed something predatory about him and wanted to protect me. Counterbalancing that, however, was her vacant response to Alan's repeated sexual abuse of me. It left me feeling that if George were in any way a reason I went on the tour, I couldn't rule out that my mother might have perceived me a sexual threat and wanted me gone for the summer. George left their marriage and our house after less than a year. Afterwards, my mother never mentioned him again.

Not long after George's departure, my mother informed me that she had scheduled me to take an IQ test. It was another of my mother's actions that didn't make sense to me. I was in tenth grade, my first year of high school, and doing well in school. I asked her why. She told me that she had requested the test for Patrick and Gillian, siblings on either side of me, because they were having some difficulty in school. She paused, waiting for me to express sympathy for them, which I did, then said, "Nikki, you are doing well in school, but I want you to take this test, because I don't want Gillian or Patrick to feel there is anything wrong with them." I knew very little about the IQ test, but I knew it was not typically administered to children who were performing well academically, and getting along with their teachers and peers. I also knew it was not administered as an intermediary for other children's hurt feelings. Remembering my poor academic performance in fourth grade with Mrs. Harry, I instantly leaped to my own conclusion about why my mother had signed me up. There was something wrong with me—I had a low IQ.

My worry seemed borne out. After I finished the initial writing section of the IQ test, the examiner told me that for the next section he would ask me a question, and I was to give him my best answer. After asking me several questions, which I answered easily, he asked, "What is glass made of?" I didn't know the answer and with some embarrassment told him so. I felt a little ashamed but assumed he would move to the next question. He didn't. He responded, "Oh, come on. You know this. Everyone knows this!" I told him again that I didn't know the answer. He again instructed me to give him the answer. Barely audible, I stammered again that I didn't know the answer. "It's sand," he said. "Everyone knows that!" The confidence and buoyancy I felt at the start of the exam evaporated. I shut down for the remainder of the test. For weeks afterwards, I asked my mother for my score, afraid it was so low that once my school knew it, I would be forced out of the advanced high school classes I was taking.

The day my mother received the IQ test results—a letter she eagerly opened—she approached me, barely able to conceal her excitement. She knew something I didn't. In a honeyed voice she said, "Nikki, I know all three IQ scores (referencing mine, Gillian's, and Patrick's), and I know mine, which is *very* high. But, I have decided that I am not going to tell you your number." She went on, "Actually, I am not going to tell anyone their score. It's not important.

All you need to know, Nikki, is that *you* use everything you have."

It was a sideways punch, and it felt wrong. I couldn't tell if it was her dismissive words, her saccharine tone, or her face cleverly molded into an expression of counterfeit compassion that left me gasping for air. She managed to simultaneously confirm my low intelligence, with a slight nod to my overachieving spirit, while congratulating herself on her own incomparable innate abilities. Years later Gillian told me my mother had told her what her IQ was. It was high. Discerning the true motivations for what my mother said, did, and believed was impossible. Whatever her reason or reasons for requiring me to take the IQ test— to confirm that I was intellectually disabled or that my IQ was lower than hers—she knew my Achilles' heel, and exploited it forever after with minimally costumed references to my intellectual inferiority. I became what she thought I was. After the IQ test, I underperformed on every standardized test that I took, including the SATs.

Not long before we packed up from the Colonial and moved again, my mother decided to try her hand at establishing a few traditions. The short-lived rituals included breakfast after Christmas Eve Midnight Mass, attending the annual Philadelphia Easter Parade en famille, and birthdays. The early Christmas morning breakfast appeared mysteriously one year, held steady for a few years, and then petered out. It consisted of creamed chipped beef and toast. The pièce de résistance was that my mother made it. While a few of us braved the winter cold at midnight to

120

go to mass, my mother would fall asleep on the living room couch with the TV on full volume. When we returned a few hours later, she would groggily get up from the couch, pull out an electric skillet, and begin cooking. I waited all year for the breakfast. The prettiness of the moment wasn't our religious beliefs or connection to the Catholic Church—both were haphazard and fleeting—it was that my mother was taking care of us.

The second fleeting family tradition was the Philadelphia Easter Parade. We started attending the parade because my mother's television station was covering it, and my mother decided we should all go. Once we physically made it to the parade route in downtown Philadelphia, we had a good time. It was fun watching people preen and prance about in their Easter finery. But getting there was another matter. Leading off the list of challenges was finding suitable clothes to wear. For some reason, I don't remember this being a problem for my mother; she always seemed to have a thrift-shop outfit and matching hat squirreled away somewhere for the occasion. The rest of us, who by that time lived in jeans we bought ourselves, were not so fortunate. With tension mounting, fights erupting, and the clock ticking, we scoured the maze of laundry that filled the back of our house.

When we at last all found something to wear, a motley and mismatched crew, the next challenge was getting us all in the car. Older, independent, and rarely together, we couldn't be easily corralled. This prompted my mother to begin screaming at us. We screamed back. More fighting. The fighting escalated. It was difficult to breathe. Before we had even left the driveway, we had nearly asphyxiated each other with hate. After the fights, I tried to let go of the anger and hurt, but it was hard. At the parade my mother drifted about with no memory of what had come before. She delighted in introducing herself and her six children to anyone expressing interest. Pageantry and being in the spotlight seemed to matter most; everything else was immaterial.

Our final irregular tradition in the Colonial was birthday dinners. I don't recall birthday celebrations in either the Ranch House or Tudor, but for a few years in the Colonial my mother would buy us what we wanted to eat for our birthday dinner. My sixteenth birthday is the only birthday I remember from my childhood. It may have been memorable because I asked for steak, an odd request to me now because I have never been a big meat eater. Somehow my mother scrounged up the money to buy cake and steak, which Michael cooked. Sitting at the dining room table, cleared of junk for the occasion, waiting for my birthday dinner, I remember . . . I was happy.

My sixteenth birthday marked another significant development in my life: I decided to get my driver's license. Having a license, I determined, was my ticket to greater independence, although mostly in the future, since we didn't have a car I could use. I enrolled in an inexpensive driver's education class, which I paid for with babysitting money, and started studying for my written and driving tests. Months before the tests I realized that I would need my birth certificate to get my license, so I asked my mother if she had it. As expected, she didn't and had no idea where it might be. Luckily she remembered the name of the hospital where I was born in Colorado, so I wrote them to request a copy of my birth certificate.

When I opened the large brown envelope and pulled out my birth certificate, I was confused. Listed for the name of the baby was my first name, Monique, and my last name, Parrish, but instead of the two middle names, Maria Andrea, the ones my mother had always told me were mine, the name on the certificate was listed as Mari. I asked my mother if she knew why they put Mari as my middle name, assuming the hospital had made a mistake. As though she had been preparing to answer this question all her life, she immediately said with great theatrical flourish, "Oh, yes, that is your middle name; it is pronounced, Mar-ee." "What about Maria and Andrea, the middle names you told me to put on all my school forms?" I asked. "Oh those, well, those are, I guess, your Baptism and Confirmation names, but I'm not sure," she said. She thought for a second and asked, "Well, what did you take as your Confirmation name? Whatever it was, it probably wasn't the one on your baptismal certificate." I told her I wasn't sure about my confirmation name—I was only seven years old when I was confirmed. Fuzzy on the details of my name and without any certificates in the house to check, my mother lost interest in the discussion. Without any ripples of embarrassment or guilt that she didn't know my middle name, she successfully transferred the responsibility of knowing my name to me. I promptly dropped the subject, as well as the middle name, Maria Andrea, that I thought was mine. From that moment on, I only used my birth-certificate name, Monique Mari Parrish.

We stayed in the Colonial until after my sophomore year of high school. Without any explanation that I can recall, although I am sure the primary catalyst was that my mother could no longer afford the rent, my mother announced that once again we had to move. In addition to packing up the house, she tasked us with excavating the basement. The state of our basements haunted me. Superficial differences aside, mostly having to do with the different physical layout of each, the content of the interiors was always the same: gigantic dunes of clothes no humans ever wore, innumerable boxes of past-due bills, newspapers, books without readers, and broken contorted objects whose original purpose was only a guess. I was terrified of our basements, and my mother's subterranean collections were the fuel for another recurring dream I had throughout my adolescence. In the dream, I was locked in one of our basements unable to escape. On cue, mountains and mountains of clothes ghoulishly floated toward me, threatening to strangle me. Behind them, evil king rats controlled their movements. I always escaped, but just barely—another dream worth psychoanalyzing.

When we left the Colonial to move into a rental row home, only three of us went with my mother: Patrick as a sophomore in high school, me as a junior, and Gillian as a senior. My older three siblings had already moved out and into their adult lives. Our new house was much smaller than our previous two homes, and because it was the first in a series of row homes, we were fortunate to share only one wall with neighbors. I remember thinking that was a strong plus. When the screaming broke out, we would only impact the tenants on our right. It turned out I didn't need to worry about that. Much of the high drama of our lives had abated with the decrease in our population. With more calm in our lives, I began taking on more responsibility around the house. Between school, sports, and babysitting, I started shopping for food, cooking dinners, and trying to keep communal areas clean. My mother and brother and sister didn't seem to mind my quasi-parental role, or that I made more than a few inedible dishes. My cooking was the trial-by-error learning approach. Someone was sort of in charge and that appeared to be a comfort to them.

During this last phase of my home life, the ricochet fighting and constant crises of my childhood had slowed to a trickle, but I entered into a new twisted dynamic with my mother. About a year before I went off to college, she started telling me intimate stories about her life. To entice me to serve as receptacle of her secrets, she dangled the promise of greater closeness. "Nikki, have I ever told you the story of my Aunt Charlie, the one who was so horrible to me when I was a child? She didn't treat my brother and sister the same way, and I don't know why. Maybe by telling you what happened, Nikki, I can learn more about myself. I actually think you more than anyone else might find it interesting," she said. Because of the opportunity for intimacy with her, and a chance to know more about her and why she behaved the way she did, I suspended the hurt and confusion I felt about her and grabbed the bait. She reeled me in. For more than a decade, whenever the mood moved her, she whispered confidences to me when I was alone in the house or car with her.

Her first tutorial was on the origins of her victimhood. I thought I knew the whole story. In the version my mother had made sure I had known from the moment I formed conscious thoughts, it began with my father and ended with us, her children. But in her first top-secret discussion with me, my mother asserted that her true mark of suffering occurred before she entered the world. Solemnly and with perfected breathiness she revealed that she had been conceived out of wedlock. It was a family secret she said few people knew, since her parents married immediately after they discovered that her mother was pregnant. Eight-and-a-half months later my mother was born. I silently agreed with my mother that because the time between her parents' marriage and the date of my mother's birth was just a few weeks shy of nine months, most people probably didn't know that her parents had a shotgun wedding. I was thinking about this when my mother launched into a giddy description of how egregious her parents' "illicit" act of intercourse was for the time, 1929, and the place, Omaha, Nebraska. Seconds later her mood changed again. She soberly stated that knowing how she came into the world was a heavy burden that only she carried. It was both a confusing and riveting story.

I was mulling over the burden point, which I didn't quite understand, when my mother expanded the story, telling me that throughout her childhood her parents had treated her as their shame. Moved with compassion, I was ready to relieve her of the weight of this burden—although how exactly I wasn't sure—when I realized that she had given no examples of how she had been mistreated or treated differently from her siblings. Similarly, there was no mention of the impact of her parents' dishonor on the few family members who apparently did know about her mother's pregnancy, or the slightest hint of a family cover-up. The latter would have at least placed it in the exciting category of covert lives and affairs.

My mother continued, "I have always known that I was the black sheep of the family, and that my parents never really liked me. I know they never would have gotten married had it not been for me. Think of the shame my mother experienced, Nikki. But what could she do in 1929 in Omaha, Nebraska? In the end, if it weren't for me, my parents would not have stayed together, which means of course, that without me, my brother and sister would not have been born." Believing in her absolute power over her parents and siblings apparently didn't clash with my mother's concurrent belief that she was and always would be a victim, a sure sign that she did not subscribe to Spiderman's belief that *with great power comes great responsibility.* My mother lived comfortably with the duality. The victim mark she wore so proudly throughout her life just took on deeper hues the older she got. From being the disgrace of her family, to abandoned wife of a physician husband, to single mother of six thankless children, her victim sensibilities were amply rewarded by the sympathy she won for each starring role.

If there were ever a "victims' group" structured along the lines of an Alcoholics Anonymous meeting, I imagine my mother would proudly join. I can see her walking into a meeting and unobtrusively taking a seat. It was her way not to call outright attention to herself; she preferred to wait until the curtain went up before dazzling a crowd. When the facilitator asked her to introduce herself, I can see her standing slowly, reeling in her audience. Coyly and with the right touch of theatrical gravitas, I can hear her state with perfect enunciation, "My name is Maria Russell [Russell was her maiden name] but call me Ria, and I am a victim." Her belief in her victimhood was remarkably stable. It didn't change as I grew older or as her circumstances changed.

My mother's tutorials with me continued. With the origin of her victimhood firmly established, she moved on to describing her exquisite mental gifts, asserting without hesitation that she was an undisputed intellectual virtuoso, the belle of the Mensa ball. With her prodigious memory and knowledge of multiple subjects spanning theater, art, books, history, and politics, she believed she sizzled with smarts. Even her vocabulary and comprehension of the English language, she more than implied, rivaled the expertise of English scholars. Her braininess, she said, had opened important educational doors when she was a teen.

She was awarded an academic scholarship to attend a prestigious private girls' high school in Omaha and another to attend a private university.

"I won so many academic awards in junior high that my teachers recommended that I attend a private high school," my mother told me. "My teachers were the ones who helped me get the scholarship to Duschene Academy, a private girls' high school. Our family had no money so it was a really big deal for me to attend. Nikki, you have to understand, we were from the poor side of town. I loved Duschene, especially the theater classes I took, and the opportunity to be in plays. I know my mother felt envious of me. Her life was so small and contained at home, taking care of my brother with polio and my younger sister, and keeping the house clean. Good thing that it all worked out for me; my top grades at Duschene gave me a full scholarship to Creighton University."

As a coming-of-age young woman with an ability to draw inferences, listening to this story I was sure that my mother's entrance into the world of academic privilege gave her respite from a home that lacked a warm and central core. She was the oldest of three children born to a salesman father and stay-at-home mom in Omaha, Nebraska. Beyond describing her own mother as especially clean and neat, she said little about her, other than to allude to her as a sometime competitor with her for the attention of teenage boys. This short summary of her mother was odd. In the mood, my mother could talk for hours. But as she described it to me, their mother-daughter relationship seemed like the rest of my mother's relationships: barely there. Even the sudden death of my maternal grandmother from an enlarged heart when my mother was fifteen—complications from a previous bout of rheumatic fever—was described to me in minimal detail. But she did talk about one aspect of her mother's death that saddened me: her guilt. She admitted to me that she had been a very difficult, selfish, and messy child and later teen. With honest emotion that I rarely witnessed from her, she said she fervently believed that had she been neater or more helpful, her mother might not have overexerted herself and died. I wished someone in her life back then had told her she was not responsible for her mother's death. It broke my heart thinking about what she experienced—a child filled with grief and guilt desperately trying to emotionally reconcile the loss of her mother.

After my grandmother's death, it must have been an anguishing and difficult time for my mother and her family. Her father and other extended family members may have expected her, the oldest child, to parent her two younger siblings, a brother eighteen months younger than she with polio and a sister only seven years old, but my mother never mentioned stepping into a nurturing role with either of them. Snippets of her life from that time only chronicled her completing high school and college, and then after college, marrying my father.

The picture my mother painted of her father was even less detailed than the one of her mother. While her mother seemed focused on keeping house and caring for the children, her father came across as aloof and detached, hovering somewhere in the background of their lives. She implied, although never explicitly stated, that he was not a particularly skillful salesman. From what I could discern, her father supported the family but only barely. At one point my mother told me her father had trouble keeping a job. And there was something else about my grandfather, something that didn't seem quite right. Nothing was ever directly said to make me feel this way, but I got the impression from my mother that there was a dark secret about my grandfather. My gut told me not to trust him.

During one family visit to Omaha when I was seven or eight, I was inexplicably chosen as the grandchild who had to spend an afternoon alone with him. I begged my mother not to make me go. I told her I didn't like her father and wanted to be with my cousins, her brother's children, or my paternal grandparents. They were safe. But I was forced to go, and for an entire afternoon, I felt nothing but terror. Both my grandfather and his house were dark and depressing. For hours, my grandfather said very little to me. Sitting quietly in the house with him that day, I believed the only reason he didn't hurt me was because he didn't want me to be there either. Relief came when my mother eventually showed up and swiftly redeposited me at my paternal grandmother's house.

Years later when my mother's hoarding was finally recognized as a grave and debilitating problem, I asked her about her father, thinking there might be a connection between his scary persona, as I experienced it, and her hoarding problem. With a distant look on her face, she told me that after her mother died she began piling books, clothes, and other objects on the landing in front of her room to discourage her father from entering her bedroom. That was it, nothing more.

My mother did occasionally allude to having been the victim of brutality by more than one family member. There was Aunt Charlie, who gave her forced enemas for no reason, and the uncle whose interactions with her didn't seem so innocent. Without detail or explanation, her tales resembled twisting roads that led to a destination we never quite reached. I remember wanting to know more about each of these anecdotes, as well as all the others she forgot to mention. Without knowing it, I was looking for clues that linked the injustices done to her to how she mistreated us. Despite my persistent inquiries, I could never pry more details loose.

Throughout her one-sided tête-à-têtes with me, my mother educated me intimately on the pain and power of being the ultimate sufferer and genius. She later told me, and I confirmed it with my siblings, that I was the only child she told these stories to, although I am not sure why. It may have been because I was the kid who chased her the most for connection, for intimacy. My need for her allowed her to use me as a release. Another possibility is that she chose me because she thought I could manage the shards of internal madness that seemed to regularly cut her. Or perhaps she chose me to punish me for being everything she was not. It was probably a combination of all three. As

132

my mother downloaded all her unpublished burdens onto me, she became lighter and more energized, even happier.

The clandestine conversations never changed my relationship with my mother. Outside our conferences, she remained distant as always. Months before I left home for college, I began to wonder if after I left for school she would make any effort to communicate with me. That thought was supported by my growing awareness that I had a mother who was confusingly nice at times, but mostly aloof and uncaring. Sorting it out was as disorienting as falling into a dark abyss. And all the way down, I still craved her love.

The confusion and hurt I felt about her crested one drizzly spring Saturday morning weeks from my high school graduation. I had gone out for a three-mile run and was back in the house feeling strong and energetic, my tee shirt and blonde hair damp with perspiration. My mother was sitting in the kitchen in jeans and an old dark blue sweatshirt, dotted with pills. Her thick dark hair was pulled back into a ponytail at the nape of her neck. She was still so pretty and youthful looking, even without makeup.

Engrossed in the old newspaper she was reading, my mother didn't look up when I said, "Good morning." Then I asked her what I had been waiting to ask for weeks. "Mom, did you send in the college commitment check to reserve my spot for fall?" The $50 commitment check was the only college payment my mother was responsible for paying. Earlier that spring, CBS had awarded me a four-year college scholarship, and the school I had chosen to attend, Le Moyne College, a Jesuit college in Syracuse, New York, had complemented it with an additional academic scholarship and a work-study award, guaranteeing me twenty hours per week of on-campus employment. I asked again, "Mom, did you send in the check to Le Moyne? If you don't send it, they won't let me come." Silence. "Mom, why can't you tell me if you sent it in or not?"

Suddenly, the tourniquet of adolescent anger that was part of my everyday wardrobe went from delivering mild but constant pressure to squeezing me so tightly I could barely breathe. I screamed, "Are you kidding! You're not even going to answer me?" My mother remained mute. Blinded with fury, I did something I had never done before. Challenging her fantasy version of her mothering, I screamed, "I can take care of this house and family better than you can!"

Chapter Four

Taking Flight

Two days after I completed high school, I left home on a plane. In my suitcase, I packed clothes, a few books, toiletries, and, unknowingly, a bonus pack of emotional scars and coping mechanisms—some functional, some dysfunctional. Leaving was exciting. It was also disorienting. With high school graduation in my rearview mirror and enough babysitting and work money to cover the cost of my flight, I left home and flew to Denver, Colorado, en route to the mountain town of Estes Park, Colorado, where I had a job as a restaurant hostess for the summer.

I heard about the hostess position when my entire family assembled in Colorado earlier that spring to attend my sister Celeste's wedding—Celeste and my brother Alan had both moved to the Boulder area not far from my father. At the wedding, a friend of Alan's told me about the summer job and offered to drive me up to Estes Park for an interview. Between wedding activities, I made the quick trek there. Following a brief interview, I was offered the summer position and a shared room in a local boarding house for female workers.

I felt comfortable making the leap away from home right after high school, because the previous summer in between my junior and senior year of high school, I had flown across the country to spend the summer with mother's sister and her family in San Clemente, California. I don't remember much about the specifics of the arrangement, but my aunt and uncle had generously offered to pay for the flights and host me, and I had jumped at the chance. That summer I worked as an aide in a nursing home and as a restaurant hostess. In my free time, I hung out with Sean, a boy my age with a canary-yellow pickup truck and a gift for playing the piano. Sean played exquisitely, a combination of fierce musicality and meaning. In our adolescent love, we talked, laughed, went to the beach, and rode rides at Disneyland. My aunt and uncle took good care of me. There was plenty of food, dinner every night with the whole family—my aunt, uncle, and two younger cousins—and a clean house. I was constantly in awe at how easily I could sail unimpeded from one room to the next. My aunt looked like my mother, but they shared little else. Quieter and more reserved, my aunt was deeply devoted to her children and happily attended to their needs. No theatrics, outbursts of anger, or episodes of melancholy. And not once did I ever find her hidden in her bedroom.

There were a lot of similarities between my summers in San Clemente and Colorado, with one big difference. In

Colorado I was entirely on my own. It was a summer full of the firsts that come with venturing out on your own: paying bills, feeding yourself, and navigating more complicated romantic liaisons. For the most part I managed to avoid huge catastrophes. Several weeks into the summer, Gillian moved to Estes Park and found work. We didn't hang out together very often, but I did see her a lot around town. And while I only saw my father once, the time he picked me up at the airport and drove me to the mountains for my job, I saw Celeste and Alan a few times. I didn't appreciate it then, but my grand leap into adulthood was girded by a very unexpected sibling safety net.

As the summer drew to a close, I faced a practical and symbolic decision: how should I get from Colorado to my freshman orientation at Le Moyne in Syracuse, New York? For both economic and emotional reasons, I decided to fly directly from Denver to Syracuse, bypassing Philadelphia and my mother. My mother didn't object.

I got out of the cab in the late afternoon summer sun and stepped directly onto my new college campus into a scene that resembled a Brueghel painting. Activity exploded everywhere. Hundreds of people, including new students, mothers, fathers, kids, and school personnel, stretched across an area of the school that included a large square parking lot and several dormitory buildings. Everyone, it seemed, had a place in the snap portrait that day. Dads hauled heavy trunks up dorm stairs, moms scurried to pick up scarves, shoes, and Frisbees that had fallen from boxes packed with love, and younger siblings ran in frenzied circles on the lawns outside the dorms, momentarily liberated from long car rides and the gathering emotional tenseness of saying goodbye to the one who had kept their secrets. In the middle of the picture were my peers—freshman—standing on foals' legs they hoped would hold them up as they took their first steps toward independence. Rounding out the scene was school staff pink faced with the strain and excitement of orchestrating another physical move into young adulthood for an entire class of new students.

My eyes floated from motion to color. The reds, browns, greens, and blues of suitcases and duffel bags met the pinks, yellows, and whites of stuffed animals and overstuffed pillows. Standing alone I watched the frenzy. I heard choked sobs from parents as they watched their children walk away and step into their new lives. I saw people my age looking nervous but ecstatic at being released. Feeling self-conscious and sad, I suddenly realized I wasn't part of the painting. I didn't come with a mother or father who would lovingly cut the umbilical cord for a second time. In an act of symbolism that I didn't quite get at the time, I cut my own cord. Over the summer I decided that I no longer wanted to be called by my family's nickname for me—Nikki. I wanted to be called by my real name, Monique. It was my new beginning.

With my one suitcase, I stood in front of the dormitory where the freshman orientation letter said I should go, trying to quell my fears, then I walked into my building hoping for the best. Luckily it didn't take long to settle into school. Because of my work-study award, in less than a week I was employed in the library checking out and filing books. That gave me something to do right away. Libraries had always spoken to me. I enjoyed everything about them: the quiet, the earthy mustiness of books shelved long ago, the electricity of intellectual pursuits past, present, and future, and the opportunities to meet people through soft whispers. While I launched into my job, classes, and other social events around campus, my roommate, Cindy, a quiet beauty, preferred to stay in our room. She ventured out only to go to classes or the cafeteria. But that didn't stop the boys. In no time our dorm room was a rest stop for many of her suitors. I was used to living where I didn't sleep, so that didn't bother me. Usually I didn't come back to my room until curfew time—Le Moyne was a Jesuit college with a weeknight 10 pm curfew—and by then, Cindy's beaux-in-waiting weren't allowed to wait any longer in our room.

Cindy loved the initial attention she received and seemed to be thriving because of it. Two months into the semester, however, she precipitously changed and moved into a darker space. She stopped going to class, rarely got out of her pajamas, ate little boxes of cereal she had taken from the cafeteria, and spent all her time watching cartoons. Understandably, the young men who had sought her affection redirected their attention to other possibilities. Soon the petting zoo of stuffed animals piled high on her bed became her only daytime companions. After a few weeks of this lackluster schedule, I came back from class one afternoon and decided to have a heart-to-heart with her, hoping to raise her spirits and encourage her to return to class. In the middle of our conversation she confided that she missed a boyfriend at home and wanted to drop out of school to be with him, but she was afraid to disappoint her parents. In the next breath, she revealed more.

Cindy told me that she had never wanted to leave her hometown to go to college, but felt pushed by her parents to go away to school, something only a few other kids in her town were doing. I suggested she speak to the resident advisor on our floor. I thought it would help her to have the perspective and support of someone older and wiser. Cindy said no, she would be fine. The last part of her statement seemed unconvincing. Turning my eyes away from her for a second and looking down, I caught the end of a thin red line on the inside of one of her wrists. It was a cut, raw and fresh. Too neat for an accident. Glancing at her other wrist I saw the same line. Alarmed, I asked about the cuts. Cindy began crying. Between sobs she told me she didn't want to kill herself, she just wanted to dull her pain. I put my arms around her. Afterwards I told the resident advisor what I had seen. The next day Cindy packed up her belongings and returned home.

For weeks, I could not stop thinking about Cindy's departure. I felt anxious, unsure of my actions. I turned the events over and over in my head, alternating between thinking I had done the right thing with thinking that I had betrayed a friend. I talked to the resident advisor about it, but nothing helped. Then out of the blue one day, I realized that Cindy's deep depression and retreat from the world reminded me of my mother. Still years away from capably analyzing their similarities, the revelation helped me. Although I didn't know what Cindy was suffering from, the name or all the symptoms, I knew from experience that it was beyond my ability at age eighteen to solve. Knowing that made me feel a little better.

Like most college kids I found a group of friends that fit. My three closest girlfriends were effervescent brainiacs with big hearts. Together we were four studious, pretty-straight-laced Musketeers daring one another to have fun. The one group challenge that captured our goofy brand of playfulness was to jump on the cafeteria food tray conveyor belt and ride it into the dishwashing area. I did it while lying on my side; hand on my hip in a laughably sultry pose. I looked silly and the dishwashers were happy to let me know that. I didn't mind. I loved being on my own.

Everything was going well those first few months of school until the call from my mother. "Something has happened to your brother." My mother's voice on the other end of the line was small, but vibrated with excitement. Her call to me that evening on the dorm floor phone was a first. Over the summer when I was in Colorado and into the first few weeks of school our pattern of communication had a fixed sequence, and it never included my mother initiating phone calls. The typical drill was every few weeks or so I would call her, usually at night to be sure she was home. After the tenth ring I would hang up. Moments later, I repeated the pattern. If she didn't pick up on the second or third attempt, I gave up.

Days or weeks later, I would try again. When she finally answered the phone, I felt conflicted, angry at her unalloyed indifference toward me but happy to finally get her on the phone. Once on, my mother followed her own script. It began with no apology and segued immediately into taking the wrinkles out of my anger, "Honey, I am so glad you called. How are you? It must be freezing up there at school but I know you are taking care of yourself. I miss you so much and just can't wait to see you when you come home." All calls with my mother ended the same way, with her sweetly, emptily pledging to continue our call and relationship the next week.

That night when my mother called *me,* I took a moment to register that fact before I could respond. "What, what happened?" I asked, alarm in my voice. With pride in the size of the drama and that she was first in line to play "telephone" with me, she said, "A few days ago Michael was sleeping in the trailer he was sharing with Alan, who was at work, when some men broke in and demanded drugs. Michael didn't know anything about any drugs and told them, but they kept asking and threatening him. When Michael didn't give them what they wanted, they beat him with hammers and tied him up. Somehow he untied himself and crawled to a house next door and banged on the door. Neighbors took him to the hospital. He's in intensive care."

Stunned by the enormity of the assault on my brother, I gasped, and then said, "Are you leaving for

Colorado?" My mother didn't respond right away. Then, carefully stacking her words to ensure the crescendo would stay behind long after we had hung up, she said, "Your brother Alan just told me about this yesterday. He and your father, I guess, decided that it would be too much for me. They weren't sure Michael was going to make it. They wanted to spare me." I heard her words, jiggled them around in my head, and felt no less baffled. "But Mom, Michael needs you. Even if he is a little out of the woods, don't you think you should go see him?" "No," she said. "No, I think it's better for me to stay here and get reports on how he is doing. Alan doesn't think I could handle it."

It was useless to try to persuade my mother to go and be with my critically-injured brother. She couldn't go. After a lifetime of closely observing her behavior and trying to understand it, I think her decision not to go, which at the time felt so unexplainable, so unconscionable, was probably influenced by her inability to feel much emotion for anyone other than herself, and by her sizeable and constant fear that by going she would be expected to assume some amount of responsibility. Faced with expectations that she *do* something that she likely couldn't manage or sustain, my mother withdrew. And there was one other reason I believe factored into her physical and emotional retreat: imagining her life as theater, not going provided a better arc to the drama for her. Indeed, throughout the crisis, neighbors, coworkers, and her children called her daily to make sure she was OK. It was the beginning of a brand-new theatrical role: Emotionally

143

Fragile Mother from Afar. She played it with relish for many years. Sadly, my brother's grave injury and agonizing recovery took second place to my mother's martyrdom.

Many years later Michael shared with me the story behind his assault. It began his freshman year of college. Michael had done well in high school, and with help from his high school counselor, but none from either my mother or my father (despite my mother having a master's degree and my father a medical degree), he applied and was accepted to Colby College, a strong liberal arts college in Waterville, Maine. From the beginning, Michael struggled to make tuition payments at the expensive private college. The first half of his freshman year my mother helped minimally, but whenever Michael tried to engage her on the issue of his tuition, either for funds or to sign off on financial aid or loan forms, he fell into her inverted life, which invariably required weeks out of his own to escape from. Exhausted from the unhealthy dynamic, in the second half of his freshman year he decided to declare himself financially independent. By that spring he was working several jobs to pay his tuition and room and board. He kept up that pace for another year before concluding it was too much. After his sophomore year at Colby, he transferred to the University of Colorado Boulder, which he could afford, and moved in with my brother Alan, who was working as a hospital orderly and living in a trailer on a large ranch near the university.

A few weeks into his fall semester at CU-Boulder, Michael decided to stay in on a Friday night to catch up on some of his course reading. He was sitting in the living room reading *Plato's Republic,* ironically the section discussing the definition of justice and the just man, when he heard the trailer's backdoor window break. Groggy from reading, Michael didn't have time to react to the group of men who suddenly surrounded him shouting, "Where are the drugs?" Michael told them he didn't know what they were talking about. They didn't believe him and started punching him in the chest and slapping his face and head, pausing occasionally to demand the drugs. When no drugs surfaced, they further communicated their fury by switching from using their hands to various metal objects, including hammers and hatchets, to beat Michael about his head, face, neck, and hands. The assault continued until Michael fell to the floor and passed out. Before they left, the assailants gagged him and tied him to a chair.

Barely alive and losing blood rapidly, Michael managed to untie himself and crawl out of the trailer and to the house of neighbors on the ranch, several hundred yards away. As soon as his neighbors saw him they weren't sure what they were seeing. It was dark, blood was spurting everywhere, and Michael's face and head were grossly swollen. Slipping in and out of consciousness, Michael managed to tell them he had been attacked by a group of men who had broken into the trailer. He then asked if they would take him to the university student health center. He didn't want to go to the hospital because he didn't have insurance. The neighbors carefully put him in the back seat of their car and drove as fast as they safely could to the center. The center medical staff took one look at Michael before rushing him into an ambulance for the nearest hospital.

Michael stayed in the intensive care unit for almost a week before transferring to a medical-surgical floor. It was touch-and-go the first few days, as doctors struggled to keep him alive. It was only after he was stabilized that he underwent multiple surgeries: doctors inserted metal plates in his head where his skull had been cracked, reset the fractured bones in his orbital lobe, and performed microsurgery to save his nearly severed finger. Although my mother never went to see him, Alan, Celeste, and her husband visited him daily. Twenty-four hours after hearing about the assault my father swooped into the hospital. Before conferring with Michael's medical team, he made a beeline for Michael's bed in the intensive care unit. "Michael," he murmured under his breath, "I brought your textbooks. You don't want your grades to slip."

Within days of the attack, Alan realized the intruders had broken into the trailer looking for a former roommate who had moved out just before Michael moved in. Alan knew the roommate smoked marijuana but hadn't known he was dealing harder drugs. Figuring out that he was, Alan immediately moved his and Michael's belongings out of the trailer. The vengeful posse could return any time. When Michael's date for his hospital discharge approached and my father valiantly offered, within earshot of more than one medical staff person, to have Michael come home with him to continue his recovery, Alan was relieved. He was couch surfing at a friend's apartment because he hadn't found a new apartment yet, and Michael still needed significant care. In addition to his many physical injuries, Michael had suffered a brain injury and severe emotional trauma.

Michael, too, felt some relief that my father would take care of him and wondered if the upsetting experience he'd had with him several weeks earlier was an aberration. Michael described the incident: within days of arriving in Boulder to start his fall semester, he realized that he needed a good pair of warm winter shoes but couldn't afford them. All his money had gone to tuition and he hadn't yet found a job. Financially autonomous, Michael seldom asked my wealthy father for anything, but decided this ask was urgent. Before he completed his appeal, my father interrupted him. With no emotion in his voice, he told Michael he would buy the shoes, but only if Michael first completed repairs on his roof.

When Michael was discharged from the hospital, my father picked him up at the hospital in his Lamborghini and drove him back to his luxury home. Within hours of settling into my father's beautifully decorated guest bedroom at the back of the house, my father poked his head in. "I really need to have quiet for my patients," he admonished Michael as he lay in bed not making a peep. Not once during Michael's brief stay did my father check on him or bring him food or water. When Michael eventually hobbled to the kitchen with a cane to hunt for something to eat, he found the expected: a few boxes of crackers and cereal, some baby food, a container or two of brewer's yeast, and bottles of medicine. Less than three days after he arrived, my father ordered him to leave.

Disturbed by my parents' disconnected response to Michael, and frustrated that I didn't have money to fly to see him, I felt guilty about being in school. But as Michael began to make progress, I relaxed into my freshman year. It was a heady time. I felt flush with the possibilities of life ahead—what I could do, who I could be. At the same time, I noticed I had more than a few quirky behaviors. I pushed myself relentlessly in school, constantly put myself down in front of people, and often withdrew from fun just as I was beginning to enjoy myself. Something about these things that I did made me uncomfortable, but I made no effort to explore them—I wasn't ready to know more about me.

Weeks into my first semester at Le Moyne, I began attending campus Catholic Mass and Young Catholics club meetings. As a shiny-faced freshman with more questions than answers, I was eager to explore my spiritual beliefs and relationship to the church. It helped that the Jesuit priests and nuns who led the student mass and volunteer activities were youthful and willing to incorporate fun into their devotion. Impressed by them, I began entertaining the thought that perhaps I was being called to become a nun. Thoughts of teaching underserved children in inner-city communities or going overseas as a religious to help the sick and dying felt real and important. Inspired by the electricity of caring for people who might need me, I began volunteering at a soup kitchen connected to a church in downtown Syracuse. Each Sunday morning a group of Le Moyne students would caravan to Unity Kitchen, an extension of the Unity Acres, a program for homeless men, which was affiliated with the Catholic Worker movement.

On the first Sunday I volunteered, we arrived at the soup kitchen in a white school van early in the morning. Huge aluminum pots and pans were spread out on an industrial-looking metal counter in a kitchen in the back of a small Catholic Church in downtown Syracuse. Gigantic bags of rice and monster cans of beans were parked off to the side. Everything looked prepped and ready to go, except me. Before I knew it, a group of gently-worn older men and women dressed down in flannel shirts and jeans, with denim aprons that had been through hundreds of washes, gathered around us, softly nudging us into a circle of safety and tutelage. The teaching began. Within a few weeks, I became adept at making rice and meatloaf for fifty, scrubbing baked chicken skin off the sides of broiling pans, and synchronizing my assigned duties with those of my fellow team members to meet our Sunday goal of getting a meal from concept to reality in under three hours.

What was not so easy was seeing so many faces of need. That changed when I met Hank, who slouched into the soup kitchen one Sunday in layers of brown—brown workman's pants, brown long-sleeved plaid shirt, thick brown corduroy jacket, and a well-worn pair of brown Timberland construction boots, all accented by a broad smile. I thought he was probably in his seventies, but that was the view of an eighteen-year-old. In truth, he was probably no more than fifty. Hank came up to the serving line whistling.

"Hey, bright eyes, what you got cookin' today?" he said, looking straight at me. "Chili, is that OK?" I nervously responded. "Girl, that'll work. Food's food but it's even better when it has the touch of class that you sure done given it." I chuckled and responded, "Not sure I did much. I'm just learning." "Well, life's like that chili, a bit of this and a bit of that. And in the end, it always comes out the way it's s'posed to, ain't that right?" My shoulders came down a full three inches. This was going to work. Hank and the other men in line were just people, some trying to make a better life for themselves, some just trying to hang on, and some able to connect to a young coed with small talk that wove a sturdy hanging bridge between two seemingly different worlds.

Six months after I started at the soup kitchen I had a flash of insight. My desire to become a religious, I realized, was connected to my thinking that I should pursue a life of restriction and self-denial, not a passion for my faith. And, I couldn't sidestep that once I became a nun, I would invariably chafe under a prescription of rules and regulations that demanded exacting adherence. The sisters at Le Moyne were selfless and hugely devoted to serving poor and disenfranchised members of the community. I admired that. But I couldn't ignore that they were answerable to a Church hierarchy that didn't include women. Entering an organization where I believed I would be powerless and largely ignored by leadership seemed to

150

mimic the dynamic of my childhood. That didn't feel right. The more I thought about it, the more I understood that my reasons for becoming a nun were safety-pinned to my belief that I didn't deserve a husband or children. As this connection materialized in my head, a visceral force within me pushed back. I wanted a family.

While I successfully changed my career choice to allow myself the opportunity to find love and have a family, there was no change in the belief I held that it was my fault that my mother didn't love me. Two interactions that freshman year reinforced this thought. The first happened after I fell at the school gym. To do battle against my first Syracuse winter blues and escape from the bone-chilling outdoor temperatures while breaking a sweat, several friends and I decided to run a few miles on the school's indoor track. Afterwards, I went to the weight room to do sit-ups. When I finished my mat exercises, I pulled a chair over to one of the freestanding cross bars athletes use for pull-ups and kicked the chair away. I wanted a good stretch. The running/stopping/hanging sequence, however, caused a precipitous fall in my blood pressure. I blacked out and fell face first onto the cement floor below.

When I regained consciousness, my nose was OK but I was bleeding from my mouth. Frightened, my friends bundled me into a car and took me to the hospital, where the emergency room doctor checked out my teeth—still intact—and stitched up my lip. A month later, however, I noticed my front left tooth was turning an unsettling shade of gray. I quickly got a referral from the student health center and went to a dentist. He x-rayed the tooth and told me the fall had killed the nerve and that I would need a root canal and a cap on my front tooth. He also suggested that I cap my other front tooth, which was not injured, so my front teeth would not look dissimilar.

Upset about losing my front tooth I called my mother. Once I reached her, I told her what the dentist said about capping my non-injured front tooth, and asked, "Mom, what I should do?" No response. I never got used to my mother's silences. When they filled the space between us, an image of her falling helplessly into darkness with no bottom would pop into my mind. Even though I was asking her for help, she seemed to be the one in need. I waited a few minutes for her to say something, to connect with me. When she didn't, I changed the subject. Released from any expectation that she help me, she immediately reengaged and chattered amiably away about nothing important.

With no guidance from my mother, I followed the dentist's suggestion and had both teeth capped. Later I learned that was unnecessary. What bothered me most about the experience was not my teeth; it was that no injury, physical or emotional, not even Michael's horrific beating, seemed significant enough to elicit my mother's compassion and attention. How had she sat vigil during Gillian's multiple childhood hospitalizations, flourishing, it seemed, on the urgency of each crisis? Many years later I discovered a likely answer. I was replaying the movie of my mother in my head, starting with my earliest memories, when suddenly a few forgotten parts emerged. The most compelling was that she had always been hugely incapacitated in her ability to care for us. Throughout our childhood, we had no regular parental, medical, or dental care. When I walked myself back through the maze of our medical emergencies, I couldn't miss that any involvement on her part was the direct result of someone outside our family physically and emotionally guiding her to the crisis. Once engaged, however, she seduced the medical staff with her abundant charm, fluidly working the room until the last glimmer of excitement faded. This longitudinal perspective on how she parented us helped me understand her disinterest in our adult medical injuries. She was long past wanting to pretend she could or would take on any responsibility for us, and there were no longer any friends, teachers, or neighbors to nudge her along. Besides, playing Florence Nightingale to a grown child wouldn't garner half the attention of a single mother at the bedside of a critically ill young child.

The other memory I have of not being a deserving or good enough kid for my mother took place when she came to watch me in the play *Barefoot in the Park,* in the spring of my freshman year. Up to that point, I hadn't much acting experience. Following my acting debut as the Six of Hearts in my elementary-school production of *Alice in Wonderland,* I had one follow-up role: Hermia in a junior high school English class production of *A Midsummer Night's Dream.* With nothing to lose, I auditioned for *Barefoot in the Park* and was astounded when I was cast as the mother, Mrs. Ethel Banks, with more than a few lines. I only have vague memories of the play but cannot forget that my mother made the four-hour drive from Philadelphia to Syracuse to see it. I was doing something she valued, and she rewarded me by showing up.

After the play my mother told me my performance was good but saved her superlatives for how much I looked like my grandmother, her ex-mother-in-law, in my character's box-cut jacket and matching pencil skirt. "Oh, my gosh, Nikki, you look just like your grandmother. Honestly, I can't get over it. It's incredible. That outfit, the way you moved on stage, you could be her," she said moments after the play was over. So pleased with herself that she had discovered my paternal grandmother's doppelganger, she kept going. "I just can't get over it. That could have been your grandmother up there on stage, you two look so much alike."

When I was growing up, my mother often told me I was similar in personality to my grandmother. She would enthusiastically emphasize that we were both organized and energetic, qualities she said she did not have. After highlighting these "positive" attributes, she would slyly intimate that we shared some less desirable characteristics: "Oh, and you two share other similarities too. Well, I don't need to tell you, Nikki, that your grandmother is very judgmental. She always made me feel inferior, lower class." At the time, I didn't fully understand the reference. Now that my mother thought I physically looked like my

154

grandmother, that in fact I was she, I was distraught. Every fortune cookie said the same thing: "Your mother will never love you."

The big open sky that changed colors with the seasons in Syracuse was captivating but not enough to help me cope with winter, which was long, freezing cold, and gray. Ten-foot high snow banks flanked campus sidewalks in January and February. Coming from more temperate Philadelphia, I struggled to adapt to the raw cold. Making my adjustment even harder, I would not allow myself to buy the clothing I needed to stay warm. I had plenty of money from my work-study funds and could easily have bought proper winter clothes, but I was afraid to use it. I also remember thinking I shouldn't spend $25 for a warm coat. It seemed way too much to spend on myself. Instead of purchasing a coat, I wore layers of wool sweaters underneath a thin, used jacket that I bought at a local thrift shop. On my legs, I wore a pair of navy wool sailor pants also from the thrift shop, a bargain at a dollar. With an average winter wind chill of many degrees below zero, I wore multiple sweaters under the shell jacket and sailor pants over long underwear every day for months.

On a warm day in May close to the end of the spring semester and my first year at Le Moyne, I was musing over how I had barely survived my first frigid winter in Syracuse, while looking at a collage of colorful brochures on a school bulletin board near the cafeteria. Most of the brochures advertised exotic study abroad opportunities in France, Italy, Spain, and England. A few dressed up the opportunity for chemistry and math scholarships for the quantitatively gifted with photos of smiling students in white coats wielding beakers and test tubes. Then my eye settled on a lone brochure advertising opportunities for students attending Jesuit colleges or universities to transfer, for a semester or permanently, to a sister Jesuit college or university. Immediately intrigued, I read on. The brochure said students requesting either kind of transfer would first need to be accepted by the new school. Admission was based on the student's high school and college transcripts and motivation for transferring. Once a student was accepted, the school would determine which college credits it could honor for completed course work. Underneath this text was an italicized sentence that made my heart flutter. It said course work credits within the Jesuit college-university system were generally transferrable.

At the bottom of the brochure was a list of all the four-year Jesuit colleges in the country. As though guided on a Ouija board, my eyes went directly to another brochure on the bulletin board, one advertising the University of San Francisco (USF), a Jesuit university in the city I had fallen in love with at fourteen on the teen tour. The next thought arrived even faster than the previous: San Francisco was warmer than Syracuse, far away, and had an open, welcoming vibe. I instantly knew that I would transfer to USF. It didn't even bother me that I had missed the transfer application deadline for the fall semester and would have to apply for the spring. I was going.

When I returned to Le Moyne for my sophomore year after working as a waitress over the summer in Hyannis Port, Cape Cod, I moved into a dormitory apartment suite with my *Three Musketeers* girlfriends. Before I had even finished unpacking my suitcases, I stepped into a dizzying schedule of activity. Movement kept me from the quiet necessary to tie a tighter knot between my thoughts, feelings, and actions. I resumed my twenty-hour per week work-study job, my Sunday volunteer position at Unity Kitchen, and my intensive study schedule to keep up with my classes, which had become more demanding, because the previous spring I had accepted an invitation to join the school's honors program. At the same time, I began preparing my transfer application.

As I waited to hear whether USF would accept me and assume the academic scholarship and financial work-study award Le Moyne had given me, I tried to understand my decision to transfer. Deep self-analysis escaped me. I wasn't able to fully decode why I was leaving a school that offered me emotional, intellectual, and financial support. Keeping things simple, I settled on one reason for my transfer—*I can't stay because I am too cold; besides, I don't have the right winter clothes.* There was truth in this explanation, but I was emotionally too immature and too young to understand that the fuller reason was that I felt out of place at Le Moyne. The feeling wasn't conscious, but occasionally, I felt a confusing sting of not belonging.

The most painful experience of feeling like an outsider at Le Moyne occurred not long after my friends and I had moved into our sophomore dorm suite. We were lounging in the suite's shared living room, when AnneMarie, one of my roommates, nervously told me that over the summer her family had expressed strong reservations about her living with me. I had met her parents several times and even spent a weekend at their house with AnneMarie during our freshman year. I thought they liked me. "Why?" I asked, trying to conceal my hurt feelings. AnneMarie slowly responded, "I don't really know why." After an expanded pause, her face now a bright red, she stammered, "Well, I think it's because they think you might be too wild for me."

The memory of Angela, my childhood friend, and her father's rejection of me came roaring back into my mind. I was stunned by yet another negative assessment of me by a friend's parents. Feeling hurt and upset, I wanted to call AnneMarie's parents to tell them that of the two of us, they should be more concerned about *their* daughter. AnneMarie had been far more adventurous than I our freshman year. Unlike me, she naturally and uninhibitedly pushed back at boundaries that had given her comfort and stability when she was younger. Her world would not punish her if she drank a little more one night or skipped a class here and there. Making mistakes, for her, was part of being young, part of growing up. I never called AnneMarie's parents. In the end, I realized that my fantasy about calling them was a kneejerk reaction to feeling

158

judged. In truth, they didn't have anything to be concerned about with either of us.

Indulging my habit of ruminating, for weeks I wondered what it was about me that set off alarm bells for AnneMarie's parents. At first I thought it was my appearance. Of course. They were uncomfortable with the way I looked, with my thrift shop clothes and unruly curly blonde hair that tumbled in a billowy mane halfway down my back. Next I mused that it must be my unconventional habits, like running daily outside until the temperature dropped below zero. Both were possible factors. Then it hit me. What probably upset AnneMarie's parents the most was that I had no family to speak of, no mother fussing over me, no father guarding my virtue. Translated, I was a risk for their daughter. I knew that judgment. I also knew that in the Monopoly game of life, I had been given a *Free Chance* card with the opportunity to go to college. That was more important than what some people thought of me. I let go of their judgment and held on fiercely to my card.

In early November, I received a letter from USF informing me that I had been accepted as a transfer student and that the university would continue my academic scholarship and financial work-study award. The school also confirmed that all my credits from Le Moyne would transfer: I would not have to make up any additional course work to complete my political science major and French minor. It was fantastic news. "I'm going, I'm going! USF gave me the scholarship!" I yelled to my roommates, AnneMarie and Carol, seconds after opening the letter.

Both squealed back in excitement. "Monique, that's great. Wow! Congratulations!" AnneMarie said. So giddy about the news, I willfully chose not to fully register the shadow of sadness that passed over their faces.

At the end of the semester, full of emotion, I said goodbye to my best friends and took the bus from Syracuse to Philadelphia to spend winter break with my mother, secretly happy that I would soon be unchaining myself from her backyard. Visits home from Le Moyne were distressing and unchanging. Weeks before I made the typical six-hour bus trek from Syracuse to Philadelphia, I would begin the telephoning exercise to tell my mother I was coming home. Once she picked up the phone, she assured me she would get me at the bus station on the scheduled day and time. That was important: the bus station was in a dicey part of Philadelphia, and because I typically arrived in the late evening hours, I was anxious to be picked up as soon as I got off the bus.

Stepping off the bus my first visit home from Le Moyne my freshman year, I looked for my mother. She wasn't in the parking lot. After walking around the depot and checking the bathrooms, and still not finding her, I dug up a few dimes and dialed her home number. I let the phone ring for one minute, two, then three, before hanging up and trying again. An hour later, my anxiety rising, I decided to call the mother of a close high school girlfriend, waking her up. Hearing my scared voice and unspoken *I don't know what else to do*, she jumped into the car to get me. Driving to my mother's house she asked me why I

160

thought my mother hadn't answered her phone. Embarrassed, I told her that something had probably come up. This kind woman rescued me several more times late at night from the bus station, but never again asked me that question. If she had, I couldn't have answered her.

My mother never explained why she didn't pick me up. She met gentle questions and harsher interrogations with her silence response, which had become more finely tuned since she had first unveiled it to me before I left for college. It now appeared tied to a strange highly stylized game of hide-and-seek. She was the hider and we, her children, were the seekers. Not easily dissuaded and always hopeful, I was a natural seeker. My mother knew this and seemed to take pleasure in my desperation for her. Before the end of every phone call she earnestly pledged to be at the bus station, always signing off with a breathy, "Love you so much, honey!" Seduced by those words that sailed through the receiver with such affection, I believed she would come through. I believed so many times. Positioning herself within sight but never within reach must have been deeply satisfying to my mother—she had control over me.

When I told my mother about my decision to transfer to USF, her response was benign disinterest. Another day in someone else's life she barely knew. Days before my departure from Philadelphia to San Francisco, though, she became sweetly emotional about my leaving. The morning before my departure, I skidded into the kitchen of her row home rental thrilled that my new adventure was beginning the next day by Greyhound Bus.

My mother was standing motionless by the window, staring out the window. She was supposed to have left for work. The mug of instant coffee that she held upright with an index finger looped through the handle looked like it was about to fall. Dishes were piled in the sink and on top of the dishwasher, which had been moved from its regular place next to the sink into the middle of the small kitchen to give the machine's thick black rubber hose attached to the faucet a better angle for the water to run. "Mom, hey, are you OK?" I asked, worry in my voice. She turned to me. "I am going to miss you so much," she said. Then she began to cry. "Mom, it's OK, we can talk on the phone and I really want you to come out to see me. San Francisco is beautiful. And you can stop to see Celeste and Alan in Colorado on the way out," I cheerily said, hoping I was turning the tide of the dark mood that had swallowed her whole.

"I don't know what I am going to do without you, Nikki," she whispered. Taken aback by her words and surprise emotion, I put my arms around her and held her, certain her tears were a sweet expression of love and affection for me. "Mom, I love you so much," I responded soothingly. "I'm so sorry I'm going—I'm really sad to leave you too."

While I was a young adult, my mother repeated these sentiments of loss and despair several more times, and I was increasingly baffled by them. Like so many of her incomprehensible behaviors that I felt compelled to track and deconstruct so I could understand them and her, I noticed a pattern. They always coincided with my moving from one city or place to another but were never anchored by or a reflection of any measure of intimacy between us. Not only were we not living in the same city or state—before or after these emotional presentations—we rarely saw or spoke to one another. With distance and time, I wonder if they reflected other feelings my mother struggled with: ever-present sadness, fear of being alone, fear of being abandoned. It's also possible that believing herself a theater actress, she took each opportunity of my moving to act out her portrayal of loss.

The next day, I boarded a Greyhound bus for the cross-country ride from Philadelphia to San Francisco. Again, I showed up at college solo, but this time with two suitcases in hand instead of one. When I stepped off the bus in San Francisco, I felt good about my decision. The air, the people, and the city's Victorian houses painted in a rainbow of colors seemed to grant me immediate permission to be myself.

Within days of organizing my spring classes at USF, I jumped into the task of selecting my work-study assignment. Le Moyne work-study options were limited. Most were in the cafeteria and library. But USF offered a wide range of opportunities on and off campus. After looking through pages of possibilities, I found an organization and position that intrigued me: Rafiki Masada, a short-term group home for teens who had experienced run-ins with the law, was looking for a student to help them with filing and other administrative functions. Working for a nonprofit dedicated to giving troubled kids a second chance sounded just right. Plus, the home was located near USF, just on the other side of San Francisco's Golden Gate Park, a thirty-minute walk from my dormitory. I submitted my name for the job, interviewed, and was hired.

My assimilation into Rafiki happened quickly. Days after starting at the group home, I was knee-deep in my twenty-hour-per-week administrative assistant job, answering phones, organizing client files, updating resource listings, and helping the executive director and counselors with correspondence to and from the courts and youth agencies. The group home was in a standard single-family home on a street just north of the University of California, San Francisco Medical Center. An average of four to six teens—boys and girls, from age thirteen to eighteen—lived in the house at any given time for a few days to six months. Before committing to the program, the teens were given the choice of participating in Rafiki's six-month, co-educational rehabilitation program with a dedicated counselor, who became the resident's mother, father, therapist, probation officer, and headmaster, or staying in the city's juvenile detention center. The house was seldom empty. On my first day of work, I was struck by how much the house and the lives of the residents resembled a snow globe that never stopped shaking; it was constant activity and intense drama in blizzard conditions.

When I started working at Rafiki I was nineteen, just a year older than the oldest teens served by the program. I worked at Rafiki for two-and-a-half years, until I finished college. Initially, my duties were limited to administrative functions, but after my first year, I was given more responsibility. Sometimes when residents were feeling upset, because of a put-down by friends or a parent, a fight at school, or a negative court ruling, I was given permission to talk to them to help them blow off steam. I discovered the best listening-talking sessions happened when I took the resident out for a walk or down to the basement, where they could hit a punching bag while telling me how they were feeling. That's when I learned to listen. What I heard made me think that many of the teens in the program had been born and raised in petri dishes of parental neglect, mental illness, and despair.

Rafael punched the bag in the musty basement hard. "This is so fucked up," he hissed. "I go to get this bag of pot, and I get busted. My mother couldn't give a shit, and my father ain't never shown up, like not even one day. Like I'm fuckin' not worth it or something." I asked Rafael to come down to the basement and punch the bag a few times as a distraction. He and another boy, Enron, were circling each other and a nasty fight was on the verge of erupting. Once we got to the basement, not knowing what else to do, I encouraged Rafael to talk. "What happened after the police picked you up—what did your mom say?" I asked. Rafael scrunched his face, and told me, "I was selling but I wasn't making much and besides, coming home there was never any food, so I just used the money I made to take care of me. Besides, I couldn't even find my mother, so she said nothing. She was out with her friends, drunk as usual or usin'." Rafael hit the bag hard and then harder. "I don't want to be in this hellhole with all these stupid rules, comin' up against other stupid kids and their issues. I want to be someone, man." Sweat stains spread under his arms on his gray tee shirt. Rafael hit the bag for a long time, throwing in a few kicks to be sure I could see he had the moves. While he talked nonstop, I listened. A half-hour later, he didn't seem so angry, so tight.

On my way to and from Rafiki my first few months, I often passed an old man sitting alone on the front stoop of his small studio apartment, a few doors down from the group home. He resembled a beloved old coat: comfortable, patched, and wholly defined by a lifetime of use. Whenever I passed him I said hello; his name was Harold. My hellos soon became small chats and then lengthier exchanges, each of us sharing more about who we were, what we thought about, how we defined ourselves in a world both wondrous and inscrutable. My favorite Harold story was his description of his birth. "My mama had me early. I guess you would say I was a preemie, but back then we had no preemie this or preemie that. I was maybe three or four pounds. Everyone gave up on me and said to my mama, 'Leave the boy alone, he's going to die.' mama wouldn't give up. She stuck me in the oven. She didn't close the door or nothing; she just put me in there and kept me in there every day for a month till I was bigger. Mama saved me."

Harold was a retired shipyard worker who had dropped out of high school. At age thirty, he married a

Russian immigrant for a time he described as a wink. She divorced him shortly after their only child died hours after being born. Harold's only relative was a sister around the corner. She rented rooms from an old Victorian house she owned and kept an eye on Harold. Other than minimal interaction with her, Harold spent all his time alone, most of it studying science, politics, and current events. Every week he sent a summary of his latest scientific theory to *Scientific American* or *National Geographic*, diligently typed out two-finger style on a manual typewriter. Each theory seemed plausible, although the magazines never thought so. That never discouraged him. Sometimes mispronouncing the five-dollar words scientists used to explain their research, he would eagerly introduce his latest idea to me. Refreshing and novel, my friendship with Harold grew from stoop-side talks to the occasional game of chess to dinner once a week.

The first time I stepped into Harold's apartment I panicked. Like my mother, he was a hoarder. Scanning his closet-size studio apartment filled with the tinkering of his ideas and interests, I wasn't sure I could tolerate the mild mayhem or dirt. But I did. Unlike my mother who pretended the goat trails you had to carefully thread between ceiling-high swaying walls of junk were not actually there, or threw a blanket over a swollen pile of clothes and discarded bric-a-brac in her shower so you wouldn't guess what they really were, Howard played it straight. He didn't apologize; he didn't disguise; and he didn't hide anything about himself. His hoarded hovel was

167

his home. He acknowledged his studio was junky but defended it as his own, proud that his handprints and thought prints made it so. That I understood. That I could accept.

One late afternoon I was standing in Harold's tiny kitchen filled with grease-stained walls, dirty cast-iron frying pans, stacks and stacks of *National Geographic* and *Scientific American* magazines, and empty vegetable cans, when Harold clumsily grabbed my arm and tried to kiss me. I pushed him back, bewildered. "What are you doing!" I demanded. Harold's weathered, lined face looked confused and then mournfully chagrined. "Well, I don't know. You were coming around here and I didn't know why, so I thought maybe you wanted that," he said, with one hand on a chair to steady himself. "No!" I stuttered, confused as he was, "No, I didn't want that!" Shaken, I left.

The relationship had been so clear in my head. I had noticed a lonely older person, felt sorry and responsible for him, and befriended him to make him feel better. The big surprise was that I enjoyed Harold. He had become a genuine friend and sort of father. It never occurred to me that my intentions might have been confusing. Harold's attempt to kiss me made me feel bad. I wondered if I had unintentionally led him on in some way. Unsure of how to deal with my embarrassment, I avoided him and began taking a much longer roundabout route to work so I wouldn't pass near his apartment. The ice broke one day when he saw me entering the group home and yelled my name from several doors down, where he was sitting on his front step. I walked over to him, apprehensive. He was nervous too but managed to push out his question, would I stop by after work? "Yes," I told him. When I came back down the hill several hours later, he was still sitting on the step, waiting for me. In an awkward halting voice, he said he was sorry and, if I wanted, he would like me to still visit with him. I was not used to adults who apologized. "Sure, but please don't ever try to kiss me again. I just want to be a friend, that's all. I'm really sorry if I confused you," I answered. Harold smiled at me, clacking his ill-fitting dentures.

Romantic confusion out of the way, Harold treated me more like a daughter, happy to give me lots of advice, solicited and unsolicited. We continued playing chess, talking politics, and sharing a weekly meal that alternated between grilled cheese, tomato soup, Chinese takeout, and pizza. Our get-togethers continued for almost two years until I graduated college and left for Peace Corps. In his first letter to me in Peace Corps, he had some fun responding to a letter I wrote him telling him I had begun eating meat because it was one of the few foods available with protein.

I have wondered how you were going to handle that diet problem of yours over there. What sort of eating facilities do you have there? Is it a cafeteria where you get individual meals or is it family style where you all eat the same thing? Anyway, I am glad that you are learning to eat meat as I think you need it, lots of it. It is the best known source of protein and the human race has developed eating it, and America was built on it in the early days of the country. You always did look like you were about half-starved, so maybe that will put some meat on your bones.

Thinking about the honest and caring friendship I had with Harold, it occurred to me that from junior high school on I had three consistent relationship patterns. There were toxic people I ran away from, although it sometimes took me a while to figure out they were noxious before I bolted; there were nourishing people I ran toward; and there were people in between, broken but not severely disturbed, who wanted me to make them whole. Eventually I ran away from those people, too. Happily, Harold was one of the people I ran toward.

I was lucky to have Harold in my life, because there were a few people I had to run away from in San Francisco. "Monique, I can't take it anymore!" The voice came through muffled and pitchy on the phone.

"What, what? Who is this?" Panicking at the alarm in the voice on the other end, I mentally tried to make sense of the words, but I had been asleep and needed a few seconds for my neurons to connect.

The voice came on again, odd in tone but firm in message. "I can't take it, Monique, I've had it. I'm going to the Golden Gate Bridge and I am going to jump!"

Synaptic connections finally activated, I responded, "Please," I pleaded. "Please, whoever you are, don't do

170

anything. Who is this? Steve, is that you? Steve, please don't do anything! Where are you? What's going on?" Silence. Then the voice, woozy but determined, said, "It's all over." "Wait—please!" I shouted back. The phone went dead. Disoriented from the exchange, I gripped the receiver, my anguish stretched tight. I was in my junior year of college and the person on the phone sounded like a guy I had been dating, Steve, a student at the nearby California College of Podiatric Medicine. I met Steve on a sunny afternoon walking through USF's quad on the way to class. Steve was sitting on a bench, the best place, he had told me, to meet a coed—the podiatry school was mostly male.

I immediately dialed Steve's number.

"Steve, hi, it's me, Monique." It was late at night and Steve answered the phone with a harsh voice, one that I imagined seconds earlier in a dream had been commanding troops into battle. I quickly blurted out, "I'm calling because I just got a call from a guy that sounded like you. He said he was going to kill himself. I thought it was you. I am so sorry, but are you OK?" With the why of the call out of the way, I hurried to backfill the rest of the story, my heart thumping. I gave Steve details about the man who called me and threatened to commit suicide at the Golden Gate Bridge. Steve's response was swift and angry. "How dare you think I would ever commit suicide, and by the way, thanks a lot for waking me up in the middle of the night. I have a big test tomorrow morning!" Trying to calm him down, I gently told him I was sorry I had upset him. I explained that the person who called me had sounded like him, and I just wanted to be sure he was OK. He didn't budge. I tried another angle; I told him earnestly and with a conviction that I still feel today that anyone is capable of having suicidal thoughts. What is important, I added, is that we help rather than judge people who at any moment in time might feel like life isn't worth living. That didn't work either. Steve's fury continued to ooze through the holes in my receiver. I told him I needed to go.

After I hung up, I chose not to think about Steve or his reaction. Someone was on the verge of hurting himself. That took precedence over an angry boyfriend. I contemplated calling the police but rejected that plan. I had a vague suicide threat by a person with no name and no reportable location, other than the Golden Gate Bridge. Dread kept me awake for the rest of the night. The next morning, I told my roommate about the call. She suggested I contact USF and report it. So I did. The school administration took down the information, contacted the police, and called me back. The police confirmed there had been no reported suicides or attempted suicides earlier that morning at the Golden Gate Bridge. I exhaled. On the follow-up inhale I wondered, *who made the call to me and why? Was there still someone out there who was hurting? Would that person call me again?*

Two weeks after the suicide threat phone call I got a call early one evening. Two guys I knew from the USF Speech and Debate Club that I had joined earlier in my junior year were on the line. With no buildup as to why they were calling, they immediately blurted out that they were sorry. "For what?" I asked. I could hear air being sucked in. It made the same sound as air whooshing upward into a vacuum cleaner. "We played a joke on you," one of them said. In a knot of words, they confessed that they had been drinking a few weeks back and as a joke decided to call me up, with one of them threatening to kill himself. I was speechless. When I recovered from my shock, I asked why they or anyone would do something so horrible to another person. Admitting to feeling some shame about their backfired joke, they told me they both had a crush on me, and the call was payback. They perceived me as unattainable. Rattled by their lack of human decency, I told them that because of their "joke," I had truly believed that someone was going to end his life and there was nothing I could do to stop that from happening. I hung up the phone.

My relationship with Steve didn't last. Some part of me knew I was already hanging onto one person in my life lacking empathy and compassion, and two would be unbearable. Still, recovering from the fake suicide threat proved immensely difficult. I continued to run and to write in my journal, but neither could displace the thought that I was to blame for the joke played on me. After perseverating for several weeks about the call, I began thinking maybe I should get some help. Weighing my discomfort about talking to a stranger against the fear that the negative tape I had been playing in my head had no stop button, I decided to speak to someone.

At my first counseling session, I carefully examined the woman sitting across from me. I was on guard. Not only did I mistrust my psychiatrist father, I vividly remembered the male family therapist who had devastated me at thirteen with his insensitive and inappropriate comment. I wasn't holding out much hope for this therapist. The pleasant middle-aged college counselor met my cautiousness with a face softly lined in compassion. I felt safe enough, and my account tumbled out slowly, finally molding itself into a story with a beginning, middle, and end. For the first twenty minutes of the fifty-five-minute session, I discussed the actors who took top billing in my tale, the guys from Speech and Debate and my boyfriend, and my circling negative thoughts. Before long, though, I began talking about my mother. I didn't know why she upstaged the men. I talked about her nonstop until the end of our session. In minute detail I described her inaccessibility, distance, manipulation, and coldness, giving example after example. When I took a breath, our time was up, and I sat back in my chair dazed and drained.

I met with the counselor six more times. Each session the story of my mother trumped the suicide threat drama. Before therapy, I sculpted the anger I felt toward my mother into the palatable emotion of frustration and labeled it a byproduct of normal parent-child tensions. Similarly, I recast her profound neglect of us as the result of not having a father. My mother deftly encouraged these interpretations. Intentional or not, they normalized her behavior and our deprivation. After the sessions, however, the narrative tapes in my head about her were no longer playing so smoothly. They had begun to skip and jerk in

174

parts. My mother was more of a central character in what ailed me than I had thought. Years later I understood why: she was my first betrayal, the first person to behave indifferently toward me, and to communicate that her needs took precedence over mine. The men in my counseling story were just copycats.

The phone-call game with my mother that had started at Le Moyne continued while I was at USF. The counselor suggested that I tell my mother how I felt when she didn't answer my calls or call me. Nervous, I followed her suggestion. On the next call with my mother, I slowly and tentatively told her that her emotional remoteness felt like rejection. "Oh, my phone was disconnected, that's why I didn't call you," she responded sharply. Pause. Confident nothing more really needed to be said, she added, "Well, honey, there is another reason too. Sometimes I just don't have the energy to speak to you or anyone." Even when her explanations seemed reasonable, I had trouble juxtaposing them with a mother who seemed competent at her job and rarely missed a day of work. Nothing changed.

The relationship I had with my father during college was of a different stripe. Because I hadn't spent any extended or meaningful time with him as a child, I felt little need or obligation to interact with him as a young adult. He felt the same way. A favorite refrain of his was, "If any of you kids want a relationship with me, then you need to call me. I'm here; I've always been here. I am not the one who should have to make the effort." And he didn't.

After I transferred to USF, I spoke occasionally with him by phone and visited him once, arriving with a beat-up travel bag, hoping this would be the visit where he found me appealing, someone he deemed smart enough to keep up with him. That didn't happen, but I did make him laugh with offbeat stories of my life in college, always making sure that I was the butt of the joke. I instinctively did this to assure him I was not and never could be a threat to his belief in his superiority. He loved the story about my being the second fastest runner on the USF Women's Cross-Country team, just ahead of a self-proclaimed chain smoker, and a woman who was sure she could beat me if she lost thirty pounds. That visit, like all visits with my father, was a continuation of my childhood playdates with him: I rode shotgun in whatever fancy car he had at the time, while he ran his endless series of errands.

Throughout my early childhood, the chasm between how my father lived and how we lived remained consistently deep and wide: he indulged in excessive luxury while we coped with chaos and daily struggles with scarcity. As a teenager when I walked into his Colorado home for the first time, it was hard to breathe. The divide was even bigger. From a small but stylish apartment in Philadelphia, he and his new wife, Alicia, had relocated to a large custom-built French provincial home overlooking Boulder with a view of the Rockies. The house included a state-of-the-art kitchen; several beautiful bathrooms tastefully furnished with elegant fixtures—in one, a bidet proudly took residence alongside the toilet; a master bedroom suite; a guest bedroom; and an office suite where he saw patients. French antiques were everywhere, along with paintings, small sculptures, and a wall of my father's own black-and-white photographs. I was one of the faces in those photographs—a black-and-white photo he had taken of me when I was four, part of his photography period, a time in his life when he aspired to become a famous photographer. Strangely, my mother's face was also in the collection next to Alicia's. Parental dismemberment and divorce apparently never got in the way of art for my father.

The house also included an upstairs open loft that ran the length of the house. It was the resident art studio for my father's photography and painting, as well as for Alicia's cloth art. Granular details of how Alicia created her art escape me. Vaguely what I remember is that she arranged human models and other objects in various poses on top of enormous pieces of cloth stretched across the floor. Once her models and objects were in place, she directed strong lights onto the tableau. As I recall it, she had treated the cloth with something that interacted with the light to create an outline of whatever was placed on top of it. After a prescribed period, the light was turned off and the models and objects were removed. What stayed behind was an eerie outline of everything that had lain on the material. In post-production, Alicia used different dyes to color in the various outlines. The finished murals reflected movement and depth. Many were good. I especially liked the ones with vibrant color. Alicia and my father's marriage didn't last, but the art studio lived on as the creative space for my father and several more female companions, those who were artistic. My father married twice after Alicia. In between his marriages, he had several long-term relationships but never had any more children.

While I was staying with my father on that first visit to his Colorado home, unsurprisingly nearly all our time together was spent in the car. As always, my father's life was large and important. When he wasn't seeing patients at his house or at a small private psychiatric hospital, we ran errands in Boulder and Denver. The car we rode in was his everyday car, a souped-up BMW. His truer love, the one he kept hidden away in the garage for special occasions, was his Lamborghini. Like a child who wants to show you his newest shiniest truck, forty-eight hours into the visit my father decided I was worthy of a very brief spin in the Lamborghini one late afternoon. My father had always been lustily affectionate with his sports cars. When physically in reach of them, he talked to them and slid his hands along their bodies in long slow caresses. Whenever they were in the shop, as expensive cars often are, their absences were never considered a transgression. Tune-ups and repairs were treated as rejuvenating spa periods critical for the cars to remain youthful and appealing.

With zero interest, I dutifully crawled into the passenger seat of the ultra-chic racecar for my test drive, seconds before my father rocketed out of the driveway and up and down the streets of his fancy housing development. I didn't like the ride or the car or how I spent time with my father. I felt like I had been dipped in and out of opulence, and I was angry. Why didn't it bother him that he lived in a pricey house, wore expensive clothes, bought designer skis, and drove high-end sports cars while we struggled in poverty? He looked past the thrift shop clothes I arrived in and seemed to see no difference between his tony life and ours, not even a smidgeon of irony. Once free of him, I ran back to my unfettered thoughts and life in my universe, a place where people and events made a little more sense.

One day fresh from running the mile from USF to Rafiki for my afternoon work shift in the fall of my senior year, I launched into some leftover filing from the previous day. While I was moving back and forth between various filing cabinets, one of the house counselors came in to the office. Holding a magazine journal in one hand with her index finger as placeholder on one of the pages, she said, "Here, I want you to read this article. It's really good. You seem to be getting it about our kids, so I think this will help you understand even more, where some of our kids are coming from—what kinds of mothers more than a few of them probably have." Intrigued, I sat right down and began reading, *Superkids: Competent Children of Psychotic Mothers*. In seconds, I experienced a strange feeling; I was reading about me.

The article profiled a small study of children with psychotic mothers. In the study group there was, as expected, a significant number of less competent children, defined as children with emotional, social, and behavioral problems. There was also a surprise small subgroup of competent children. *Superkids*, as they were called, were reasonably well-adapted, high-performing children who reported having a best friend and extensive and positive contact with an adult, as well as a relationship with their mothers that was supportive and empathic but not intrusive. Not all the characteristics matched my experience, but there appeared to be enough similarities between me and the subgroup that when I finished reading the article, I whispered to myself, "I'm a Superkid." Tingling, I wanted to tell someone but didn't dare. I had stumbled on a partial explanation of me that made sense. Before placing the moment in long-term memory inside a box marked "Secret," I savored the tiny feeling that there was more to me than I could understand at the time.

As I finished my senior year of college, I applied to serve as a volunteer in Peace Corps. My reasons were simple. I wanted to help others and I wanted to do it speaking French—I had remained enthralled with French since kindergarten at Montessori. I hoped my background at the group home would match up with a volunteer need in one of several French-speaking countries, where Peace Corps had volunteers. Luckily that happened. Before I graduated, Peace Corps accepted me as a community development volunteer in French-speaking Central African Republic. I was excited, nervous, and hopeful.

Weeks after graduation I packed up my belongings and said goodbye to San Francisco, the city where I had flourished in school and work, and in friendships. I flew first to Denver to say goodbye to my father, then to Omaha to see my paternal grandparents, and finally to Philadelphia to visit with my mother, who had agreed to drive me to John F. Kennedy (JFK) airport in New York City in mid-July to join my cohort of volunteers flying to the Central African Republic.

During the two-day visit with my father, en route to Africa, his weirdness seemed to have become more glaring. No longer a child who needed to shut out what felt so wrong to guard my sanity, I started to look at his behavior with greater curiosity and concern. It began with his habit of bartering with some of his psychiatric patients, providing analysis to them in exchange for art and various services such as dog sitting, house cleaning, and yard work. As we walked into his house, just back from the airport in Denver where he had picked me up, he told me the woman vacuuming his living room was a patient of his. Not knowing much about payment protocol for mental health services, I asked him about the arrangement. As usual, he had a persuasive explanation for everything he did. He told me that because he primarily treated very wealthy patients in his private practice he could not see artists and the occasional tradesperson referred to him, since they could not afford his sessions. His generosity, he said, led him to provide treatment for a select group of patients who could not afford his fees, but who could provide specific services he needed and wanted. Believing in his infallibility, he saw no problems with the practice. From my vantage point, it seemed like a great exchange for him, but not such a good one for his patients—on many levels.

Shortly after we arrived at the house, my father said he had to go to the small inpatient psychiatric facility where he worked to do rounds. The plan was that I would find a quiet corner to read in while he saw patients. Just before we split up, my father ran into some fellow psychiatrists. After chatting with them in the hallway for a few moments, he turned back to me, and with a wave of his arm motioned in my direction. In a loud voice he said, "This is my sister, Monique." I instantly shot back, "Oh Dad, that's so funny!" Indignation flared up in his eyes. His mouth quivered and twitched with fury at me. How dare I expose him, his paternity and age, to his colleagues? I'm sure it never occurred to him that he had just lied in front of his peers or devalued me as his child. After a nervous group laugh, my father changed the subject. Years later one of my sisters told me that once she became a teen, he routinely introduced her as his sister. And one of my brothers told me that he didn't even make the sibling cut: my father regularly introduced him as his friend.

After we returned home from rounds, my father bounced into the guest bedroom where I was staying. With no apparent shame or discomfort over his recent treatment of me, he loudly announced, "Nikki, I thought you might want to know that I have been doing some cutting-edge research on children and their use of transitional objects [blankets, pieces of cloth, pacifiers, and stuffed animals that children use to comfort themselves during times of stress or change]. I am working alongside some of the best and brightest people in the field to understand the relationship between children and their transitional objects." Full of pride, he handed me a hardcover book. "Here, I want to show you this. Look there." He opened the book and pointed to his name in the table of contents. "I authored that chapter. It describes my research on twins and transitional objects." To be sure I understood the value of his work he added, "Transitional objects play a very important role in child development, in children's emotional security." I was proud of my father but couldn't quite wrap my head around his accomplishment, given that he had fantastically ignored his own children. It was a thought heavily complicated by the fact that I was sitting on a bed in his guest room filled to overflowing with teddy bears of all sizes and colors.

That wasn't the only strange moment during my visit. At least two or three other times my father came into my room and begin waltzing about talking in baby talk to me or to one of his bears. My self-important father, generally disappointed in the inadequacies and failings of human beings, repeatedly transformed himself into a frisky toddler in front of me. It made me wonder if he were developmentally stuck and hurting in some way. Did my grandmother withhold her love from him or forbid him a transitional object, a teddy bear? Even more disturbing to me than his dancing and baby talk was that I never knew how to respond. His performance art came across as a plea for me to mother him, a tough request since he typically treated me as though I didn't exist. Handcuffed to his paradox, while he babbled and wheeled about I smiled and waited for him to stop.

My father came back into my room one last time. Dressed only in boxer shorts he began twirling around in circles again speaking baby talk, but this time he held out the bottom hem of his shorts, like a little girl pirouetting before an adoring crowd of grownups. At that point, instead of fascination or concern, all I felt was wet, cold embarrassment, for him and for me—*he* was my father. Madness, I thought, sometimes wears boxer shorts.

With Africa beckoning me, I said goodbye to my father and flew to Omaha to see my grandparents. During the visit, I asked my grandmother if she would tell me about her life. She was getting older and I hoped to fix her in my mind with more color and texture. Bolder with her than I had been when I was a child, I was ready to ask questions about her and my father. Where did she grow up? What were her parents like? What was my father like as a child? How did he behave? With a tentativeness that made her look like a cow being nudged toward the slaughterhouse door, she said yes to my request. I ignored her reticence, richly imagining that once she started telling me her story, it would be a special moment for both of us. I bought a small notebook for the interview, and sat down across from her in her living room, excited to finally meet my grandmother's deeper self. A quarter of an hour later she declared she had nothing more to say.

In those fifteen minutes, I filled less than two pages, front and back, of my undersized notebook. Altogether, I added only a dash of extra details to what I already knew about my grandmother. She was born and raised in Dodge, Nebraska, one of eight children. Her father was born in the United States, mostly of German ancestry, and her mother immigrated to the United States from Germany. She described her mother as a good cook and her father, who was initially in the livery and then car business, as moody. In 1926, my grandmother married her first husband, my biological grandfather. His family had immigrated from Czechoslovakia.

After their Omaha wedding, my grandparents—and my paternal Czechoslovakian great-grandmother, who was a widow—moved to Galesburg, Illinois, where my grandfather had a job as a pharmacist. My father and aunt came along several years later, and the three generations lived together until my grandfather's death in 1942 from leukemia. He was thirty-eight years old. Moving on as though we were speed dating, my grandmother quickly summed up the rest of her life: when her husband died, she took my father and aunt back to Omaha, moved in with her sister (she added that my great-grandmother also relocated back to Omaha), found work, and then met and married the grandfather I knew and loved, Gramps.

Before firmly shutting down, she said a few things about my father. He attended a private preparatory high school in Omaha, and college and medical school at the University of Nebraska. As a young man, he worked in a meatpacking plant. That was it. There were no details about him as a boy or adolescent, his interests or personality, or their family life. No mention of friends or school activities. When the interview was over I felt a little cheated. The lack of inside information about my grandmother and her life were disappointing, but the blankness about my father as a child meant I couldn't tie his contempt for us, or his oddities, to what had come before. His willful withholding of both parental and financial support would never be explained. Nor would his many peculiarities, the bottles and bottles of prescription pills lining his bathroom and kitchen counters, the baby food, his decision to change his surname Peatrowsky to Parrish after my older sister Celeste was born. My father never discussed his name change, although my mother happily implied it was part of my father's wily plan to reinvent himself as less ethnic. On my father's life map of extreme and unusual behavior, I couldn't find the starting place. That seemed fine with my grandmother. With silent but steely devotion to her son, she ignored his expanding list of misdeeds and the people he had abused, in one way or another.

After my grandmother's taciturn interview, I approached Gramps hoping for more connection. Turns out that was not a problem. For several hours Gramps roamed around in his memory vault, delighting in coaxing out the smallest of details of his life. I learned that his thick mane of fast-growing hair, silver white when I knew him, had been a lifelong problem: he couldn't keep up with the costs of cutting it. His least expensive cut was fifteen cents, his most expensive was eight dollars. One of eleven children born in 1910 in Omaha, Nebraska, to Polish immigrants, he began doing odd jobs to help his family out, while still in "short pants." After high school, he pushed aside his dream of becoming a doctor to go straight to work, so he could add his earnings to the family kitty. He worked for ten years as a printer before joining the Omaha Police Department, and eventually meeting my widowed grandmother. Deeply respected by his peers—for being smart, fair, and caring—he was with the department for thirty-four years. Unlike my non-emotive grandmother, Gramps was open and unabashedly sweet. Kindness above all was what mattered to him.

Hours after speaking with me, Gramps came down to the basement where I had sequestered myself with a book. Unprompted he told me he regretted never playing a bigger role in my father's life or reining him in when it was warranted. With great sadness, he noted that my grandmother had forbidden him on both fronts. In his flickering retrospective, my grandfather wished he had given my father limits and consequences, even a low dose of tough love. If he had, he said, my father might have developed some empathy for others, some remorse for his actions. His words felt like an apology to me and to my brothers and sisters.

On that visit I came across a photo of me from my father's photo shoot of me when I was a child—the time we trespassed into someone's backyard in his attempts to become a world-famous photographer. There on my grandmother's dining room wall, in an elegant oval wooden picture frame, was a photo of me from that sunny afternoon, now faded. I am sitting on the grass; my right thumb is tucked into the corner of my mouth and my fingers are holding my black patent leather shoes. My feet are bare. My head is cocked sideways and my chin is resting in the half fist of my left hand. My face is framed by blonde hair falling out of a high ponytail in wisps. I look sad. The pretty maroon velvet pinafore I am wearing, paired with a pink cotton blouse with a bow, is pulled casually over my knees. After commenting about the photo, my grandmother decided to give it to me along with a contact sheet of black and white photographs that my father had taken of me when I was four years old.

The contact sheet photos appear to be another set of photos my father took for his photography portfolio. In each small photo square, the camera captures just my face and bare chest from different angles. In one I am twirling my hair; in another I am looking over my shoulder. I am not smiling in any of the photos. In the only enlarged photo from the group, my head is down so you see my crown and a glimpse of my eyes, nose, and mouth. My arms are folded at the elbows with each hand tucked under my face on either side. On the back of the photo is a typed label with my father's name, David D. Parrish, the initials MD after it, and his address. Below is a handwritten description of the camera he used, the film, the exposure, and a title, "I AM FOUR." Underneath this information is written "Please Return," underlined. My name appears nowhere.

Reeling from my visits with my father and grandparents, I arrived in Philadelphia to spend a few days with my mother before leaving for Peace Corps, bracing for the worst. To my amazement I was greeted at the airport by an avatar—a loving mother passionately concerned about her offspring. Suddenly my mother was vibrating with affection for me. Before I could figure out why, she graciously volunteered to drive me wherever I needed to go to get supplies for my trip and to help with my preparations. In between our many stops, she told me how proud she was of me and how much she would miss me. As though to further demonstrate her new feelings, she gave me step-by-step instructions on how to wash clothes without water and what to do if I became sick far from medical care. Her unexplained devotion to my survival was mysterious. Ever optimistic, I accepted the change hoping it was the warm embrace I had been missing for so long. To show my appreciation I tidied up her home, cooked dinner every night, and cleaned and scrubbed the kitchen and bathroom. Both were barely accessible when I arrived.

The night before I flew to the Central African Republic, my mother took me to see *Fiddler on the Roof.* The play was an exciting and unexpected gift. Just thinking about my mother taking the steps to make the evening happen, selecting the show, purchasing the tickets, and getting us there on time, was mind boggling. But I pushed aside my incredulity, and focused instead on my certainty that somehow she had turned into a real mother. That feeling rose even higher in my chest during the song, "Sunrise, Sunset," an ode to the passage of time and the need for parents to let go of their adult children. The father,

Tevye, sings, "Is this the little girl I carried? Is this the little boy at play?" and his wife responds, "I don't remember growing older. When did they?" As the last words of the song floated up to us in the upper balcony, my mother and I burst into tears. I was the little girl leaving, growing up, and she was the loving parent saying goodbye, with wistfulness and pride.

Arriving at JFK the next morning I was bursting with happiness: I was headed for an adventure I knew would change my life, and my mother appeared ready to remember my middle name. The care and concern she had shown me felt so genuine I was sure they came with a lifetime warranty. I finally mattered to my mother. Moments before we parted my mother told me, "Nikki, there is a special bond between us, but I don't want you to think I love your brothers and sisters any less. It's just that we have harmony." As soon as I was on the plane, I wrote those words down in my journal. Underneath, I wrote that I was embarrassed by them.

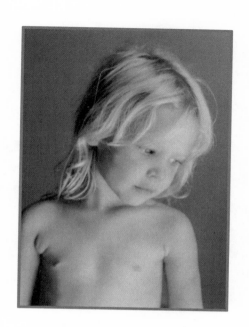

I Am Four

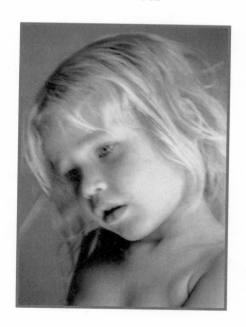

A Day of Trespassing

Age 8

5th Grade Class Picture

Volunteering at LeMoyne College

My Father

Chapter Five

L'Afrique

Vibrant heat pulsating with humidity and the smell of burning charcoal welcomed me to the Central African Republic. As I walked down the stairs from the plane and into the terminal, dozens of other smells helicoptering in the air registered deep in my brain. Colors floating up from richly-patterned dashiki shirts worn by men and traditional wraparound skirts worn by women rounded out the sensory smorgasbord. I had journeyed to a beautiful and very different place.

So much was different so fast. I chronicled my transition in a journal. Early entries record my first impressions and daily life during the three-month in-country Peace Corps training called "Stage." The training, held in an educational facility nestled in a luscious rainforest west of the capital, Bangui, entailed a high-speed introduction to local culture, classes in French and Sango, the country's two official languages, and orientation specifics for each volunteer's assignment. Enhancing the indoor cerebral training was a world outside fluttering with the sounds of tropical birds and smells of fragrant rainforest flowers. Regular rain showers added a dewy freshness to the training, inspiring an anything-can-grow attitude among us newbies.

Between demanding daily classes and the unfamiliarity of everything, I felt overstimulated but nervously happy. The one slim journal that survived my two-year stint jumps around with descriptions of my first impressions, my hopes, my deep longing for my family, my fellow volunteers and trainers, and my village, often in text infused with religious sentiments. It also discusses the brain-fatiguing advanced French and introductory Sango classes I took during training. Peace Corps wanted us to become proficient in both languages as quickly as possible, so we followed an immersion approach. During Stage, we could only speak French and Sango, no English.

Rereading my journal entries, I understand my youthful hopefulness but cringe at how stiff and formal my writing is, how controlled I am.

> *I'm feeling more calm about being here. It has just dawned on me that no matter how much I try to assimilate myself, I am—and always will be, an American. This is not by any means negative. In fact, it is rather positive, since from this position I can explore fully my potential to adapt without losing my identification. This is of true importance, as I delve deeply into my interior, exploring my raison d'être.*

*Today I am thankful for my family.
They are good and kind, and I love them. I
miss my mother so—such a part of me she is.*

*In the marketplace I had the good
experience of learning in depth the making of
a community social situation. I spoke a little
Sango, French, and sign language. I suppose I
realized more than anything that people are
people the world over.*

*I have been blessed with diarrhea today
and unfortunately a missing wallet. I hope one
gets better and one is returned. Ainsi (so), I
am feeling good.*

A month before leaving for Africa, I attended a
weeklong Peace Corps pre-invitational staging in Saint
Louis, Missouri—a screening week for recruits. There, I
was told that my community development post would be
in a very small village called Bokiné, close to the
neighboring country of Chad, and that I would be living in
a tiny house on a modest UNICEF training compound just
outside the village. I would work with my Central African
counterpart, who lived in Bokiné village, conducting train-
the-trainer classes on the compound for village-appointed
leaders from the surrounding region. Classes would cover
nutrition, disease prevention, and building wells for clean
drinking water and ovens for cooking and baking. Because
transportation was difficult for trainers in remote villages,
my co-worker and I would also have to periodically travel
to outlying areas to conduct trainings for leaders who could
not make it to Bokiné.

When I arrived in Africa, I was relieved to find that a good chunk of my training in the country would include intensives on most of the subjects I would be teaching. That was critical. I knew next to nothing and felt wholly anxious about my volunteer assignment. I worried whether I would even be mildly effective as a volunteer. I was also concerned about the isolation of my post. I would be living alone on the UNICEF compound, a half mile from other homes in Bokiné village and thirty kilometers from the nearest town and other Peace Corps volunteers. Not sure what else to do to manage my anxiety, I studied hard during the Stage training, rationalizing that since I couldn't control the future, I might as well improve my French, learn Sango, and know as much as I could about everything from how to build a fuel-efficient mud brick oven to reducing malaria.

Like the journal entries from my student days at USF, the anxiety I recorded during my training jumps off the pages of my Africa journal.

> *Feelings of home pervade my thoughts. Already I am noticing the difference in me— positive changes. Will I still be able to realize these changes upon my return home? During the Stage so many thoughts swirling as I try desperately to get a firm grasp first of the languages used here. My interest in community development is certainly alive, but it is being pushed into the background some—due to a slight case of fear.*

My anxiety seemed to serve two masters—one a commander of paralysis and fear, the other of inspiration and hope—and the two were symbiotic. I couldn't have one without the other. A constant companion, my anxiety waxed and waned: sometimes it was overwhelming and disruptive; sometimes it motivated me and helped me focus. Rereading my journal, there's no doubt that my anxiety and I share a birthday. I have been anxious for as long as I can remember and have written about it since I could hold a pencil. It has always been there, barely disguised, in school assignments, diary entries, and later in my poetry. It's hard not to wonder if it took its first breath with my mother's likely postpartum indifference toward me.

A lot of what I wrote in my Africa journal was young and naïve, even when the subject was my anxiety, but at times it reflected weightier, more searching questions and observations. In one entry, I reflect on a country still quivering with colonial vestiges, writing, "I will never be comfortable with the French colonial precedent of Central Africans addressing white men as 'patron' [the French word for boss]. That disgusts me." In entry after entry, I examine race, privilege, and the gumball chance of life, each of us spilling down a gumball chute, the random result of a quick turn of the handle. I pose questions about people's ability to change trajectories seemingly ordained at birth, and whether individuals can reverse the effects of circumstance, of where, how, and to whom one is born.

Years later, it's not clear who was the intended focus of these questions: my Central African friends or me.

In the middle of my Stage training period I took a brief trip to my post at Bokiné with Julie, the volunteer I was replacing, so she could introduce me to my Central African coworker, Jean-François, and the village before she returned to the States. Julie spent two years in Bokiné, and she and Jean-François had done a wonderful job building up the community development program. Confident and comfortable, Julie moved easily and respectfully in and around a culture I was still learning. As I tagged alongside her for a day trip to the capital Bangui, she arranged, in flawless French and Sango, our four-day, four-hundred miles round-trip to Bokiné. Preparations entailed securing a Peace Corps jeep and driver, purchasing provisions, organizing lodging, and sending word ahead to Bokiné about our visit. I couldn't imagine that I might ever be as competent. Reminding myself that I had another six weeks of training, I took a deep breath but kept every digit crossed.

The Peace Corps jeep we took for the trip survived hours of driving on dirt roads with more holes than road. We bounced, jostled, and made more than a few sudden jerky swerves to avoid chickens crossing the road. Somehow, we avoided breaking down and getting a flat tire. Only after the trip did I learn that was rare. Most journeys of any length in country involved at least one major vehicle problem or road catastrophe. A key benefit of our accident and drama-free trip was that I had a chance to closely observe the changing topography and village life as we drove north. Unlike the southern rainforest canopies that crowd you like relatives swarming to embrace you after a long absence, trees in the north were standoffish and often alone. Broad-leafed African oak, red cedar, mahogany, and imperial mango trees, standing singly or in twos or threes alongside the road, were the reigning trees, offset by scrub forests and scrappy vegetation. Only plants with moxie survived the North's climate of six months of rain and six months of drought.

All along the country's main road leading from Bangui to Bokiné we passed evenly-spaced villages neatly lined up on both sides of the main road. Years before I arrived, the government had issued an edict that required most villages in the country to move to roadside perches. Before, many were hidden away in forests or huddled in groves of thick vegetation, purposefully positioned away from the road to increase villagers' proximity to their fields and water sources, or for protection of one sort or another. As we whizzed by villages of varying lengths, some just a few houses long, others extending for a mile, there was plenty of distinction among the sameness of mud brick houses with straw thatched roofs. Some had new straw roofs, extra windows and doors, or small gardens in front; others were painted brilliant white, a dramatic contrast to the more ubiquitous golden brown of mud bricks.

Driving along I noticed that quasi-domesticated village animals—goats, wild pigs, and chickens—happily cohabited with people, although their housing arrangements differed by family and village. My Central African friends later explained that they were accepted as valued freeloaders, because when the time came, they served a vital function: breakfast and dinner. Ignorant of their fate, they behaved imperially, only moving from the road where they were foraging when the threat of being skewered by the grill of a jeep or truck was imminent. Children, however, were the center and best part of every village scene.

Whether playing or working—carrying firewood, cooking, or caring for babies and toddlers—children were the village's natural first responders. They attended every village event, arrival, and departure, and they acknowledged every car and truck whizzing past. From far off down the road the kids would hear our jeep coming long before they saw it. As soon as they caught first sight of the vehicle, they started running full sprint running alongside the road, enthusiastically waving to us and singing out hello in a mixture of French and Sango. From that first trip until the day I left Africa, I treasured their running welcomes.

My early days as a Peace Corps volunteer were intense, hard, and heady. Soon after I completed training I moved upcountry and into my two-room, two-hundred-square-foot house on the UNICEF compound at the edge of my village; the only other people living on the compound were a guard-groundskeeper and his wife. For months, I found it difficult to do much more than connect with the villagers and learn my new job. The transition was huge. I went from being a college student with four roommates living in a San Francisco Victorian flat and working with high-risk youth, to a Peace Corps volunteer living in the bush, alone, without electricity, running water, or plumbing, and teaching villagers a medley of skills that I had yet to master. Getting comfortable required a perfectly titrated blend of energy and patience. Just staying current with the supplies I needed to function in my job and live alone without crisis initially felt like a fulltime job.

Because my village was physically isolated, I quickly learned to carefully calculate how long food and supplies would last before I had to travel to Bossangoa, the town closest to Bokiné with an open-air market and several stores. I went in about every two weeks for staples: dried milk, coffee, cocoa, dried legumes, canned sardines, and rice. Cheese too, but only when my kerosene-powered refrigerator was working. Vegetables and wild meat I bought in the village.

Besides calculating the amount of food I needed, I had to carefully manage several other supplies. Kerosene turned out to be one of the most important. To keep my home lit for a few hours each night and keep perishable foods from spoiling, I needed enough kerosene to fuel one large lantern, one small lantern, and a finicky refrigerator for a two-week period. The lanterns worked like a dream using little kerosene; the refrigerator was another matter.

I had a strong love-hate relationship with the refrigerator. It sucked kerosene like an old gas-guzzling car and was equally undependable. The little blue flame that I carefully lit and kept burning through constant manual readjustments to the tank, wick, and burner would randomly burn out. No explanation. For days it would work beautifully and then it would stop. It reminded me of a boyfriend who whimsically stops calling you for a reason he can't articulate. When the fridge worked, I ate rich creamy yogurt made with a yogurt starter given to me by the French nuns in Bossangoa, and Dutch powdered milk. It was a delicious dish I didn't get too used to eating.

After my first year in Bokiné I planted a garden next to my house that took off in the rainy season and produced a panoply of vegetables: carrots, squash, zucchini, and lettuce. It even created an accidental papaya tree. One day after breakfast I threw the seeds and the rind of a papaya into my garbage pit, a deep hole in the ground located about ten feet from my garden. Somehow the seeds migrated from the pit to the garden, possibly carried by birds. Within a few months I noticed a tall tree growing in the middle of the garden. By six months I recognized it as a papaya tree and it was bearing fruit. It was Jack and the Beanstalk, but without Jack and with more than a few creative overrides to the original fairy tale.

A young woman I hired from the village prepared one meal a day for me and kept me supplied with water from a local well located about a half-mile from the village. She also did my laundry and swept out my house, which freed me to focus on my community development job with my co-worker, Jean-François. It helped too that my bathroom and shower required no cleaning. My toilet was a hole in the ground covered by a large flat rock, encircled by a wall of woven straw four to five feet in diameter and six feet high to protect my privacy. A second circular straw wall with the same dimensions guarded my adjacent bathing room. Inside my "shower," I had a small stool that I sat on next to some rocks that kept my soap and several calabashes that I used to dip into the bucket of warm water I brought in each day for washing.

Monday through Friday and until noon every Saturday I worked with Jean-François in an office we shared on the compound, either planning or conducting trainings on site. As expected, we periodically conducted trainings in remote regions when it was difficult for trainers living in far corners to get to Bokiné. Jean-François was extraordinarily patient with me as I sputtered to get up to speed with our work. I often wondered what he thought of me, such a young, inexperienced, American woman living in the middle of nowhere. I was twenty-two, unmarried and had no children. My community development position was financed by Peace Corps. He was a Central African man from the Bokiné area, in his early thirties, married with several small children. His position was funded through a community development grant from UNICEF. At first our worlds seemed far apart. If he was Earth, I was Pluto. Gradually though, the space between us shrank. Misunderstandings became opportunities for growth or redemption, depending on the severity of the incident, and over time we developed genuine respect for each other. After six months, our relationship had the formality of a smart tweed jacket paired with the informality of a pair of jeans, shrunk to fit of course. Not only did our relationship work, it worked well.

During the week Jean-François and I talked about work, our families and our different interests. Outside of work we didn't socialize; it wouldn't have been appropriate given cultural mores. My social time was mostly spent with a few women in the village, especially two midwives, both of whom were named Monique. The surprise of having a shared name with my friends was wonderful. It made me feel less of an outsider, and hearing them pronounce my name with a throaty musical Sango accent gave me a tickle. I also spent time with the village chief. The chief was a tall willowy man. For two years, I never saw him in anything but his pastor outfit—black slacks, white dress shirt, tie, and black suit jacket. His dress, regal manner, and dual role of chief and pastor meant that he was a one-stop-shop for the village—leader, judge, and spiritual advisor. And he took his responsibilities seriously. Always calm, he mediated conflict between villagers and meted out punishment to the guilty in a rich baritone that projected authority but resonated with compassion. Grand master of every village festival, and lead haranguer of every church sermon, he was Bokiné's president, chief justice, and pope all rolled into one beautiful black suit.

Because I was considered a guest of the village, it was expected that I would walk every evening to the chief's house in the village after work and sit with him by his fire for a half-hour or so. It was a combination sign-of-respect and daily-check-in. Whenever I was not on the road—

hosting community development trainings, attending meetings in the capital, visiting volunteer friends—I made the trek to his house in the early evening and sat with him on a small wooden bench in front of his house. A fire burning less than a foot away kept us warm. Our visits were pleasant and interesting. In French, I gave him a quick update on how I was doing. From there, our discussions veered toward international politics, religious education of youth, and the future of the CAR. I enjoyed our tête-à-têtes, but some days didn't want to go; I wanted to curl up on my bed inside my mosquito net and read. But I always went. When I left Africa, I realized I had misunderstood the deeper reason for our daily meetings. It wasn't at all about honoring him as the village elder; it was about his responsibility to keep me, a young woman alone without family, connected to him and to the village. Sitting with him by his fire every evening, talking about what I had done that day, what I thought about village life and Africa, he made sure I did not drift off, isolated from him or the village. He treated me like family.

Growing accustomed to the quiet and the enormous expanse of sky that accompanied my life in Bokiné took months. Both spread across me until I often felt like a tiny dot in the middle of silence and space. Although I visited with friends in the village and made trips every few weeks to Bossangoa, where I hung out with other Peace Corps volunteers, I struggled with my new solo life. My routine was basically monastic except for work and a little socializing in the village. To ease my loneliness, I wrote long detailed letters about my life to my mother, and poetry chronicling my internal thoughts. One of my poems summarizes my heartache and hope.

I have become a woman
shedding awkward garb

it is hard and painful at times
to grow and change

the freckled spots of yesteryear smooth over
but still a whole world of unknowns

I struggle to connect
but all seems so distant and unobtainable

tears of joy and pain take me by surprise
but the salt that remains is comforting
… it reminds me there is still so much to learn

That first year in Bokiné was tough. I was lonely and homesick. Occasionally I thought about why I had traveled so far from home. All the reasons were a bit murky except one, and I thought about it a lot: I was determined to be more than nothing.

Notwithstanding the ebb and flow of loneliness that came with my living alone, distant from other volunteers, lots of comical and serious things happened during my Peace Corps tour. The most entertaining was my dance with a Suzuki 125 motorcycle. Most of my fellow volunteers lived in towns or large villages. For local transportation, they were offered a bicycle or moped. To travel large distances, Peace Corps expected all volunteers to use public transportation. At first glance, the local public transportation system seemed hugely improbable. Souped-up jeeps, trucks, and buses, typically called Occasions, were so full of people, possessions, and livestock they looked unable to budge, like women way past their pregnancy due date. Incredibly, they managed to keep an entire country moving, despite the usual breakdowns and occasional collisions. Like most volunteers, I took Occasions to travel between Bossangoa and Bangui, typically an eight-to-ten-hour trip to cover less than 200 miles. Because my post was considered remote, I was one of a small handful of volunteers given a motorcycle instead of a moped. The Central African Peace Corps office wanted to be sure I could travel quickly and safely between Bokiné and Bossangoa for emergencies.

The buildup to receiving my motorcycle was intimidating. At Stage, my Community Development supervisor repeatedly told me how lucky I was to be given a motorcycle. I was one of the chosen few, he said. To be sure I didn't hurt others or myself, I received several lessons on how to ride the bike. Ironically, I had exponentially greater enthusiasm for the book *Zen and the Art of Motorcycle Maintenance* than I had for an actual motorcycle. Although the Suzuki 125 is considered a learner bike, and compared to its bigger cousins rides almost like it has training wheels, I was terrified.

Fortunately, a Peace Corps friend drove my new motorcycle from Bangui to Bokiné for me, enjoying every minute of it. For three months, I toughed it out. I rode my new motorcycle back and forth between Bokiné and Bossangoa, but fell on nearly every trip. My falls were not, however, the crashing results of going top speed; they were slow motion, molasses-like descents to the ground that occurred because I didn't go fast enough to keep the bike upright, as I maneuvered in and out of deep potholes in the dirt road created by coffee and cotton trucks. For some reason the worst moonlike craters were clustered right in front of a few villages on my route. I would approach these lunar sections trembling. My goal: get in and out of each hole and onto the tiny sliver of flat road that threaded its way between the holes without falling. I surrendered to holes constantly. When it happened in front of a village, several children watching the show would invariably run to my aid and lift the bike off me.

One early morning trip home to Bokiné from Bossangoa, I approached a village with neatly lined up houses flanking both sides of the road. All the front yards were swept clean of the previous night's chicken and goat droppings, a sign that most of the adults had gone to work in the fields—village women tended to sweep the areas around their houses before leaving for the fields. My eyes went from the bucolic scene to the road running right through the middle of the village. I groaned. It looked as though it had been the victim of an aerial bomb raid. Dozens of holes three to nine inches deep and a foot wide lay ahead of me. There was no flat part of the road I could safely ride on for more than a foot or two. I could feel my heart lurching into overdrive. Going back to Bossangoa didn't seem reasonable with only ten kilometers to Bokiné, so I inched forward. Within a few feet I could feel the heavy, hot machine move to the left. I instinctively moved my torso to the right hoping to balance the bike, but already the front tire was below the crust of the deep hole. I was too scared to gun it to launch the tire forcibly above the rim, so the bike listed slowly to the left. Not wanting to crush my left leg, I managed to lift it up just as the bike slowly put itself down. Neither the bike nor I was hurt. A group of pre-adolescent girls and boys who had been watching my Suzuki death spiral raced over and lifted the bike off me. After getting me right-side up, they gravely walked me and my bike to the end of the holes section of their village road, hoping, I'm sure, that I would make it to Bokiné without any more anemic misadventures.

When my falls were repeated in front of the same village and the same children, I noticed my embarrassment had company. A few of the children who had rescued me more than once had a look that seemed to indicate a subtle change in their original thought bubble, from "I wonder how she fell? Well, let's help her up and get her on her way," to the more pitying, "Poor girl—she shouldn't ride a motorcycle." After months of physically embracing the dirt, I decided humility and defeat should meet. I made the decision to trade in my 125 for a moped. It was a decision that left the heads of every single male Peace Corps colleague in the country shaking in disbelief. Who in her or his right mind would willingly abandon a sleek riding machine with decent horsepower for a donkey? Apparently, me. But I was extremely happy with my small and nimble moped. I never fell again. And, when I passed through pockmarked road stretches, my former nemesis corridors, the village children looked very relieved.

Interspersed with comedy of my own making were experiences that shifted me from impermanent two-year observer to more engaged community member. Within a few months of arriving in Bokiné, I met an active group of French Catholic nuns in Bossangoa spearheading a variety of women and children's education and health projects. I was immediately taken with one member of the religious order, Soeur Émilie, the medical director of Bossangoa's children's nutrition hospital. Soeur Émilie was in her early fifties, petite, no more than five feet tall, with a mass of curly black hair that elevated around her head. Her untamed hair seemed to keep the disciplined part of her—the modest striped shift dress, bookish glasses, and sensible shoes—from taking over and defining her entire look. The result was a non-threatening, unassuming, very kind, intensely interesting woman. Soeur Émilie was different from other nuns I had met in Central Africa. Self-assured and independent, she was an immensely talented physician, passionate about providing the best medical care possible to malnourished children and their families. From hours of conversations with her, I learned that because she was of African descent (her family came from Algeria), she respected all faiths and revered the people and country she called home for nearly twenty years. Humble and unafraid, her spiritual mission was to serve her African family.

For the first six months at Bokiné, Jean-François and I conducted a series of community development trainings at the UNICEF compound. During this period, we repeated a few of these trainings in a handful of remote villages. Once I met Soeur Émilie, I began looking more closely at children in these outer villages. Invariably, I saw or was told about at least one very sick child suffering from malnutrition. In the middle of one of these trainings, it occurred to me that because we traveled in a UNICEF truck, we might be able to take the most malnourished children to Soeur Émilie's hospital when we finished the training. I mentioned the idea to Jean-François and we both decided to go for it. At the end of the training we bundled a very ill boy no more than two years old with marasmus, severe undernourishment, into the truck. Since families did the day-to-day care for loved ones in the hospital, leaving the medical care to nurses and the doctor, we also brought the boy's parents and an older sister with us.

Because I wasn't sure if I had acted properly bringing the child and his family to the nutrition hospital before speaking to Soeur Émilie, it was a long ride to Bossangoa. When we arrived, Soeur Émilie welcomed the child, his family, and Jean-François and me with open arms. No derision, anger, or indifference. I had done something good and right that day. Afterwards, whenever Jean-Francois and I trained outside of the compound we brought every malnourished child we saw and his or her family to the hospital. And on almost every trip to Bossangoa I squeezed in time with Soeur Émilie. In her soft nightlight glow I felt safe.

The most memorable experience I had with Soeur Émilie happened the afternoon she asked me to come and accompany her on rounds at the hospital. Gliding through a large ward of sick children, wearing a faded blue shift dress, thick black walking shoes, and a stethoscope, Soeur Émilie stopped by each bed and crib. Before reading the metal patient chart, she lovingly stroked the head or hand of the boy or girl in the bed. We were almost through the ward when a male nurse soundlessly approached us, his green cotton nursing uniform rippling as he walked. His look implored Soeur Émilie to politely step away from the group. In gentle whispers, urgency was perfectly communicated. Soeur Émilie absorbed the message and then quietly turned around and walked away with the male nurse. Nervously I followed.

At the other end of the hospital, Soeur Émilie joined a group of nurses and assistants gathered around the metal crib of a young boy. Standing back to give them space, I could only see the child's silhouette. He looked to be about ten months old. A few moments later I noticed that his body was older and wizened. His face lacked the soft still-forming features of an infant. A nurse reporting on his condition stated he was four or five years old. I stifled my shock. Surveying the child carefully, Soeur Émilie's face promptly changed. The slightly lopsided winning smile she used to comfort children was tucked away, saved for a later time. All her power seemed concentrated in her eyes, and they seemed to tell her brain what she needed to do next for the fragile life in front of her barely registering a pulse.

From the hushed high-speed conversations going back and forth at the bedside, I could make out that the boy was extremely malnourished, his skin stretched so tight across his frail body and enlarged stomach that staff could not find a viable vein to give him medications and life-saving fluids. He was deteriorating rapidly. Barely audible, Soeur Émilie asked the nurse to fetch something. Seconds later he returned and handed her a utensil wrapped in heavy blue muslin. When she opened the sterile bundle, inside was a very large, barbaric-looking needle filled with something. With no time to waste she plunged the needle into the child's chest in the direction of his heart. "Oh, my God!" I thought. While I stood watching incapacitated with fear for the child, Soeur Émilie found a vein and successfully inserted a line, starting the flow of medicine. Hours later the beautiful boy died, but the sacred intersection of the child and Soeur Émilie lived on in me as a breathtaking twinning of heroism.

Over the course of eighteen months, my friendship with Soeur Émilie deepened. In her kind, shy way she became a steady mentor and mother to me. She wasn't mercurial, like my mother. Her universe was real. No pretenses, no theater. Her dedication to her patients, her brothers and sisters, and her religious community never muted her joy of the simple, even the mundane. Her impassioned lectures about the merits of her favorite cheeses over the ones whose flavors and textures she judged altogether inferior were quirky and fun. So too were her step-by-step instructions on how to make exquisite lemon herbal tea. *Go to the garden, pick a fresh bunch of lemon verbena leaves, give them a quick dip in cold water to wake them up, then kiss them goodbye before gently immersing them in a battered teapot filled with steaming water. After five minutes, enjoy nature's gift: lemony ambrosia steeped to perfection.* I loved the big and small parts of Soeur Émilie.

Africa gave me the gift of Soeur Émilie and a pinwheel of other meaningful moments and experiences. Some twirled by slowly granting me strictly observation privileges; others flew at me demanding participation and heart thumping action. "Come, come fast, we need you!" two teenage girls from the village yelled in Sango as they sprinted full speed toward me, their wraparound skirts almost coming undone as they ran. I was surveying the pokey growth of a few vegetables in my garden when I looked up and saw them. Their young and determined faces signaled something terribly wrong had happened. It took me a few months of living in Bokiné to realize that by age ten all villagers are on a first-name basis with crisis. By that time, everyone has experienced illness, accidents, and death—of a loved one or member of the village. That may have been why the teens hurtling toward me were not hysterical. In clipped but precise Sango they did their best to communicate the dire nature of their message. Only the words 'man' and 'hurt' ricocheted around my head. Heart pounding, I took off running with them. Just before reaching the village I realized I didn't know what I was running to or what exactly was expected of me.

We crossed the threshold of the village and I followed the girls to a house set further back from the road than its neighbors on either side. At first glance it looked like a typical village house. Up close, though, I could see there were pieces missing. The straw thatched roof had turned solidly gray; its comb-over no longer hid the bald spots. Bricks from the walls were chipped, a few were gone, and the front wooden door hinged on one side was so much smaller than its frame that it seemed to float in darkness on three sides. It was a tired house. Off to one side I saw several teens kneeling over a young man on the ground. He looked to be in his early twenties. Covered in blankets he was noticeably shivering and struggling to stay conscious. A smoldering fire not more than five feet from his body looked guilty.

Suddenly everyone was speaking to me. The adults in the village were away for an event and the young man had fallen into the fire during a shaking episode he couldn't control—an epileptic seizure. After registering the information, I asked if I could see the injury. The blankets were gently lifted. With the covers off, I saw the villager was rolled on his right side. Along the left side of his body, from underneath his armpit to just above his left knee, was an uninterrupted very severe burn line of charred flesh. Sweeping my eyes up and down his trembling body I noticed something white glistening in the middle of black and red thigh muscle tissue. It was his thighbone.

The victim's agony was palpable, but I wasn't sure what to do. When I arrived in Africa, Peace Corps gave all volunteers in my group the book *Where There Is No Doctor*, an easy-to-read health education manual that describes common medical conditions and diseases. I remembered the section on treating burns, and there was no doubt the young man in front of me had sustained a severe burn, the kind requiring immediate medical help. I also remembered that the section outlined a few helpful steps to consider for severe burns, including elevating the burned part of the body to prevent the victim from going into severe shock. I quickly asked several people kneeling by the man to fetch some blankets. When they came back I gently tried to insert them under the young man's right side, to further elevate the left part of his body that was burned, but couldn't. His burns were so extensive that he was in extreme pain. Afraid to touch or move him very much, I asked the two teenage girls to keep talking to him softly to keep him from losing consciousness completely. They did that and more, speaking words of encouragement in soothing tones.

After the elevation and preventing shock steps, I knew what I had to do next: get him to a doctor as quickly as possible. The problem was no one in my village had a truck (the UNICEF truck I used for trainings was kept in Boassangoa), and I was the only one with a moped. I spent a few valuable moments wondering if I could take him to the hospital in Bossangoa on the back of my moped. It was a ludicrous idea clearly generated by my growing fear for the young man's life. Thirty kilometers of an unforgiving dirt road made it even more absurd. The choice was clear. I had to leave for Boassangoa immediately by myself. I would ride straight to the town's main hospital and then ask, beg if need be, hospital staff with a truck to drive me back to my village to rescue the young man. It was a long shot. By the time I returned with help, he might not be alive. Then I heard the distant rumble of a truck.

Trucks and traffic of any kind passing Bokiné were infrequent, maybe one or two a week—and it was the Central African cotton and coffee trucker's code of the road not to stop for villagers in need. The math was simple. If trucks stopped each time they were flagged down by a villager, they would be late with their loads and the result would be a loss of wages for the driver. And stopping to help a villager had another built-in risk; it nearly always involved a complex human drama that required more involvement from the truckers than they were generally willing to commit to. Money and compassion were always dueling in this part of Africa. As soon as I heard the big lumbering machine in the distance I decided to see if compassion would hold advantage over money this one time. Leaving the young man moaning in excruciating pain, I ran to the road, my heart beating like a hummingbird's wings. As the huge cotton truck approached I stood squarely in the middle of the road and manically began waving my arms.

The driver stopped. He might have stopped anyway or maybe he stopped because was curious about why I was standing in the middle of the road pinwheeling my arms. Whatever the reason, I was grateful. I hurriedly explained that we had a severe burn victim in the village who needed to be taken to the hospital in Bossangoa thirty kilometers away immediately, otherwise he would likely die. To my surprise, the driver agreed to transport the young man and even helped several villagers carry him into the truck. As he sped off with the young man and two of his friends, I slumped to the ground. Then, I waited for the young man's family to come back to the village, so I could tell them what happened.

Six months or so later I heard a knock on my door during siesta time. Standing in front of me was the young burn victim, nervously fingering something in his hands. Happy to see him, I smiled and said hello, looking past the quilt of burned scar tissue that flanked the entire left side of his body. Without a word, he thrust a hunk of honeycomb at me, dripping with dark amber honey. A gift of honey with a few bees still attached, buzzing with life.

By my second year as a Peace Corps volunteer I had experienced more than a few faux pas and heartaches. But I had grown up a lot. Unanticipated joys hugely outnumbered difficulties. I was the guest of honor at the wedding of a couple from a nearby village, and until the bride and groom were joined at the end of the ceremony, I was given a seat in the front of the church . . . next to the groom! On the dirt floor of a house in my village I held life, a just-born mewling baby, seconds old. For four worrisome weeks, I watched a child I had brought into the nutrition hospital near death struggle, then regain her strength and future. And, I learned how to read twenty-four-hour weather patterns just by looking at the sky from the groundskeeper for the UNICEF compound. With a touch of magic all his own, he could accurately read the forecast for a week. I had changed.

I wanted to tell my mother about what I had seen and done; I wanted her to be proud of the person I had become. Because she had stopped writing just months after I arrived in Central Africa, I resorted to trying to reach her by phone whenever I was down in the capital, Bangui. During one brief call I had with her early in my second year, she announced that she was coming to Africa. I was sure that I misheard her. Through several follow-up calls that my mother uncharacteristically picked up for some reason, we made a plan. I gave her the flight information for a major airline that would take her from New York to Bangui, and we settled on a date and a specific flight several months down the road to give her time to purchase her ticket, get her passport and tourist visa, and obtain all State Department recommended vaccinations. I assured her that I would be at the airport to get her. Once the arrangement took on a patina of immutability, I shared the good news with the chief and my village.

With just a half-year to go before the end of my two-year Peace Corps program, I left my village to retrieve my mother in Bangui. I could barely keep still for the ten-hour journey. On the way, I smiled to myself as I imagined how my mother, who would travel back with me to my village by Occasion, would react to the squawks and bleats of chickens and goats, the truck's nonpaying passengers. Before I left Bokiné, I gave the chief, Jean-François, and my village friends the details of my mother's expected arrival on Air France in Bangui, and our return date to the village. The chief informed me in his proud but understated way that he would lead the celebrations for my mother. The village, he said, had been working on a welcome drumming and dance ceremony, and my mother would be the guest of honor at several celebratory meals of goat and chicken. He even noted that he had selected the goats that would be slaughtered immediately upon our return. As the patriarch of the village, his pleasure in welcoming my mother, now kin to him, was as sweet as it was foreign to me. I was a daughter who added, not subtracted, from his life.

The plane touched down. It was early morning but already an old hour for heat. Hot air rose from the tarmac, expansive and thick, and swept into everyone's nostrils without invitation, including disembarking jet-lagged passengers lumbering down the stairs toward the airport. Its heaviness instantly disabused the newly arrived from groggily thinking, for even a second, that they might be in Paris instead of the heart of Africa. With my face pressed against the airport window, I waited, thinking of my mother inhaling the colorful and aromatic life of the world I called home. I waited some more. When the last passenger descended from the plane followed by the crew, my heart roped itself in fear and disappointment. Panicked, I continued my wait. If I were patient, she would come. That was a daytime, bedtime, anytime story I had told myself for as long as I could remember. She never showed. In frustration, I walked over to the airline desk and discovered her name was not on the passenger list.

With no other choice, I caught a bus from the airport back to downtown Bangui and went directly to the post office, where most volunteers made international calls. Reflexively, I put coin after coin into the machine created to make connections, hoping I would reach my mother right away. As I dialed the ten-plus digits for an international call, I wondered if she were still in transit. Maybe she had missed the plane and would come tomorrow, or maybe I had the wrong arrival date. Underneath those possibilities were a few more. Something bad might have happened to her, or she was not coming and there was no reason. My mother's phone rang and rang. No answer. I tried again later that day. Still hopeful, I returned to the Peace Corps hostel in Bangui where I was staying, and told friends there and at the Peace Corps office, so excited that she was coming to visit, that there must have been a mistake. She would arrive tomorrow.

I returned to the airport the next day and then the next. Between my airport runs I continued my search-and-rescue phone campaign. Hope, like a garland of gardenias around my neck, perfumed my every step and made it easy to ignore what had never smelled right. Three days after my mother's scheduled arrival, I decided it was time to alert my siblings, but just before I did, I decided to try my mother one last time. My mother picked up. "Hello?" Her voice was whispery and babyish. "Mom, where are you? How come you aren't here?" My voice sounded pleading and strained, a weird alchemy of anger, fear, and despair. After a long pause, my mother answered, sugary and sweet, "I didn't make it, but I'm coming next week."

My mother never came to Africa. I told my Peace Corps and village friends she wasn't well. That was the truth. What I left out was that I was heartbroken and angry with myself. I had fallen into the trap again of yearning for the mother I thought she would be, if I pulled the right levers and pushed the right buttons. If I tried hard enough. Consumed with hoping this woman would emerge, I didn't realize there were two people who did show up for me in Africa: the chief and Soeur Émilie. I had grown so fond of the chief and our special time together that it was heart-wrenching to say goodbye to him. It was even harder to leave Soeur Émilie—she had been the mother I never had.

She was someone who believed in me. In a letter that she slipped to me after our final embrace, she reminded me that she was there for me:

If sometimes, along your path you strike a stone that hurts you, think that in a little far away part of Africa, a friend believes in you and is sure that you will never let yourself lose who you are.

Chapter Six

Swimming Upstream

Unsure how I would adjust to the people and memories of home that filled my dreams for two years, I walked carefully down the jetway at JFK. The dress I had chosen to wear, a silk 1920s vintage tea-length dress in soft peach, was a treasure I had unearthed from a pile of clothes in a Paris flea market—I had spent a few weeks in Italy and France after Peace Corps before flying back to the States. During the flight, my seat belt had ripped the dress's fragile silk, creating a six-inch long tear across my bottom. To cover the tear, I folded a dusky gray shawl with delicate pink and red flowers, also picked up in the flea market, across my hips handkerchief style. My retro urban chic presentation was nothing more than an accident.

"Hi honey! Wow! You look like a model!" my mother sang out, just seconds before throwing her arms around me in a warm hug. I immediately searched for signs of embarrassment, a half-hearted apology. None. Apparently, her failed Africa visit didn't happen. Feather-light, she skipped across the taut tightrope between us, never once wavering or losing her balance. I was

226

unprepared for her smoothness. Alone for so long, I ignored the synthetic warmth of her welcome and melted in her embrace.

On the way back to her home in Philadelphia, questions and curiosity poured out of my mother as she drove. What did I do most days in my village? What were the people in my village like? How did I manage the several episodes of malaria that I had written her about? Did I have anything more to do with Peace Corps now that I was home? The rhythm and pace of our exchange was fun and my mother was in a buoyant mood. As we motored along I thought she might still get around to asking me about the trip that never was. She didn't mention it.

Before coming home, I daydreamed about confronting my mother regarding her no-show. In each imagined scenario, the setting was the same: a truth commission and I was the lead prosecutor. Before extracting a confession—her real reason for not coming—I would describe to her and the whole court the consequences of her action. I would explain how it felt to tell my village she was coming and then return to a beautifully decorated village festooned for her arrival without her. In unsparing detail, I would describe the emotional exhaustion and anguish of showing up at the airport several days running hoping to see her. But she never disembarked from a plane. Last, I would tell about the anxiety I felt when I called and called her, unsure if she were alive or dead. Sitting in the passenger seat on the way to Philadelphia, however, I knew any attempt to excavate the truth would be in vain. I said a final goodbye to my fantasy and fell back into the one dynamic that worked best with my mother: she pretended her make-believe world was real and I went along.

Sated with a mother who for the time being appeared present, I allowed my thoughts to drift to my reentry, a subject I had given scant attention. Before I left Central Africa, I had undergone a complete physical exam and participated in an exit interview. During both I was forewarned that many volunteers struggle with readjusting to life in the States. While in Europe, I intentionally suspended any thoughts about my reintegration back home, in favor of breathing in the cathedrals, museums, and street life of Italy and France. And, I wanted to keep perseverative thoughts about my mother to a tolerable level. Feeling comfortable in the car that there was no immediate emergency with my mother, I allowed myself to look out the window.

Two yellow crayon-colored school buses traveling next to us on the freeway caught my attention. Clean, sleek, and new, they traveled noiselessly, every axle working. No careening from side to side, no heavy creaking that indicated maximum weight had been exceeded long before the last passenger boarded. I let my mind wander to thinking about what life would be like for children in Bokiné if they were transported to and from school by buses designed just for them. That could change a nation, I thought. From that, I segued to what would happen if Central Africa had freeways and paved side roads without the initials of heavy cotton trucks carved into them. Soberly, I thought it might be good, or it might mechanize, speed up, and alter a way of life for the worse. No mistake, I was back in the land of plenty.

Although I had put worries about fitting back into the States on hold, midair over the Atlantic I had decided to relocate to Philadelphia. While my dress was wrestling with my seat belt, my mind was wrestling with whether to go back to San Francisco or move near my mother. The baby voice she used with me the day I realized she would never come to Africa convinced me that she needed me. Living near her seemed doable. For two years, I had cooked food over three rocks, trekked through thick rainforests behind machete-wielding men, and seen death in the eyes of babies. It couldn't be that hard to live near her. Fresh from relationships where giving and receiving was easy and natural, I was confident that I could establish the same meaningful relationship with my mother that I'd had with my Central African and Peace Corps friends.

I waited until there was a lull in our bubbly car exchange, and then I nervously told my mother I was relocating to Philadelphia. She lit up. For more than five years she had been living alone thousands of miles from her children, her only consistent social contact a man I had met a few times before I left for Peace Corps. Their relationship, as described by my mother, was sticky. I wasn't surprised. By then I noticed that she dispatched every suitor who was nice to her, staying only in relationships where the toxic mold of conflict grew easily.

Her hanger-on beau was in his fifties, married but separated, with a very young son. And he lived with his elderly mother to whom he was completely devoted. His inability to cleave from his mother or his wife meant my mother was constantly warring with him, alternating between verbal assaults and lockdowns on her affection. Whether it was the strain of this on-again/off-again relationship or her self-imposed isolation, she seemed thrilled with the idea of having a child back in her universe to distract, entertain, and most likely parent her to keep her sadness at bay.

I burbled on about my plan, unconsciously trying to woo her with my more adult version of cuteness, fearful she would discard me once we were home. "Mom, it will be great living near you again. I missed you so, so much! We can have dinner together and go walking during the week after we both get off work, and on the weekends. You know, I never told you, but sometimes I cried myself to sleep thinking about you. I even placed your picture under my pillow. But wait, get this, I have to describe my bedtime routine and my bed. So, here I am in this teeny tiny house in Bokiné—I think I told you in one of my letters that I lived on a UNICEF compound that was built as an education center. My house was a few blocks down from my village, Bokiné. Anyway, I would finish up my work with Jean-François every afternoon, go to see the chief of the village in the evening, chat with him, then come back and make cocoa on my little butane camp stove. After I brushed my teeth, washed my face, and went to the bathroom outside, I would crawl into my bed ingeniously made from local wood and draped in mosquito netting, and think about you. You got me through a lot, Mom, more than you probably will ever know." I let out a happy, satisfied sigh—my mother wanted me near her.

As I continued chatting away, I realized I knew very little about my mother's everyday life. I had spoken infrequently with her when I was in college and communicated even less in Africa. The only details that made it into my information log about her were those she had vetted carefully in advance. Anything she didn't want known had long since been redacted from the sunny elevator speech about her life that she liberally shared with anyone willing to listen. The one update I did have was that she had left her television job and was working in an antique store. I looked forward to being closer to her.

With just miles to go before we reached her house, my mother decided to let me in on a significant change in her life. Blushing with the double glow of having done something hard and achieved the unexpected, she reported that twelve months earlier she had moved from the rental row home where she had been living since my junior year of high school to a row home that she had bought in Manayunk, a community on the outskirts of Philadelphia. Floored, I didn't know which was more surprising: that she had completed the necessary organizational steps to physically move all her stuff or that she had structured her finances and credit to purchase a home.

As we turned off the freeway we entered Manayunk, with street after street of appealing, unpretentious row homes. Row homes in a defined neighborhood typically share the same DNA. But if you look closely, you find plenty of individuality—some windows with shutters, some doors with awnings, and house colors spanning a range of hues. Approaching her home my mother suddenly gushed, "Nikki, I can't wait for you to see the house! The people who live here are really nice working-class people, and this is an up-and-coming neighborhood. I'm not sure if everyone who lives here knows that these turn-of-the-century houses will be worth a lot in the future. The fixtures, materials, everything, date back over a hundred years. Believe me, this neighborhood is going to quickly become a desirable place to live. By the way, you won't believe the exposed brick in my living room, Nikki. It looks great! I had a guy who uncovered one wall for me, and I want him to do more but he had to stop. I can't wait till he can come back and finish the whole house." Her enthusiasm was contagious. I was excited for her.

As she prattled on about her real estate success, an alert message popped into my head. It was a reminder that the last house my mother had invested with stadium-size dreams, the Tudor, didn't pan out. If past behavior is the best predictor of future behavior, the row home didn't stand a chance. Feeling disappointed in my negative thought, I silently chastised myself. A better person, a fairer person, would be less judgmental. Now was a good time, I decided, to channel Soeur Émilie. I briefly closed my eyes and focused on being open and supportive. I had almost made it through this mental exercise when I remembered that Soeur Émilie was not only kind and nonjudgmental, she was strong and discerning. When lions charged, she didn't make excuses or rationalize their behavior. She got out of the way.

It was pitch black by the time we opened the front door and stepped into the living room. I couldn't see very well but didn't miss that my mother immediately stepped over a thigh-high pile of something to turn the light switch on. As the light came on I instinctively knew to look at her, suspending my overwhelming desire to take a panoramic mental photograph of the living room. My mother's face would tell me all I needed to know. And it did. Her eyes looked back at me gleaming with shame and defiance. She seemed to be asking and poking me at the same time, "Can you stand it?" She didn't know then that I could. She didn't know what I had seen in Africa. I had held the hand of suffering and loss many times; I was stronger than she thought. I looked at her and smiled, "The place looks great—I love the brick walls!" My response gave us both the oxygen we needed in that moment to breathe in a living room so dense with stuff there was no space for walking.

My mother's house was in terrible shape. She had lived there for only a year but every room except the upstairs bathroom was unusable, and even that was barely accessible. It looked as though her collection of things could repopulate a small planet that had been stripped of its belongings. All that was missing were animals—at least the domesticated kind. After I carried my two bags into the house from the car, a large backpack with a frame and a medium duffel bag, my mother told me where she slept. It was on the floor by the front door, in a sleeping bag. "No problem, that's where we'll sleep!" I said cheerfully. That first night I pushed back encroaching piles of clothes and paper to make more room and unrolled the sleeping bag I had brought to Africa and back, placing it on the floor next to my mother's bag. We bedded down in that same spot by the front door every night for the four weeks that I stayed with her. Only when I went to sleep did the shock and worry I felt for my mother slip out of the cognitive headlock I kept them in during the day. Each night short films with hazy plots of murder and sabotage committed by gruesome half-human figures filled my dreams.

It took me a few days to get acquainted with the interior landscape of the row house, which paradoxically resembled an outdoor landscape after a weeklong music festival. Detritus in both environments shared the same dizzying range of stuff: dishes, plates, clothes, blankets, couches, barbecue sets, washing machines, bicycles, electric fans, radios, televisions, books, magazines, as well as food and drinks—and the bags and wrappers that tell you where their voyages began. The only real difference between the two was that rock concert groupies usually leave behind an entire inventory of unmentionables that I didn't believe my mother collected, yet. Once I acclimated, roughly the point at which I could stop holding my breath every time I walked into the house, I decided it was time to speak with my mother about her hoarding. Deeply naïve, I thought I could fix the problem, and her, once I understood why she collected.

I brought the subject up, slowly and carefully. Before I made it across the street to the next sentence, she vehemently denied there was a problem. I tried again. Reframing my concern, I mentioned it would be good to discuss her abundant collection because it posed a serious fire risk to her. That didn't impress her, so I raised the ante: I told her that her home was a fire risk to her neighbors. Only a brick wall separated her from neighbors on either side. No reaction. Desperate, I brought up rodents. I had been awakened every night by rats tearing into old food she could no longer reach in the kitchen. Knowing this bothered her too, I asked, "What about my cleaning up the kitchen so we can at least get rid of the rats?" Incredibly, she agreed to the plan. That was as far as I got. Between looking for work and trying to adjust to America, I took back the kitchen from the rats, one counter at a time.

My mother's trash-filled home was worry enough, but more surprises awaited me. At dusk one evening when the two of us were taking a walk up a steep hill near her row home, she told me monstrous, angry demons in her head were chasing her, day and night. They yelled at her, telling her she was a terrible person, a bad parent. She mentioned this casually as if she were giving me a shopping list. Horrified for her and unsure what to say or how to help, I asked her for more details. "Are they always there?" "Do they say anything else?" In a flat, tired voice she confirmed the villains were constant companions in her head. Then she stopped talking as though the transfer of classified information was complete and any additional information would endanger her. But my new role of being her appointed rescuer was just beginning. Scared by her confession, in the fading light of day I passionately told her she was a good person. With no reaction, I told her with more enthusiasm than I felt that I was the result of her wonderful mothering. Then, she smiled.

Overwhelmed by her report of demons harassing her around-the-clock, I thought about calling one of my brothers or sisters, but I had been out of touch with all of them for most of my time abroad, and my mother only spoke to them when they called her. The following day I was still musing over how to respond to my mother's confession of beings in her head, when I walked into the house and heard her upstairs angrily cursing at someone. I carefully threaded my way through the junk toward the commotion, not sure what I would find. Halfway up the stairs I realized my mother was in the bathtub by herself. I had never heard my mother curse or talk as though she were possessed. I nervously knocked on the bathroom door. "Mom, are you OK?" Silence. "I'm fine, honey," she sang out. She didn't seem fine.

Once she was out of the tub, I told her I was really worried about her. Without referencing the one-sided conversation that I had just heard, I delicately suggested that she was under a lot of stress and it might help to talk to a therapist. She looked blankly at me. When I finished,

236

she said no thanks. Nothing was wrong. I was confounded by her and her ability to ignore the state of her house, her demons, and the disturbing monologue I had just overheard. Minutes after she left for work the next morning, I called the Department of Psychiatry at Hahnemann Hospital in Philadelphia, hoping they might admit my mother as an inpatient. The intake coordinator was sympathetic, but after asking me a series of questions about my mother and her behavior, confirmed that the hospital could not admit her for treatment without her consent, because she did not pose an extreme danger to herself or others. She did suggest, however, that I encourage my mother to voluntarily meet with a psychiatrist as an outpatient. I knew my mother would never do that. I was right.

Two weeks into my stay with my mother, I began looking for work in the Philadelphia area. My first stop was the Peace Corps office in downtown Philadelphia: I heard they often gave returned volunteers job leads. During a casual conversation with the office manager about what work I might be qualified to do, I learned the New York City Peace Corps office was looking for a returned volunteer to fill an open recruiter position. The manager encouraged me to apply. In the space of a few days, I completed my application, went to New York for an interview, and was offered the position. My jubilation lasted a few seconds. I struggled with whether to take the job in New York and leave my mother. Desire beat guilt by a nose and I decided to go. Days before I started work I found an inexpensive studio apartment in a multi-story apartment building in Brooklyn. Because the place was so cheap, I signed the lease quickly, never noticing that my fourth-floor apartment was in the back of the building. Only a fragment of natural light made it down a dark airshaft and into the apartment. I was treated to light gray light in the morning and dark gray light in the afternoon. The upside of my new home, however, was that I could walk from end to end unimpeded. Trying to recuperate from my mother's strangulated home, I kept my belongings to a minimum: a small wardrobe, a used bed, and a few items I salvaged from my mother's house—dishes, silverware, towels, bedding and a lamp. Sparseness was a relief.

Recruiting new Peace Corps volunteers was a perfect job for me. Because all the recruiters were recent volunteers, I was surrounded by people who had been through a similar international experience and, like me, were transitioning back to life in America. A big bonus of my new job was that I got to travel to different colleges and universities throughout New York, New Jersey, and Connecticut promoting Peace Corps opportunities and interviewing potential recruits. With space from my mother, I focused on friendships and activities important to me. Much of my social time was spent with three friends from my Central African Republic Peace Corps cohort. Serendipitously, we had all found jobs in Manhattan and apartments in Brooklyn, making it easy to hang out together. Intent on keeping our African experience alive for as long as we could, we spoke *Franglo*, the French-English-Sango patois used by Central African Peace Corps volunteers, made our favorite African dishes from time to time, and stealthily incorporated a bit of sensuous African swaying into our dance moves when we went to clubs. I also took an English writing class, swam several times a week in a fourth-floor pool housed in a synagogue near my apartment, and once a month served as an overnight volunteer in a local homeless shelter. All the same, my whirring activity never blunted my worries about my mother.

Before I left for New York I asked my mother what I could do to make sure she would be OK without me. She thought for a moment and then said, "I'd like you to call me every morning." "What do you mean?" I asked. She explained, "If you call me every morning and speak positively to me, I don't think I will be depressed." I wasn't sure how I would manage the cost of her request, phone calls were expensive in those days, but enthusiastically agreed to give her a happy upbeat message at the beginning of each day. Fortunately, free long-distance calling available to Peace Corps employees—for recruiting purposes—supported this therapeutic plan. For an entire year, I called my mother every weekday morning to pump her up and once a month took a train to Philadelphia to reinforce my weekday affirmations.

Try as I might, I never made my mother better with my calls or visits. Sometimes she seemed hopeful but mostly she remained sad and depressed. Whatever progress

I made lifting her mood one day, telling her how wonderful she was or describing all the good things I was sure would happen to her, evaporated the next. Throughout this up and down period, I still didn't share with my brothers and sisters how anxious and concerned I was about her. I never mentioned her unbreathable house, so full of things it was hard to walk, or the strange episode of her cursing at phantoms in the bathtub or telling me about her demons on our walk. Had I enlisted help from them, I wonder if anything would have come of it.

Over the years, each attempt to rescue my mother, by any of us, had the same theme, main character, plot, and story structure. They all began with my mother playing to perfection the victim or abandoned matriarch. Inspired by empathy or guilt, one of her children would gallantly step forward to cheer her up, clean out her house, pay her bills, or organize her affairs. My mother generally welcomed each rescue, in the beginning. Then came the repeat climax. At the precise moment the intervention was deemed successful, my mother seemed to take pleasure in passively but defiantly undoing each kindness. It was a dynamic that condemned all of us to pushing a boulder up a hill only to watch it roll back down again. Sisyphus had nothing on us.

A couple of months into my Peace Corp recruiting position that fall, I applied to several graduate programs in social work for the following year. Although I had harbored a dream of becoming a juvenile court judge from the age of twelve on, after reading *Manchild in the Promised Land* and subconsciously deciding that I needed an occupation with the power to right the wrongs done to children, in Africa I had changed my mind. Working closely with people as a social worker replaced my dream of going to law school. Social work felt grittier, more real, and more me. Again, I had an opportunity to relocate near my mother, so I applied to two Master of Social Work programs in Philadelphia, one at Temple University and one at the University of Pennsylvania. On a lark, I applied to a third program, a joint Master of Science in Social Work and a Master of Public Health at Columbia University. Columbia's joint-degree social work and public health program, with the former focusing on the psychosocial needs of individuals and communities and the latter addressing the public health of populations, made sense to me. In the Central African Republic, I observed that malnourished children needed access to quality medical treatment and nutritional care. They and their families often needed social support too. Public health and social work were interwoven elements on the same Möbius strip.

That spring I received three acceptance letters. Amazingly, Columbia offered me a full scholarship for both master's degrees, as well as work-study payment for my required social work field placements. There was no question in my mind; I wanted to go to Columbia. Soon, however, a miasma of guilt engulfed me, noxious and demanding. It told me if I accepted Columbia's offer I would stay in New York City and once more abandon my mother in Philadelphia. For weeks I went back and forth between Columbia University and the University of

Pennsylvania in Philadelphia. Days before I had to make my decision I had a dream. I don't remember what it was about, but I remember that when I woke up I chose Columbia, and with conviction.

Not long after I started school at Columbia, I had trouble concentrating on my studies. I worried about my mother. After all, I had been anointed her custodian and truly thought that if I did a good job at that she would not only heal herself, she would finally love me. Since I no longer had the free long distance phone line at the Peace Corps recruiting office, I couldn't afford to call her daily, and because of school demands I didn't go to Philadelphia every month. Recalling my positive experience with the counselor in San Francisco after the "suicide joke," I decided to talk to someone about my feelings. With a referral from Columbia's student health center, I made an appointment with a clinical therapist in Manhattan.

The first session was therapy redux. Just like my counseling sessions in San Francisco, I could not control the words, feelings, and stories about my mother that came shooting uncontrollably out of my mouth. Subsequent sessions I talked about all the guilt and shame I felt: I felt guilty for choosing my future, repeatedly, over my mother's, and shame that I was not a better daughter. My relationship with my mother felt as cluttered and oppressive as her house. The therapy lasted for three months. At the end, I didn't experience an epiphany about my mother, my relationship with her, or my childhood, but the change that had begun floors below my consciousness

242

when I was in therapy in San Francisco was continuing. In the meantime, the therapist gave me permission to unchain myself from my mother's happiness. Each session she emphasized that I was only responsible for my own. That gave me enough support to refocus on my studies and my first-year social work field placement on a pediatric unit in one of New York City's public hospitals.

When I was informed that I would be working in pediatrics, images of the children and parents I had known in Africa ran like a slide show in my head. Although families in my village sometimes needed a helping hand, community was paramount, a fact evident in life and death. Whenever someone in Bokiné died, especially a child, the entire village mourned the loss and shared the pain. Village drums beat for three days straight, a percussive elegy for the departed and musical tribute for the living. The rhythmic drumming comfortingly communicated love and connection between people. Naïvely, I jumped into my work on the pediatric unit and waited to hear the drums.

I approached the hospital crib of a delicate twenty-month-old girl. She was sitting perfectly still in the middle of the crib, peering back at me through the metal bars. The genetic gods had blown her a kiss. She was breathtaking. Two large luminescent brown eyes, each outlined by a full set of long dark eyelashes, were spaced symmetrically in a beautiful heart-shaped face framed by tight black curls. Little spitballs glistened on the lower lip of a sweet button mouth still getting used to forming words whole. The toddler watched me intently as I walked up to her crib.

Conscious that I needed to reach out to her carefully, I softly called her name. She responded. Lifting her arms toward me, she curled her fingers in and out, universal baby language for "pick me up."

The little girl in front of me silently asking for a hug was too ill for me to take out of her crib. She had numerous internal injuries that were still being evaluated and only nurses and doctors could hold her. Reaching my hand through a crib bar I grasped her tiny hand and spoke to her soothingly. Pushing aside her first choice, she delighted in the touch and caressing words. As we played our adapted game of patty cake trying to touch each other's hands and not the bars, round marks on her beautiful skin came into focus. Initially I saw only a few on her arms. Then I noticed they were all over her legs. When I gently peeked under her hospital pajama top I saw they covered her torso.

I had known about the marks. My social work supervisor had assigned me to meet with the child's mother who was under investigation for child abuse, but I was wholly unprepared for what I saw and felt. How could a mother stamp out her cigarettes again and again and again all over her child, and beat her too? How had this innocent child survived the pain and insanity of each burn and assault? I started shaking.

Eventually I pulled myself away from the child and walked briskly to my supervisor's office. "I can't meet with the mother," I told her, panting to catch my breath. "I just don't think I can work with her. Who would do that to a child!" I exclaimed. In a quiet voice my supervisor said,

"This is so hard. What that mother did was truly horrific, but she deserves our compassion too. Something is very wrong with her. It's our job to get her the help and support that she needs. Speak with the mom. Try to understand her and why she would hurt her child." She went on, "Put aside your feelings and try to connect with her, understand her truth, however she defines it."

At first I had no idea what finding the truth in the mother meant. She was abusive and cruel, there was nothing to find. Since I had no choice, however, I began meeting with the mother and encouraging her to tell me her story. Our initial interactions were difficult. I didn't want to hear anything she had to share. But with each successive meeting, I went deeper into the mother's own childhood of abuse and struggles with severe mental illness. At our last meeting, she expressed affection for her child and remorse for her actions. Stamping cigarettes out on her child and beating her, she explained, were the only way she knew how to stifle all the wants her child had that she couldn't meet. The mother was subsequently incarcerated for child abuse, but was also referred for psychiatric treatment in jail.

For the rest of the year I worked with children who had been abused. I felt deeply connected to and protective of them. My feelings towards their abusers, however, were mixed. Abusers who expressed remorse and an earnest desire to stop their abuse, I could emotionally connect to. They had, I felt, some real possibility of healing for their children and themselves. But I struggled to find empathy for abusers who were uniformly unrepentant and unfeeling.

245

Children victimized by individuals in this group had emotional injuries that were often as severe, and sometimes more so, than the physical injuries that triggered their hospitalization.

Before the end of my first year in graduate school, I became engaged to Morgan Gilhuly, a fellow Central African Republic Peace Corps volunteer. Morgan was part of the small group of Brooklyn-based Peace Corps volunteers I had hung out with the previous year, when I was recruiting for Peace Corps. I first met Morgan during the weeklong pre-invitational training in Saint Louis before leaving for the Central African Republic. It was an awkward first meeting—two twenty-one-year-olds anxious about moving over 6,000 miles away trying to appear cool and together. Fortunately, the jittery parts of us melted away as we got to know each other in Africa. Although we didn't date until we were both back in New York after Peace Corps, I was smitten with Morgan. He was kind, funny, thoughtful, hardworking, and smart. Although more than a few Peace Corps friends thought we were a mismatch, I thought we fit together beautifully.

Morgan and I decided to get married weeks after we started dating the winter of our second year back in the States. I was in my first year of the joint-degree program at Columbia; he was in his first year of law school at Yale. Our engagement was not the pre-planned kind. Late one Sunday afternoon in mid-February 1983, Morgan borrowed a car from his parents and picked me up at my apartment near 125th Street in Manhattan for an inexpensive dinner at an

Indian restaurant in the Lower East Side. Walking back to the car after dinner Morgan noticed that the trunk of his parents' old Volkswagen Jetta had been jimmied open, and both our school backpacks were gone. His contained a massive criminal law text; mine had reams of painstakingly recorded social work process notes from my child abuse field placement. The theft nudged us, already happy with each other, into a future. Back at my apartment Morgan asked me, "Since we just got robbed, do you think we should get married?" I emphatically said, "Yes!"

Instead of the typical *I love you—you love me* betrothal pledge, Morgan told me he loved me, but I was unable to say the same back. It was hard for me to believe that he or anyone could love me. But I did allow myself to feel giddy with joy for an entire month. After four weeks of uninterrupted bliss, I realized that I needed to tell my mother the news, a conversation I did not want to have. For the nearly two years since I returned home from Africa, I felt locked into a zero-sum happiness game with her: if I were happy that meant she would be unhappy. Not only that, I had to tell her of a third consecutive decision that put my needs and future in front of hers. Impaled once again by confusion and uncertainty about her and our relationship, I forced myself to schedule a weekend visit.

On the designated weekend, I took the train from New York to Philadelphia and caught a bus out to Manayunk to my mother's row home. Letting myself in the house I quickly and loudly announced my arrival. Since my mother's bathtub brawl with phantoms I was nervous about walking in on her. My mother rang out that she was upstairs in the tub. I walked up the stairs and told her through the closed bathroom door that I had some news. "Come in but just give me a minute," she said. Giving her more than a minute, I turned the handle. My mother was lying in half a tub of water with a bath towel spread over her, the edges already soaking wet. She looked puzzled. I felt somber. Steadying myself I told her the story of my engagement. With all the longing of a young child, I asked her if she was OK with my plans. She didn't answer for a while; her thoughts seemed to soak alongside her body. After a few moments, she looked up at me and said, "You deserve to be happy."

It was one of only two comments I can remember my mother making to me that felt genuinely authentic. The other came later when I gave a presentation to my daughter's high school French class, in French, about my Peace Corps experience in Africa. I had invited my mother, who does not speak French, to attend. After the presentation and slides she shocked me by telling me I had a gift for communicating and connecting with people. Both comments, her support for my marriage and her compliment about my public speaking, came out straight, without the curlicues of language she normally used to disguise her deceit. All the same, I sensed her wedding comment might have an expiration date. On the spot, I thanked her for what was likely a time-limited blessing, and never asked her again if my plans were acceptable.

Six months after I told my mother I was getting married she locked the front door of her row home and moved to San Clemente, California, to live with her sister. The decision seemed to be a good one. In addition to reconnecting with my aunt, whose organization and structure I hoped might rub off on her, it seemed like a great opportunity for my mother to build a new life with more people in it. Months after leaving, my mother reported back to me that she liked the balmy Southern California climate and had decided to stay. Through my aunt and uncle, she found work as a sales associate in a furniture store and had moved into her own place, a one-bedroom bungalow a stone's throw from their house.

As my mother appeared more settled, I relaxed into my second and last year of graduate school. Feeling the burden of her lifted just a bit, I immersed myself in school and spent weekends with Morgan, alternating between my apartment in New York and the house he shared with roommates in New Haven. We had decided not to marry until after I finished my joint-degree program—eighteen months from the day of our engagement—so for the first time in a long time, I slid into a slightly less worrisome state of mind.

Before my mother left for California I asked her what she planned to do with her Manayunk home. Casually but convincingly she said if she decided to stay out west she would come back to clean it up and rent it out. I believed her. Not too long after she declared California her homestead, I began to worry about her Philadelphia home.

Knowing my mother was not paying the mortgage or property taxes, I knew what came next and none of the permutations and combinations that catastrophe was likely to trigger—losing all her belongings, foreclosure, and a lot of drama—were comforting. Not only that, the state of my mother's house had not changed from the first day I saw it. It was still jam-packed. Gas, electricity, and water had long since been cut off due to nonpayment, but the mausoleum of things heavy and willful seemed to be challenging me from Philadelphia to do something about them. Because of school and my fieldwork, I didn't have the time or money to clean out the house.

Up until my mother's house debacle, I had said very little to Morgan about my mother or my family. I had learned the art of feigning normalcy from a master. Anything dodgy in my background was avoided and answers to questions about my family life were tightly wrapped in gossamer. Not knowing what else to do, I finally told him about my mother's house, hoping he might help me think of a solution. I started with a simplified explanation of my mother—*My mother has suffered a great deal in her life—she was abandoned by my dad, and then to keep us all together, she worked at a job where she was paid less than men doing the same job, even though she was better educated. Despite our being poor, she kept us together and raised us by herself, with no help from my father.* Then, I delivered the finale: *When my mother moved to California, she left her house in Philadelphia full of stuff. She has a problem collecting, but it's understandable given what she's been through.* The story was so overlearned it joined other deeply ingrained habits like brushing my teeth and tying my shoes.

When I finished my tale, Morgan made an extraordinary proposition. He decided that he would ask his father to cover the costs of cleaning out and preparing my mother's house so it could be sold. Since his brother was looking for a renovation project, he thought his brother might be able to do the work. He paused and then said, "I think this will work and I know my dad will propose a financial arrangement that will work for everyone." And he did. It was a win-win proposition for everybody involved, especially my mother. She would be freed from a house destined for foreclosure, and would walk away with more money than her original investment. The offer was so compassionate and so contrary to the proposals that passed for social contracts in my family system, I was dumbfounded. My soon-to-be father-in-law and Morgan's brother generously agreed to the arrangement; so did my mother.

Not long after the ink was dry, the beautiful melody accompanying this feel-good story abruptly wandered way off key. I should have known.

Chapter Seven

Wedding on Its Side

Insomnia gifted me with time I never knew I had. Before I could enjoy it, though, anxiety muscled in and claimed it all for itself. As I headed into the home stretch of graduate school in 1985 with my social work program wrapping up in May, my public health program in July, and preparations for my wedding in mid-September, I joined the ranks of city dwellers desperately seeking sleep. The cause of my sleep disorder was undisguised. For months I contemplated day and night how I would complete my second-year social work internship in good standing and finish two master's degrees, while finding a job and a new place to live, and planning a wedding in Connecticut near Morgan's parents' home that neither my family nor I could afford. Two thoughts kept me awake: I must get everything right; and, if I make a mistake, I won't be able to fix it. It was like trying to complete the crossword puzzle of your life every night, in pen.

To distract myself from the fogginess in my brain and the exhaustion in my limbs, I wondered how other sleep-deprived people managed to function or at least to stay upright during the day. As I staggered off each morning to tackle the commitments of school and work, I amused myself by trying to identify kindred souls in the people I passed on the streets. Telltale signs were hollow mauve-colored orbital cavities and a weary shuffle. Before I managed to pull myself out of the tortured no-sleep phase with the help of a relaxation tape that featured a woman annoyingly urging me again and again to "R-E-L-A-X" in a high-pitched warbling voice, I was convinced I could singlehandedly start an impressive protest movement to take back sleep. My completely unscientific on-the-street study had led me to conclude New York is full of insomniacs.

My period of sleep deprivation lifted just in time. I finished both degrees and found a job. Luck held and Morgan and I found an apartment near his law school; he still had another year before graduation. One anxiety that didn't get much of a lift, though, were the wedding plans. I never had any fantasies about my wedding, what I would wear, what food we would have, my first dance, etc., but I did desperately dream that my mother would help me plan it. The moment I was engaged I hoped she would delight in singing the second half of the *Fiddler on the Roof* song, "Sunrise, Sunset," the part that celebrates the young newlyweds and their time to experience seasons of happiness and tears. But eighteen months earlier she had retracted her "you deserve to be happy" wedding comment. It hadn't lasted much longer than her bathtub soaking. Not only did she not sing to me throughout the wedding preparations, she refused to talk to me.

"I have no role in this wedding!" my mother hurled at me while I was driving her from JFK back to Connecticut for my wedding, scheduled to take place three days later. In retrospect, a full-fledged panic attack might have provided some relief to the audacity of her words. If that had happened, I probably would have seen someone immediately for help. Instead, the mild and very brief panic attack symptoms I did experience—sweating and trembling—were knocked to the back seat by my colossal anger. I was furious at my mother. How dare she scream *at me* about having no role at my wedding!

From the moment I started planning the wedding twelve months earlier, other than suggest that I look up her old television boss who might have a wedding dress I could borrow from his collection of vintage clothes, and giving me the names of a few people she wanted me to invite, my mother had unapologetically checked out. As she thundered to a full-on fight with me in the car, I removed the kid gloves I had put on when I came home from Africa out of concern for her mental well-being. "Are you kidding!" I screamed. "The entire time I was planning this wedding, you refused to help me or even discuss it!" I gripped the steering wheel hard to manage my rage. "When you did finally pick up the phone you wouldn't even answer my questions! You gave me the silent treatment." The last statement I remember throwing back at her was, "I'm sorry you feel you don't have a role, but I didn't cause that. You did!"

Our fight didn't resolve anything. Throughout several pre-wedding parties hosted by friends of Morgan's parents, my mother treated me coolly. It wasn't hard to sense that something was going to happen and it wouldn't be positive. The first indicator that my suspicions were correct was that my mother immediately abandoned her go-to repertoire of theatrical roles. Instead of flattering and charming her way into people's psyches the way she'd always done, she looked and behaved as though she were an unwanted guest at every event. To counteract her sulking, I focused on staying upbeat and making sure Morgan's parents knew how grateful I was to them for generously paying for the entire wedding reception and most of the rehearsal dinner. My father agreed to pay for a small portion of the rehearsal dinner, but only after many pleading phone calls.

Adding another small bit of wedding drama was an unexpected last-minute wedding dress switch. The day before my mother arrived, I went into Manhattan to the vintage clothing warehouse owned by my mother's former television boss to pick up the sublimely beautiful 1920s drop-waist wedding dress I had selected six months earlier as a loan. When I got there, no one could find it. Quelling my disappointment, I started hunting for a replacement. Within an hour I had found another equally beautiful 1920s style dress made from a sheer lace curtain that fit beautifully over a snug body-length slip.

With sand pouring through the hourglass, on the eve of the eve of my wedding, I decided it was time to tell Morgan more about my family. We sat down on the floor in his old childhood bedroom with his oar from his college lightweight shell hanging on the wall above our heads, and I poured out my story. "Babe, there are a few things I haven't shared with you about my family, that, well, I think you might want to know," I said in a quiet voice. "Spill the beans, can't be all that bad!" he replied, laughing. "Well, actually, I am not sure what you consider bad, but there are a few things about my parents that aren't that good," I said. Morgan gave me a hug and said, "Nothing you say is going to make me change my mind about you!"

I started. "Well, I know you have probably wondered what's going on with my mom. Why she's been so weird since she got here." Morgan had noticed that my mother had been unhappy since she had arrived for the wedding, but was willing to take it all in stride. "Well, you remember I told you when your dad bought the house that she . . . she has suffered a lot in her life. That explains some of why she acts the way she does, and maybe her hoarding, which you know about. But there's more. I need to tell you my mother is not like other mothers. I need you to know that I couldn't count on her, really, ever." I took a big breath and went on.

"All my life it has been this strange pattern, where like one moment I feel a connection with her, and the next, she's totally out of sight, out of mind. When you're not directly in front of her, she makes no effort to call or write or even, it seems, think of you. There's something wrong with her, but I don't know what." Morgan watched me intently. I continued, "Remember last year after you and I announced our engagement, and she came to visit me in the apartment on the 23rd floor that Anjani and I were subletting over on 125th and Broadway? Well, my mother and I were talking about something in the living room, but then I had to go get something in the kitchen. When I came back, she was gone. It wasn't a big apartment but I couldn't find her. I was frantic. I don't know why, but I had this strange feeling that she might have thrown herself over the balcony—you remember we had that little outdoor patio off the living room. I ran to the patio door, opened it, and found her, standing outside on that tiny little patio, super close to the railing with a strange expression on her face."

I continued, unable to keep many of the frayed threads of my origins from unraveling more, "All my life she has been like that. She seems wonderful and dialed-in, all sweetness, but there's no carry-over of caring from one day to the next, or even of one minute to the next." I started to cry, but was determined to keep going. I filled in more about my upbringing—the lack of food, the sibling fighting, constantly moving houses, the lights off. I didn't get to everything but did share enough that I felt Morgan knew more about me. Not wanting to skip my father, whose life and behaviors were sure to wreak havoc in some way on my and Morgan's future life together, I added, "My dad has done some really bad stuff too. We rarely saw him growing up, but when we did, he was a big bully. He physically and emotionally pushed everyone around, he even threatened my brother with a gun. What he did to us is a long list, I don't want to go into all of it. Just know that he's not like your dad, at all. He was rich and spent his money on cars and all kinds of toys, while we lived hand to mouth. If this is all too much for you, maybe," I paused, "Maybe, I'm too much." I slumped down on the bed, feeling crushed by the weight of my story.

Morgan took me in his arms and told me he loved me, with or without my family. He didn't reject me or construct an impossible passive-aggressive obstacle course that I had to successfully complete to win back his affection. His response was exactly what I wanted, and exactly what I needed. To this day, I am not sure if my last-minute disclosure was a test to see if he would stay with me, or a gift, a chance for him to get out before it was too late. That night, for the first time in our relationship, I told him, "I love you."

My big reveal to Morgan was seismic but didn't include my growing fear that our wedding, this good thing happening to me, would go sideways somehow. As we gathered in the church for the wedding rehearsal the night before the wedding, I was consumed with anxiety. Leading up to our nuptials my father had told me loudly and firmly he could not commit to coming. Up until the moment he walked in, or didn't, I wouldn't know his plans. It was vintage my father. Whenever he was invited to a family event, which wasn't very often, he melodramatically told whoever invited him that it was his policy to avoid family gatherings. He acted as though they were war crimes tribunals and he was a defendant without friends. In my mind, all my father had to do was show up at the wedding, an act I equated with his finally caring about me. To relieve him of any burden that he *do* something, I told him that he wouldn't be giving me away. Morgan and I had decided to walk down the aisle together.

Forty-five minutes after our two families and members of the wedding party had gathered in the church to start the rehearsal, my father opened the heavy church doors and walked in, making sure they closed behind him with a dull thump, loud enough to be heard. Not knowing where to go, he haughtily stood against the back wall of the nave, half slouching. Morgan and I were standing at the altar pretending to exchange our vows with the priest; everyone else was seated in the front pews. Seeing my father's indiscreet grand entrance out of the corner of my eye, I glanced at my mother. Her face was a tapestry of strained facial muscles in a brand-new background color, her natural olive skin tone had morphed into an unsettling shade of blue-white.

During Morgan and my *do this next* practice cues, I quickly glanced at Morgan's parents to see how they were sizing up my father. They had met my mother soon after Morgan and I announced our engagement but had never met my father. From the look on their faces they seemed unfazed by his late entry or his look—business casual with oversized glasses and his classic blondish-brown toupee. Over the years the quality of his toupees had steadily improved; earlier iterations could pass for an Andy Warhol wig on loan. Those hairpieces resembled straw in both color and texture and always included Warhol's signature hair flourish—random tufts of hair that stuck straight out. I sighed with relief: the toupee my father had on was still noticeably a toupee, but the time it took for someone to recognize it as one had moved from seconds with just a glance, to a full minute or two with scrutiny.

When the rehearsal wrapped up, my father surprised me by graciously greeting everyone in attendance. Unlike my mother, who continued to act as though she were being primed for surgery without anesthesia, my father seemed relaxed. Despite his apparent wealth, he showed no embarrassment or discomfort that my future in-laws were paying for nearly everything related to the wedding. With the pesky question of paternity out of the way, after all he only considered me a "sister," he proceeded to feel free to fully enjoy the wedding he had decided to attend at the last minute. So free that immediately following the rehearsal he began pitching an investment opportunity to Morgan's aunts and uncles regarding a company that he had become involved with in Colorado, M & L Business Machine Company.

"Hi, I am David, Monique's father. How are you?" I heard him say to his unsuspecting prey. "So, what do you do for a living?" He paused with the impatience of someone forced to sit through a timeshare presentation for a discounted resort stay. The moment his quarry finished describing their occupations and interests, he continued,

"I'm really glad I met you, because I want to tell you about a truly incredible opportunity to double and triple your wealth. I'm a physician and vice-president of a first-rate business, M & L Business Machine. Our company sells computers and other business machines, and we're growing like crazy. We are looking for some smart early investors. I'm telling you about this because, honestly, this is an opportunity you can't pass up!" I groaned.

Nothing about the company or the touted exorbitant return on investment rate seemed legitimate to me. Months before the wedding while I was trying to extract a commitment from him to pay for some of the rehearsal dinner and attend the wedding, he tried to sell me M & L stock—via long-distance phone calls. Aside from the fact that I was broke, I declined any involvement. I knew my father's manipulation up close. Trusting him with even a penny of my money was out of the question. After the rehearsal dinner, I was relieved to learn that none of Morgan's family had signed on as investors. Undaunted, my father was at it again the next day, during my wedding.

At the same time that my father was cheerfully trying to lure new investors to M & L at the wedding and stay clear of my mother, my mother alternated between two dramatic roles: the pained He Did Me Wrong Ex-Wife and The Overwrought Mother of the Bride. The latter was particularly galling given her complete absence of involvement in all aspects of my wedding. On the positive side, watching my parents circumvent each other all night might have provided entertainment for anyone watching.

Their most interesting performance of the evening was their unexpected decision to walk out of the church together after our ceremony. It was a no-touch angry tango that broadcast in unsparing detail their shared human agony.

Halfway through the reception, when I allowed myself to think I had survived my wedding intact and that guests had actually enjoyed themselves, I headed for a quick bathroom stop, unable to scale back the smile a climber feels right before reaching the summit. Celeste, my matron of honor (Gillian was also a bridesmaid), joined me, and I looked forward to quickly chatting with her about how excited I was that the wedding was going well. She made it clear, however, that she wasn't there to celebrate. She was upset. Before I could say anything, she angrily whispered to me that she couldn't believe I didn't include our brothers in the wedding party, especially since all my husband's siblings, his three brothers and one sister, were groomsmen and a bridesmaid. Feeling my way through her words to her hurt, I realized that she thought I had not included them because I was embarrassed by them. That wasn't it at all. Devastated, I immediately apologized and tried to explain.

Tearing up, I told her I had made a grave mistake but the arrangement was not an intentional slight. I explained that when Morgan and I were discussing our wedding party, we decided to have five bridesmaids and five groomsmen. My bridesmaids included my two sisters, Morgan's sister, and two friends. Because Morgan already had three brothers and wanted two close friends as groomsmen, adding my three brothers, we thought, would make the party off balance. We weren't sure what to do until I came up with the idea of spreading my brothers out in the reception room, each seated at a table with attractive single women. At the time, they were all in conflict with each other, so it seemed like a terrific idea. Not only would the arrangement reduce the potential for sibling friction, it would give each of my outgoing brothers an opportunity to be a table star. To be sure that my idea wouldn't offend anyone, I told Celeste that I had run the proposal by our mother, whose knowledge of etiquette do's and don'ts was vast, a vestige of her private high school education. But she refused to comment on the appropriateness of the arrangement, or discuss any possible repercussions. In keeping with her passive-aggressive protest over me, the wedding, and my in-laws, she chose silence over helping or guiding me. If my mother had helped me a little with the wedding plans, I might still have made the same mistake, but I wouldn't have born the weight of my inadvertent sin alone. Or so I thought.

I left the bathroom and walked back into the reception room and immediately went to each of my brothers and Gillian to apologize that I had not included Alan, Michael, and Patrick in the wedding party, and emphatically told each that my error was the result of my ignorance about wedding etiquette, not because I was embarrassed or ashamed of them. I was devastated. I understood how hurt my siblings were. We were raised in an incubator of not good enough. The rest of the wedding was painful.

The morning after our wedding, Morgan and I headed over to his parents' house for brunch with our two families, minus my father, who had made a quick getaway. Since it was Patrick's birthday, I picked up a birthday cake to bring to the brunch. I was hopeful the intimate brunch would provide an opportunity for me to right my wedding wrong. As we pulled into the small parking area above my in-law's home, I heard yelling near the house but couldn't make out whether the exchange was playful or angry. As I walked over to the set of stairs that led down to the house, Gillian and Patrick were bounding up them, furious. When they reached the top, they tried to communicate to me in angry snippets the argument they had just had with my new mother-in-law. They believed she had slighted my family during the wedding and was responsible for Alan, Michael, and Patrick not being included in the wedding party. Seconds later they stormed out. The party was over.

While we honeymooned in Portugal, a gift from Morgan's grandmother, I occasionally took breaks from crying about the wedding to delight in the huge life step I had just taken. When we returned home, I jumped into a new job counseling pregnant teenagers in Bridgeport, Connecticut. The job and adjusting to married life at home kept me busy, but neither stopped me from replaying the events of the wedding in my head. To cope, I started imagining a different version of my nuptials. In my recast version, all my brothers were groomsmen and my mother was a loving and supportive mother-of-the-bride. Swapping out what happened with what I wanted to happen, like cutting out and folding the tabs of a new paper doll outfit onto a paper doll, helped me re-experience my wedding and the day after as less agonizing. Cutting off my shoulder-length curly mop into a pixie helped, too.

A couple of weeks after my honeymoon I called my mother, impatient to talk about how I could smooth over Alan, Celeste, Michael, Gillian, and Patrick's hurt feelings. To my surprise she was thrilled to chat about the post-wedding blowup. "I can't believe that Gillian and Patrick behaved so badly, Nikki. Honestly, they embarrassed me beyond anything I thought imaginable. I thought I had raised all of you with better manners. I still cannot get over it. I feel so humiliated." She never mentioned the misbegotten wedding party arrangement involving my brothers or that I had specifically asked her whether that was a good plan before the wedding. As the ultimate victim of other people and events, her behavior or role in our conflicts would never be discussed or dissected—as usual, we operated with the unspoken proviso that *she* was off the table.

Morgan and I settled into young married life. Without much modeling on how two people conduct the give and take of intimacy, it took me a while to trust that he would be there when he said he would and that we could work together to solve our differences and challenges. In the meantime, I wrote letters and left phone message apologies to my siblings, reiterating that I had not intended to exclude my brothers or slight my family at the wedding. I simultaneously begged my mother to intervene on my behalf. Ignoring my requests, she cheerfully said, "Oh honey, there isn't anything I can do. I'm sure this will all blow over soon." Two of my siblings didn't speak to me for two years; two didn't speak to me for three years. My period of banishment didn't seem to bother my mother. Perhaps she found the resurrection of a familiar family dynamic comforting: sibling conflict and no one pointing a finger at her.

Ripples from the wedding saga continued to spread out for a while. Several years after I was married, my father's incredible investment opportunity was revealed to be a Ponzi and check-kiting scheme. In 1990, M & L declared bankruptcy. By that time my father had been vice president of the company for several years. The *Denver Post*, which followed the case closely, reported in February 1991: "Investigators peeling back the layers of what appeared to be a simple company bankruptcy in Westminster have uncovered what they suspect is one of the nation's largest investment fraud schemes. The investigation of M & L Business Machine Co., Inc., is definitely a multi-state, national problem. It is much bigger than just the bankruptcy, said Christine Jobin, the Denver attorney appointed as trustee to manage the case." The article further stated that when Ms. Jobin went to the company warehouse to inventory the company's remaining assets, she discovered more than 500 boxes filled with bricks and dirt. No computers or computer equipment.

Many people, including my father's own mother and stepfather—my grandparents—invested significant sums of their life savings at my father's urging. In 1992, my father was indicted in connection with the fraud scheme, but federal prosecutors later dropped the charges. A 1994 *Denver Post* article titled "M & L's Parrish Settles Suit: Ex-VP to Pay Trustee $300,000" reported: "David Parrish, a former Boulder psychoanalyst linked to the M & L Business Machine Co. investment fraud, has agreed to pay the defunct company's trustee more than $300,000 to settle a lawsuit." The article later states, "Parrish filed for personal bankruptcy in 1991, leading M & L trustee Christine Jobin to file suit against him to recover money she believed was owed to the company's investors."

In a separate legal matter, my father appealed tax deficiencies levied against him by the Commissioner of the Internal Revenue related to tax on his M & L income. The following excerpts from a February 1999 United States Court of Appeals Eighth Circuit decision describe the court's assessment of the matter:

> *Reconstructing Parrish's taxable income using the bank deposits method for 1988 and 1989 and the specific items method for 1990, the Commissioner concluded Parrish had unreported income of $72,415 in 1988, $236,834.27 in 1989, and $163,822.31 in 1990. The Commissioner assessed tax deficiencies based upon this unreported income, adding on self-employment tax on*

the entire amount plus negligence, late filing, and accuracy related additions and penalties. Parrish commenced this action to challenge the deficiencies. After a one-day trial, the Tax Court upheld the Commissioner on all issues except it reduced the amount of unreported income subject to the self-employment tax.

At oral argument, in response to a question from the court whether Parrish was a participant in, or a victim of, the M & L Ponzi scheme, his counsel replied that as an investor Parrish was simply "a consummate doctor." After reviewing the record, we conclude that was an insult to the integrity of the members of the medical profession. Parrish used M & L as a huge, undocumented piggy bank, while he encouraged friends and relatives to squander their savings on this worthless venture. His resulting tax problems are a predicament of his own making, not the product of overzealous enforcement of the federal tax laws.

As the M & L case continued to wind its way through the courts in the early 1990s, my father decided to move from Colorado to Nebraska. The move, he told me, was in response to death threats from defrauded M & L investors in Colorado.

Training Village Leaders in Nutrition

Chief of Bokiné

Soeur Émilie and Medical Staff

Helping at Soeur Émilie's Nutrition Hospital

Learning to Ride My Suzuki at the Stage Training

My Beloved Moped

My Wedding

Chapter Eight

The Slow Build of Anger

After Morgan's younger brother cleaned out my mother's Manayunk row home he placed everything salvageable in a storage unit, directed by my mother from California. Although it was my mother's unit and the monthly bill was sent to her, my brother-in-law had to list himself as the secondary contact to secure the storage unit. Since my mother didn't open her mail or pay her bills, he called me every month to report that he had received another past due notice. I would then try to reach my mother to plead with her to pay her bill. It was a gnarly information pass-through. Within a year, my mother lost possession of everything in the unit. Not wasting any time, she immediately blamed my brother-in-law.

Travails with my mother continued and so did my attempts to help. When Morgan finished law school, we packed all our belongings into a 1973 Volvo wagon with over 200,000 miles on it and headed west to San Diego, California. Morgan had been selected for a one-year clerkship with a San Diego federal judge. On our way, we briefly visited with my paternal grandparents in Omaha before driving to Boulder to see my father, a visit that left Morgan unnerved. For two straight days, my father gave us a tour of his favorite luxury stores and art galleries, while aggressively hawking several get-rich-quick schemes. The fact that we were penniless and couldn't invest in anything didn't deter him. At dinner, he had each of us read an affirmation card from *A Course in Miracles*. The thrust of the cards and the Course was "everything involving time, space, and perception is illusory." As my father explained it, what matters in our existence called "life" is transcendent love, forgiveness, and the soulfulness of existing without envy or material wealth. After forty-eight hours, Morgan told me he couldn't stay another day.

From Colorado, our nearly dead Volvo limped across the Mojave Desert and into San Clemente. I had asked my mother if we could stay with her for a week or two while we looked for a place to live in San Diego, about an hour south of San Clemente. She enthusiastically said "Yes!" and seemed genuinely excited that we would be living so close to her.

Walking up to her tiny one-bedroom bungalow, I groaned. Crowding the front door were dead plants in too many planters to count. Old bikes, a wheelbarrow, a collection of rusted gardening tools—spades, trowels, hoes, pocket pruners—covered in spider webs, and an off-season artificial holiday wreath yellowed by the sun accented the horticultural graveyard. The scene reflected one of my mother's signature hoarding penchants: excessive clutter posing as decorative or functional.

When my mother opened the door, I was greeted by the familiar smell of decay. Thrilled by our arrival she welcomed us in and hurriedly exclaimed how hard she had been working on her bedroom, so Morgan and I could sleep there. "I have been working all night so you two can have my bed and stay in my room. I want you to have some privacy!" she said, adding, "I'll sleep on the couch." Like her Manayunk row home, her Southern California mini-bungalow was chock-full. Narrow footpaths connected the living room to the bedroom and the bedroom to the bathroom. Pushing disappointment to the back of my throat I focused on how happy she was to see us, hopeful it would be a positive stay.

With a year of marriage behind us, Morgan and I had moved into a phase in our relationship where we had begun to identify links between how we approached married life and how we were raised by our parents. Everything, it seemed, from preparing food to managing money, cleaning house, and negotiating relationships, was either an extension of or reaction to what we were exposed to in childhood. As I stood on my mother's threshold, I felt jittery. The state of my mother's bungalow was a pretty big link between the world I grew up in, with my mother in command, and my overwhelming desire to have control over my life and my environment—even in my marriage.

To my surprise Morgan didn't recoil at his first visual sweep of my mother's overstuffed San Clemente home. He remained calm and interacted gently with my mother. Twenty-four hours into our stay, he approached her debris much the same way he had approached a fallen tree that once blocked his way on a rural dirt road in Central Africa; without a fuss, he methodically chopped up the tree, removing it piece by piece from the road. Relieved and grateful for his optimism and compassion for my mother, we slowly unburied her kitchen. As soon as it was accessible and clean, we shopped for food and began cooking. My mother seemed pleased. Thinking we were on the right track, we decided to keep going. While my mother was at work at the furniture store, we began sorting sky-high piles of refuse in the garage. Between drives to San Diego to look for housing, we made runs to the local landfill with our lumbering Volvo packed to the roof with waste, first from the garage and later from the bungalow. After a week of intensive cleaning, we felt like we had achieved the impossible. You could physically walk from one end of the garage to the other and see the walls in the bungalow. My husband and I felt immensely proud. We had made my mother's life easier. We had done a good deed.

Since my mother never said anything to me about our very obvious cleaning effort, I assumed she approved. I was wrong. When the weekend came she angrily confronted both of us. I can still hear her words. "You had no right to touch, move, or throw away anything of mine!" she screamed at us both. Her response was bewildering. Not only did I think we were helping her, for an entire week, her house had been losing weight at an aggressive pace. It was inconceivable to me that she hadn't noticed before the weekend.

After two weeks of living with my mother, Morgan and I found a small house in San Diego and swiftly moved in. Morgan began his one-year clerkship for a federal judge. I found work managing a social services department in a small hospital on the outskirts of San Diego. I continued to drive back and forth to visit my mother in San Clemente on weekends, and soon reconnected with one of my sisters, who had moved to San Diego. In October, just three months into our new life, I became pregnant. I was thrilled. It was a very exciting time. At the same time, my mother began sagging heavily with depression. Unhappy at her furniture sales job and feeling snubbed by her sister who lived around the corner, she started withdrawing, complaining of fatigue and hopelessness. There was, however, one bright spot in her life. Earlier that fall she had begun volunteer teaching English as a Second Language (ESL) in the evenings to immigrants. Disorganized class lessons aside, she loved teaching. It gave her purpose, she told me, adding, "I also get the chance to use my acting skills. It's like being on stage with a live audience."

Through her volunteer work, my mother learned that the Los Angeles Unified School District was looking for ESL teachers, and because they had so many students with limited English proficiency, they were hiring individuals with graduate degrees to work as provisional teachers under an emergency credentialing program. Given her Master of Arts degree and ESL teaching experience, I encouraged her to apply, certain the opportunity would be the perfect antidote to her depression. Despite expressing strong interest in the job, she didn't follow up to obtain the application. Desperately wanting her to see how much I loved her and wanting her to find a job that matched her skills and interests, I called the district and requested the application. After it arrived, I drove to San Clemente and filled it in for her, while she dictated her information. Days later when I discovered she hadn't mailed it back, I took a day off from work, picked her up at her bungalow, and drove her to Los Angeles, so she could physically hand it in at district headquarters minutes before the deadline.

After an expedited interview process my mother was hired as an ESL teacher for junior high students at a school southeast of Los Angeles—with an immediate start date. Morgan and I jumped into action. We spent several weekends cleaning out her bungalow before moving her and her belongings to an apartment we helped her find near the school where she would be teaching. Moving her was not easy. More than once we gently asked her about the logic of boxing up clothes she couldn't possibly wear or old yellowed newspapers she probably wouldn't read. Each time, she responded with furious indignation, "Other people's children help them move, why can't you help me!" My mother's possessions were her friends, her protectors, her children; she wasn't leaving without them. We packed everything.

Taking a step back for a moment, it's clear to me now that my never-ending quest for my mother's love was a form of lunacy. Somewhere on the long list of reasons why I didn't stop pursuing her were two that provide the richest insight into my folly. The most important was that I wanted the person who gave birth to me to love me, to treat me as though I mattered to her. The second was that after years of her manipulation, lies, and distorted reality, I identified with my mother and her view of the world. So much so, I often didn't know where she began and ended in mine.

Remarkably, my mother not only managed to become certified right before the stated deadline in her provisional teaching contract with the Los Angeles Unified School District, she taught for close to ten years before retiring. During her decade teaching, she moved several times: from the apartment my husband and I moved her into before she started teaching, to a trailer, to another apartment, and then finally to a two-bedroom condo in Long Beach, California. The condo purchase was made possible with the funds she received from the sale of her Philadelphia row home—thanks to my father-in-law.

Weeks after Morgan completed his yearlong clerkship, we moved to San Francisco with our first child, a months-old baby boy. Two more children came along, and we made the Bay Area our home. As my mother hopscotched from one home to the next, my communication with her resumed its highly irregular schedule. Each time I discovered she had a new address I struggled to imagine how she had physically moved the gargantuan amount of stuff that gave her meaning. By contrast I never had any difficulty imagining what she left behind: weakened floorboards sagging from months and sometimes years of supporting overweight stuff; dirt, insects, and animal droppings embedded in soiled carpets complete with their own ecosystems; and piles of forlorn, unopened mail addressed to her. Changes of address represented little deaths to my mother, so she rarely submitted a change of address form at the post office.

Just before my mother retired from teaching, I had an experience that foreshadowed significant change in my relationship with her. When I was in my late thirties, my brother Michael generously invited and paid for my mother, my sister Gillian, and me to attend his wedding to a Brazilian woman in her hometown of Jacareí, Brazil, and spend a few days afterwards touring the countryside with them. One of our first sightseeing stops was Campos do Jordão, a beautiful mountain hamlet dotted with Swiss- and German-style homes. While my brother and his new wife went off for a hike, Gillian, my mother, and I decided to explore the town and its quirky architecture. It was a breathtakingly sunny day with a temperature so perfect, the sweet sugar smell of pink cotton candy cones lightly touched the corners of the town square.

As we ambled into the square, locals breezed by us, using the courtyard as a shortcut to home or work. We were the only tourists that early afternoon. Sweeping her eyes around the courtyard, my mother spied a lone cotton candy vendor in the middle of the cobblestone expanse and strode quickly over to him. Ignoring his battered and worn cart, she smiled and skidded into a disconnected exchange. In droplets of limited Spanish, she attempted to ask the vendor about his craft and confection. The vendor smiled back and answered, in Portuguese, the questions he imagined she was asking; responses he thought were necessary to make a sale. Neither understood the other. From across the courtyard the two looked as though they were engaged in a lovely duet.

With each passing second, I noticed my mother becoming increasingly animated. She chirped on in manic fashion believing her wit and charm, expressed in some undecipherable code, had no peer. Disappointment, however, was spreading across the vendor's face. He was beginning to sense there would be no exchange of money for cotton candy. Then I saw him tilt his body away from my mother, with a bewildered look on his face. He wanted to get away from her. Coming out of my hypnosis, I realized that what at first had seemed so innocent between the two of them was gone. My mother didn't notice. She kept delivering her lines indifferent to the scenery that had turned moody and gray. Tingles of unease exploded like little firecrackers in my stomach. Rushing over to the cart, Gillian and I disrupted our mother's performance and steered her away. The vendor took off with his cart.

It was the first time I saw my mother interact with a stranger the way she interacted with me. Indifferent to the vendor's needs and desires and the quid pro quo that governs most interactions, she had manipulated him for some strange inner need of her own. And it was done in a way that was both compulsive and stealthy. Witnessing the moment, I identified with the vendor. We both had believed in my mother's charm and innocence. After he bolted, I had the strange premonition that one day I would follow him.

Throughout my mother's teaching and retirement, I raised my three children, worked in various positions in public health and social work, and completed a doctorate in public health. During this eighteen-year stretch of my life, I tried hard to be a surrogate mother to my mother and some of my siblings, earnestly thinking that I could repair our family's damaged nerve center. I hosted holiday dinners, family get-togethers, parties to celebrate my siblings' birthdays, weddings, and babies, and my mother's visits to Northern California. When my mother visited, I took care of her as though she were my child, fussing about her, to make sure she was comfortable. I wanted to give her what I had never received, a warm, loving family that functioned. I can't explain fully how I knew how to mother; some things I learned from watching—friends' mothers, my aunt, Soeur Émilie—but most was pure instinct to protect, nurture, and cherish the ones I loved.

One visit with my mother wholly encapsulated my complicated relationship with her—the one where I parented her, hoping in return she would mother me. I was in my thirties with three elementary-school-age children and working as a clinical social worker for a large hospital. Typical of most visits with my mother, after arranging her flight and ticket I went to the airport to pick her up. As she walked feebly off the jetway, I noticed that she was flushed and feverish. Inching her way toward me she stopped several times to lean on a trashcan or airport chair to cough a phlegmy cough. I had never seen her that ill and was scared. After a quick embrace, I told her I would take her directly to the hospital. My mother dismissed my concerns and claimed she was fine. But once she got to my house, she couldn't get out of bed. Over the next three days her fever and cough worsened. After I begged her to see a doctor, she finally capitulated. It was close to eight o'clock in the evening on the third night of her stay when she finally agreed to go. I took her straight to an after-hours urgent care clinic.

In the waiting room my mother sat motionless. When her name was called, she weakly asked the medical assistant if I could stay with her during the exam. "Of course," the fresh-faced female assistant replied with a soothing smile. After my mother was settled on the exam table and the medical assistant had taken her blood pressure and temperature, a young female doctor came in. She introduced herself, reviewed the information on my mother's intake form—her reason for the visit—and asked my mother for her medical history. To my surprise, my mother instantly regained her strength. In a coiffed voice, she launched into an animated and detailed expository of every cough, cold, and medical problem she had ever had. She even managed to weave into her personal bio that she had been married to a doctor and had raised six children, alone.

At first, I appreciated my mother's thoroughness, but as the narrative dragged on I began feeling agitated. She was ignoring the serious illness that had brought her to the doctor. Just as I thought my mother was wrapping up the historical part of her medical record and would shift to describing her present condition, she told the doctor that she had nearly died from Legionnaires' disease in the 1960s. With this touch of the exotic, the spellbound doctor began plying my mother with questions. I felt confused. In the flu story I knew and remembered, my mother was hospitalized and gravely ill from pneumonia, but not the kind associated with Legionnaires' disease. Although I couldn't recall the exact date of the Legionnaires' outbreak in Philadelphia decades earlier, I recalled that it had rocked the city. Not only had people died from the disease, the outbreak sparked national fears of a pandemic. Why, I wondered, hadn't my mother ever mentioned that she had Legionnaires'?

I was grappling with my mother's Legionnaires' disease statement, unsure if it was true or if she had made it up, when I noticed it was getting late. Our evening medical odyssey meant I would not see my children before they went to bed, and because my mother probably did have a respiratory infection, I would still have to drive her to the one pharmacy in town that had late evening hours to get her medication. More than an hour after she started her performance, she finally finished. The doctor gave her the applause she had been waiting for and a diagnosis of walking pneumonia. On the way to the pharmacy I asked my mother about her Legionnaires' disease. With great conviction she asserted that the severe pneumonia she had been hospitalized for was in fact Legionnaires' disease and she had contracted it on the job: "Nikki, you remember I was at CBS, right? Well, when I was there, I spent a lot of time at a hotel in downtown Philadelphia. You probably don't know this, but the station asked me to do the makeup of some famous people staying there, who were scheduled for a few TV appearances. It turned out that was the hotel with the Legionnaires' disease breakout."

Later I looked up Legionnaires' disease. Apparently, the organism that causes the disease, bacteria of the species *Legionella*, was first discovered in 1976, about eight years after my mother was hospitalized for pneumonia. That visit said so much about my mother and our relationship. She kept searching for the perfect audience, and I kept searching for her.

So desperate for my mother, I ignored what didn't add up, and focused instead on making sure that whenever she visited she sat down to a homemade meal every evening with my family and slept in a well-appointed guest bedroom with clean linens. Free from all responsibility, my mother was often affectionate and entertaining. Hugs didn't seem so hard for her anymore. They were fleeting moments I cherished. Her laughter, embraces, and our meandering soul-searching discussions quickly filled in the crevices of doubt that opened up between visits. Feeling full of her made me happy, but I knew it was a feeling that wouldn't last. The moment my mother physically left my presence, the next point of contact would be anyone's guess. And sometimes her *catch-me-if-you-can* game began while she was still actually visiting with me.

After setting up base camp at my house, my mother would announce that she was leaving to visit with Alan or Patrick living nearby. I understood that. We all had empty gas tanks when it came to her, so sharing was essential. After sweetly assuring me that she would be back very soon, that evening or the next day, she would return days after she said she would, no calls, no explanations. One time when she didn't call or come back for four days, I confronted her: "Mom, why would you tell me you're returning for dinner and then not show up for four days or even call me to let me know you're not coming back? You can leave for a day, a month, or you don't have to come back at all. That doesn't bother me. All I ask is that you tell me what you're going to do, so I'm not sitting and waiting for you, worrying about what might have happened, or feeling angry that you don't care enough to let me know what your plans are!" Without a tinge of guilt, she replied. "Honey, I'm probably not going to change."

Living in Northern California, I was neither immune nor unresponsive to my mother's customized crises in Southern California. When her second-floor condo was robbed, I was relieved that she had been at work and was not hurt. Curious about what the thieves might have found valuable in her impenetrable home, I asked her what they had taken, a question my mother left unanswered. That incident was followed by a 5150—California's version of an involuntary psychiatric hold. Trying to get a local phone number, my mother inadvertently dialed 911 instead of 411 for information. Because she hung up the phone the moment she heard the police dispatcher's voice, she received a police callback. When she didn't answer that call, two officers were dispatched to her apartment for a safety check. Initially my mother refused to let them in, which escalated their concerns. Once they gained entry, they found her two-bedroom condo, save the master bathroom, filled floor to ceiling with stuff.

The police recorded that my mother had electricity, water, and phone services, but no heat, working refrigerator or stove. Surveying the situation and noting that my mother was in her seventies, the police determined she was a danger to herself. They gave her two options: going with them right then to the local hospital for a psychiatric assessment, or reporting directly to crisis services the following morning. My mother opted to report in the morning. The 5150 got my mother some help. For a brief time, she saw a psychologist. Staff from a local social service agency also came out to her condo a few times to help her organize some of her hoarded belongings.

On the heels of this event, my mother received a three-month notice that her condominium association was scheduled to begin some building-wide work and would need access to all condos. She called me in a panic. Calming her down, I told her I could help. I would take time off from work, fly down to Long Beach, rent a dumpster, and hire and supervise a crew of local laborers to clean out the condo. I even threw in that I would personally safeguard her mail and other important possessions. The entire cleanup, I told her, would take a few days to a week at most. Always on the lookout for the best deal, the child who would do the most for her while not challenging her beliefs about what needed to be done, she balked. Her counterproposal and the one she went with was to have Alan do it, when he could. It didn't take much to imagine that she had sealed the deal by communicating to him that cleaning up her condo would make him important and successful in her eyes. Seeing how my mother manipulated Alan, I couldn't help but feel like he had unwittingly taken a seat on her out-of-control roller coaster…without a seat belt.

For the next year or so, Alan made more than a half-dozen trips from the Bay Area to Long Beach to clean out my mother's house—the building work had been postponed several times. To his credit, by inspection time he had made her home accessible. After inspection, he continued his efforts to construct a bulwark in her home, battling my mother's habit of replacing a portion of what he took out after each cleanup visit. He finally stopped when my mother abruptly announced she wanted to sell her condo and move to my hometown in Northern California. By then her home was in walk-through condition, a result of his hard work and double-digit trips to the landfill. When it was over my mother thanked him, and then speedily forgot that he had been her hero.

While my mother cycled between her self-induced disasters, I noticed that my adult life did not have the same carbonation as my youth and young adulthood. The fizz and pops of trauma and neglect that punctuated my early years, and the dramatic entrances and exits of my parents in my teens and twenties, had stopped. But the unhealthy relationship I had with my mother continued. I was afraid to change it. I couldn't imagine a real severing with her or a trial test even, beyond defiantly refusing to speak to her for a while after a particularly egregious act, a response incidentally that never bothered my mother. She was the queen of withholding. So, I hung onto the moments of kindness that bookended the gunk she passed off as mothering. Not far below the surface, however, I could feel my anger toward her mushrooming.

In my mid-forties, something changed. I began to feel urgency about my relationship with my mother. By then I had been a parent myself for more than a decade and was starting to see her perverse parenting game of hide-and-seek as disturbing and cruel. A sad but visceral clarity took over. My unhealthy relationship with her would never change; I had to change. At about the same time that I realized this, I began working part-time in an inner-city community clinic, providing social work support and some therapy to patients. The therapy part of my job was brand new to me. In my graduate social work program, I stayed away from anything to do with mental health. It felt too close to home. In the clinic though, I found myself drawn to the field. To develop my therapy skills and ease my anxiety about my lack of training, I pursued supervision and psychotherapy training courses. Both enabled me to see the world of mental health from a more objective perspective. Accompanying this new view was a truth I no longer wanted to deny, massage, or debate: my mother was not well.

Initial attempts to disentangle myself from my mother began with my aggressively sharing my realizations about who she was with Gillian. Unconsciously, I wanted an ally, someone who would join me in refuting her and all her injustices, before I made any big decisions. I imagined Gillian and I would do a Thelma and Louise. In dramatic fashion, we would separate ourselves from our indifferent mother by driving off the cliff together. That didn't happen.

Unsure how to extract myself from my mother, I turned my attention to my father. Shortly after my wedding, he and I began speaking by phone every few months. I wanted a dad and he, with advancing age, seemed ready to elevate my status from sister to daughter. In the beginning, our phone conversations were generally pleasant and uneventful. My father enjoyed giving me advice in the same boot-camp booming voice he used when I was a child, his tone conveying the not so subtle message I'd heard from him all my life: "I'm pretty much always right and if you follow what I tell you, you'll be damned lucky." His feelings of omnipotence additionally inspired him to frequently diagnosis the world as suffering from a slew of mental health maladies and disorders. The most common was borderline personality disorder. He asserted that all men and women were afflicted with this difficult-to-treat disorder, my father, of course, being exempt.

Because of the steady phone connection with my father, I began visiting him every year or two, still earnestly hoping to win his affection. During those visits, I noticed that even though my parents seemed so different, they eerily shared more than a few common characteristics—a bit of a surprise to me, since I didn't know my father very well. Most prominently, they both had an uncanny ability to lie without remorse. The only difference I could tell was that my mother refrained from lying about me to others when I was present. Not so for my father. One untruth he repeated to casual acquaintances with me standing right next to him was that he had "put me through Columbia [University]." I hated that lie and the little offspring lies it birthed. Parading himself as a dedicated, loving, and involved father begged correction. Each time he uttered this lie I responded, "No, Dad, I attended Columbia on full scholarship. You didn't pay for me." An awkward silence ensued until my father followed his well-known script of changing the subject and never looking back.

I thought my phone relationship and occasional visits with my father would compensate for my mother's unremitting disinterest in me. But our conversations never led to greater intimacy, and every visit required me to look past his drugstore-size collection of medication bottles, lapses into baby talk, and peddling of new products and real estate deals. When the Arizona Medical Board began

292

reviewing allegations concerning the misdiagnosis and mismanagement of a patient my father treated, and my father asserted to me that neither the hospital that had reported him nor the Medical Board knew what they were talking about, I found it harder to look the other way.

The Medical Board had conducted several hearings on the case and concluded my father had repeatedly deviated from the standard of care in his treatment of the patient in question. The Medical Board's decision stated, "The Board has received substantial evidence supporting the Findings of Fact. Said findings constitute unprofessional conduct or other grounds for the Board to take disciplinary action." The Medical Board suspended my father from practicing medicine in Arizona and placed him on probation. The lifting of his suspension was contingent on his completing a Physician Assessment and Clinical Education Program evaluation, a clinical competency assessment and fitness for duty evaluation and remedial education program. My father chose not to comply with the Board's terms. The Arizona Medical Board subsequently revoked his medical license.

This action, preceded by two things I had learned about my father, made me sit up and pay attention. The first was an offhanded comment he made to me about his mother shortly after her death, a few years earlier. In a small angry voice, he told me that when he was growing up his mother had constantly pressured him to be perfect. I was shocked. I had always thought my grandmother exalted him from birth on, firm in her belief that he was beyond reproach. Instead, it sounded like she had given him a disturbing mixed message: he was simultaneously exquisitely perfect and grossly imperfect. The second was that I learned from a family member that my father was sent to a psychiatrist when he was a child, sometime in the 1930s or early 1940s (remarkable given that the field of psychiatry back then was in its infancy and largely unknown to the public). Even though I will never know how much of his behavior was the result of the way his mother treated him versus innate characteristics, whatever was going on in his life as a child, it seemed to have had serious consequences on both his mental health and personality.

Signs from both parents merged into an unmistakable epiphany: neither my mother nor my father would ever be the healthy, loving parent I needed. All the insanity, all the want, all the hurt began to vibrate. I could feel the inevitable coming. I had to disconnect from the craziness of both my parents. Older and less afraid, I didn't want to pretend any more.

I first severed with my mother, and it came about unexpectedly. Not long after Alan's overhaul of her condo, she came to spend Thanksgiving at my house. During the visit, she asked to borrow my car to run errands. Hours before flying back to Long Beach, she told me that she had placed her name on a senior apartment housing list in my town. I was taken aback. It was a startling chess move and I didn't know what to make of it. A year later, following an exhausting back-and-forth drama about whether she would or could physically leave her condo, she moved in to my home to wait for a senior apartment in town to become available. Only then was her move revealed. I was the child she had selected to pamper, mother, and financially support her in her remaining years. Checkmate.

The plan did not go as expected. Not one to track her income or bills, it never occurred to my mother to check her income before signing up for senior housing. Years of working, Social Security, and the sale of her condo had made her ineligible for a subsidized senior apartment—her income was slightly over the eligibility threshold. Morgan discovered this after she moved in with us. Stunned that she had no knowledge of her income or assets, he offered to help her get her finances in order. My mother enthusiastically accepted his assistance. Tucking into the task, Morgan spent hours and hours methodically organizing her affairs, which included paying back taxes (my mother had not filed income tax returns in years), ensuring that she received the pension, annuities, and Social Security she had earned (most of which she hadn't received, because she didn't open mail), and encouraging her to close a half dozen duplicative and unnecessary bank accounts.

Morgan's good deeds didn't last long. For the five months my mother stayed with us before finding a mother-in-law unit in town, she passively pretended to accept his financial help, while secretly opening new bank accounts and spending money she wouldn't tell him about. It was vintage my mother. To his face, she would sweetly thank him for managing her finances and keeping her out of poverty, but behind his back created financial chaos that seemed to comfort her. Morgan persevered. He managed her finances to the extent that she would let him for several years, until she decided to move away. By the time she left, his confidence about being able to help her had evaporated.

"Nik, at first I thought this would be a piece of cake. How hard could getting your mother's affairs in order really be?" he said to me. "I see now what you have been saying about her. Every time your mom and I met to go over her finances, she would nod to me when I told her, 'Ria, you can spend your money on anything you want, none of that matters to me. Just tell me what you spend your money on, when you spend it, so I can track it for you'—and you know the only reason I said that is because when I started all this, she had half a dozen accounts, at least, and never opened her mail. And she was living hand to mouth." He was falling into a rabbit hole I knew well, rehashing what my mother did to try understand all the whys. He continued, frustration rising in his voice. "But as soon as I organized all her accounts and she had an income that she could actually live on, she started opening new bank accounts and spending money she wouldn't tell me about, like she was paranoid about me or someone. It was a never-ending battle."

The day there was no turning back with my mother occurred about a year after she had moved out of our house and into an in-law unit about three miles away. I was sitting in her apartment on a second-hand couch, resurrected by a vibrant red throw. My mother was seated in a chair adjacent to the couch. We had a coffee date earlier that morning but she had not shown up, so I had swung by to find out why. As I was settling in for another round of pin-the-tail-on-the-mother, the phone rang. It was my older brother Alan. In an oily baby voice my mother said, "Hi Alany-boy!" I had never heard her call him that. I felt ill. In a syrupy voice, she continued. "Honey, I'm busy now but I promise to call you later." Something about her manipulation of him got under my skin. Missing our coffee rendezvous and then silkily exploiting my brother's heartfelt desire for her with an ersatz mother presentation was more than I could bear. I coiled and struck.

"Why didn't you do anything when Alan molested me?" I asked. I had asked this same question of her five years earlier, when I was in my early forties and had learned that Alan had also sexually abused Gillian and Celeste in the Ranch House. The first words out of her mouth back then were, "Well, I was molested too, by my uncle." She followed this callous response with, "Well, Alan was born a blue baby. He didn't have enough oxygen at birth. And I don't know if I told you that as a toddler he fell down a steep set of concrete stairs. When I found him at the bottom he was blue and I had to rush him to the hospital." I was horrified by everything she said, including her implied explanation for Alan's behavior: brain damage.

Five years later, those words were still boomeranging around my head. With anger and force in my voice, I repeated the question, "Why didn't you do anything when Alan molested me?" I added, "I talked to him about what he did and he asked me to forgive him, and I have. But that doesn't erase your role. Both times he sexually assaulted me, I walked into the kitchen the next morning and told you. I begged you to do something. I was only six or seven, a child. You were the parent—but you did nothing! Why didn't you help me, or him? And come on, you had to at least have considered that he was also abusing Gillian and Celeste!" Time moved slowly. Finally, looking out from under the rock where she was hiding, she declared in a near whisper, "I talked to my spiritual advisor, and we both agreed that I had nothing to do with the molestation. That's between you and your brother." The statement was extraordinary for its depth and breadth of detachment and cruelty. Strangely though, it offered me something I desperately needed: an end. The chase was over. With quivering sadness in my voice, I said, "Mom, there is nothing more I can say. Goodbye."

I got up and left.

Within a week of my walkout, my mother called, frantic to reinstate the equation of our relationship where she thrived and I didn't. She told me she had found a therapist and wanted to know if I would meet with her, adding that she had already prepaid two visits for me. Before I could answer, with more pathos than usual, she said, "Nikki, I want you to see her, so our divorce is amicable." Unfazed by characterizing our relationship as a marriage heading for divorce, she continued, "Would you go see her? I think it would be good if you did." Reverting to my supple wanting-to-please self, I agreed.

I met with the therapist twice. Aside from confessing to me on the first visit that she was having trouble paying attention to me because her boyfriend had walked out on her the previous evening, the therapist unprofessionally tried to badger me into having some relationship with my mother. "Well, of course, you want a relationship with your mother!" she said. "Your mother cares a great deal about you and she just wants to be sure you are OK." Seemingly co-opted by my mother, this therapist appeared convinced that I was the enfant terrible who had caused my mother heartache and anguish, while all my mother cared about was my welfare. The session was unbearable. This person who didn't know my story or me was sitting in judgment of me. I shut down.

Perhaps discerning there was something missing on my end, during my second and final visit the therapist asked me what kind of relationship I wanted with my mother. The question startled me. Before I could answer, my brain initiated a lightning-fast download of facts and feelings about my mother, sparking an unexpected insight. When I was a social work intern in child abuse, I devoted myself to finding the truth in the relationship between abusive parents and their children. That's when it hit me; I realized that for most of my forty-eight years I had been trying to find the truth in my mother's relationship with me. In that office where I didn't want to be, I found it.

Heaving inside with bottomless grief, I acknowledged something that I didn't want to accept: my mother belonged to the rarified group of parents who for whatever reason have little to no empathy or compassion for their children. And they show no remorse. Any connection they do have with their children is all too often a contaminated and unhealthy cord.

I slowly answered the therapist's question. "Nothing. I don't want a relationship with her."

I was ready to cut the cord.

Severing from a parent, at any age, is extremely difficult and emotionally wrenching. And it takes time. It took me a full year to separate from my mother. Even after the therapy sessions and the clarity they provided, I wanted to continue my sunny supportive parental role toward her, the one I knew inside and out. It felt the most natural. But I stopped myself and settled on being kind. The change wasn't easy for my mother. Furious, she seemed determined to punish me.

When my middle son was preparing to go off to college, I invited her to attend a launch party for him with friends and family that I had arranged at our local community center. Despite our parting, I didn't want to prevent her from interacting with my children. Weeks before the event, my mother called to ask if she could help with the decorations. I told her if she had the time and wanted to stop by the party supply store to see if they had tablecloths, napkins, and dishware in his college's colors, and what the prices were, that would be great. When she offered to buy the decorations, I thanked her but told her that I didn't know whether the community center tables were round or rectangular, so I would buy the supplies. She said OK and told me she would call me back in a few days with information about the decorations.

My mother never called back. For two or three days before the party I repeatedly called her to discuss the decorations. She didn't pick up or respond to my voice messages. The day before the party, I swung by the community center to check on the tables and some other logistics. Noting the tables were rounds and because I had not heard back from my mother, I went to the store and bought the appropriate-sized tablecloths, plates, napkins and plastic silverware. Hours before the party I finally reached my mother and told her I would see her later that afternoon. I noted, too, that we were all set with decorations—I had picked them up the previous day. She erupted, "You told me to buy the decorations! I already went to the store and bought everything, including tablecloths for *rectangular tables*." Laying the conflict and the drama at my feet, she delivered her coup de grace. "And besides," she snapped, "I can't take the supplies back, they are non-refundable." For a few moments, my body began a familiar slow crawl toward anger. I wanted to defend myself, to say, "You're lying, again." But I stopped. I thanked her and said I would take the decorations she bought and would pay her back. I remembered. She had not changed, I had.

As the months went by I interacted less and less with my mother. When we did have occasion to meet up or talk, her anger was transparently revealed in under-her-breath biting remarks. This helped me widen the space between us until I knew very little about her life. About a year after I walked out of her in-law unit, I heard from a sibling that she had decided to move back to Omaha, Nebraska, her childhood home. In a letter to my siblings and me, which I received months after my siblings, she outlined several storybook reasons for going home, beginning with her brother. "One person near whom I have not lived (when we were both adults) is my one and only brother. I'd very much like to spend more time with him." Embellishing that primary reason for her decision to return to Nebraska, she added, "I would have a chance to go home after many years. The parish church would be welcoming. The medical care is great. The cost of living is significantly less. I could travel to either coast on Southwest Airlines [a reference to her four children living in California and two on the East Coast]. The arts and transportation are readily available. This seems like an experiment which can't fail." She concluded the letter with, "My dream of being in each part of the country with you and yours seems even more likely to come true so I hope you will concur that this is a positive experiment."

My reaction to the letter was amused sadness. The letter implied that my mother had to return to her brother and home pasture because she had spent so much time with her children and grandchildren, a statement that could be taken down in one quick wrestling move. Then there was the gauzy assertion, "My dream of being in each part of the country with you and yours seems even more likely to come true," referencing the ease with which she could regularly visit her children and grandchildren living on the East and West Coasts. It was a future I knew my mother could never achieve. Reading the letter, I mourned her profound inability to be truthful and how much she and all her children lost out because of it.

Just before my mother left for Omaha, we met in a local café for our final lunch. In a voice close to the ground and arced with exhaustion she declared the primary reason for her move: my brothers were stalking her, physically and emotionally. "Nikki, that's why I am moving to Omaha." Barely a mention of wanting to reunite with her brother. In our last moments together I studied my mother and felt the loss of her all over again. My mother never noticed. At the end of lunch, I tenderly kissed her, whispered goodbye, and walked out.

Within months of her arrival in Omaha I learned that my mother had secretly married a widower whom she had known when she was in her teens. The two had reconnected over a trip she had taken to visit her brother three months earlier. Their flash reunion had precipitated her decision to move to Omaha but was never mentioned in her letter to us. Sticking with her brother as the singular reason for her relocation must have seemed more acceptable to her. At the same time, she probably did want to be near her brother. Having been one of my mother's previously appointed rescuers, along with her sister, I suspected that she was running out of people to take care of her, a reality heavily influenced by her unendearing habit of taking advantage of people's desire to help her.

Knowing how generous my aunt and uncle had always been with my mother, it was hard not to wonder why they were so different from her. Both had intact marriages, children they were crazy about, and lives that were full. Standing in stark contrast to them, my mother seemed unexplainable. What caused her lack of empathy and remorse? Her frequent disconnect from reality? Was it her uncle's molestation? Abuse by other relatives? Her mother's death when she was fifteen? A spin on some genetic dial of mental illness?

In a brief call my mother made to me after she moved to Omaha, she informed me with a lighthearted giggle about her clandestine marriage. Her husband was wonderful, funny, and taller, she emphasized with a competitive rise in her voice, than my husband. And her life, she said, was fantastic. She was now her new husband's fulltime caregiver. Breathily and with unobscured pride she exclaimed that because of her caregiving, her husband, a wheelchair user, was miraculously no longer a hospice patient. She gave no other details about his condition or prognosis but managed to squeeze in that she was considering writing a book about her caregiving experience. Pausing only for a second, she exclaimed that caring for another person was exhausting. I asked only one question, "How are things going with your Parkinson's?" She had received a diagnosis of Parkinson's disease before leaving California. "Not too bad," she said, then slipped in, "I am really happy."

I don't know my mother's reasons for marrying a man whom she appeared to know only superficially and who was on hospice at the time of their secret marriage. It may be that she found her soul mate or that a new marriage and the opportunity to play an angel of mercy in the last act of her life gave her the raison d'être and attention she'd craved. For anyone inquiring about us, she very likely resurrected her role of distant but loving mother, burdened by her adult children still "having difficulty growing up." She had said those exact words to me before she left with one small addition; she included the saccharine preface, "I'm sorry, you . . . are having difficulty growing up."

Two years after that call, she called me again, this time on my birthday. I picked up the phone thinking it was the area code in Michigan where my daughter was working that summer. My mother said hello quickly: she was nervous. My guard went up, too. In a somewhat disjointed voice—perhaps a symptom of her Parkinson's—she merrily chirped on about her husband and his adult children. She asked no questions about me or my children other than a speedy how-are-you, becoming distracted before I could respond. During her upbeat prattling report, I read the news ticker running through my head. It silently challenged each cheerful assertion about her new life. By then I'd heard through other family members there were holes in her Shangri-La. Disappointed once again in her inability to meaningfully connect with me in any way, I stayed on the phone until I could comfortably end the call.

Her story was the same and it never included me, not even as a minor character. I never spoke to her again.

Several years later, I had a dream. As only dreams can, it effortlessly captured what had eluded me in real life . . . for years.

When I first see my mother, she is far away but I can make out the wheelchair she is sitting in, and her shoulder length thick black hair feathered against the neck of a loose-fitting white hospital gown. From a distance, she looks fragile. Then I see her face. It looks strange. It doesn't match her body. As she comes closer to me, her chair pushed by a young nurse, I see her face more clearly. It's glowing with satisfaction; something incredible has just happened and something even better promises to happen next.

My mother has just given birth. In her lap is a cookie tray bearing six swaddled newborns: three in pink blankets, three in blue. Amazed at her sextuplet feat, nurses and aides line up at the hospital door to congratulate her and wish her well. As my mother heads toward the doors, I see her abruptly turn around and whisper secretively to her nurse. The nurse slows down and then stops in front of the first admirer. With arched eyebrows and a warm grateful smile, my mother gazes up at the woman, lingering. This ritual is repeated all the way down the line. Each person is touched by my mother's graciousness. I am too. I am full of hope for her and her babies.

Eventually, my mother crosses the threshold of the hospital doors. Her nurse is no longer with her. She is alone. Still holding the cookie tray, she stands up and quickly looks around. Seeing no one there, she heaves the contents of the tray into a dirt ditch next to the hospital doors. She throws the babies away. She throws me and my brothers and sisters away.

I feel nauseous. It takes a few seconds for me to figure out the sick feeling roiling about in my stomach: my mother has no emotional connection to her babies—to us, her children.

As the dream begins to fade, I see my mother's face again. She looks pleased with herself. She achieved what she always wanted: she has been celebrated, highly regarded, and most of all, envied.

Cleaving from my father was less dramatic but just as permanent. It occurred within a year of separating from my mother, although our relationship had been crumbling for several years. Yearning for a responsive parent, I was grateful for the little sprinkles of support my father gave me on the phone, especially when I was in my doctoral program. That part of our interaction, which might last a few seconds to a few minutes, was positive. What I was confused by and could never quite reconcile was what always came next. Practically every call included either a brief or long exhortation on the mental health deficiencies of mankind that ended with my father's righteous assertion that forgiveness was the answer for all people and all problems. This proclamation was invariably followed by his carnie-like hawking of yet another product, company, or real estate deal that he was certain would make him fabulously wealthy. Every call felt like conversational whiplash.

In person and over the phone, both my parents exhibited a range of peculiar thoughts and behaviors, but they were also capable, for short periods of time, of playing the attentive and sometimes affectionate parent, at a price. To stay in a relationship with either of them, I had to avoid asking or expecting anything or asserting myself. I had to smother me. This pattern became clearer with my father when he asked me to write an Amazon review of a book he had authored, *Nothing I See Means Anything: Quantum Questions, Quantum Answers*. Trying to persuade me to write the review, he told me that he really appreciated my edits to the book (I had read an early draft and offered modest edits at best), and reminded me that he had cited me in the acknowledgments. Then came the pitch. My review, he told me, would help persuade his publisher to reprint the book. I politely told him I didn't want to write a review. I cited ethical reasons; not only was he my father, I had been involved with the book, my name in the acknowledgments was proof. Because of that, I reasoned, I could not post an objective review. That didn't deter him.

Over the course of several months his pressuring turned into bullying. For no reason other than to be free from him accosting me each time we spoke, I caved. I told my father I would write a review using my nickname, but asserted that it would reflect what I honestly thought about the book. Elated, he said, "Fine!"

I wrote in my Amazon review of *Nothing I See Means Anything: Quantum Questions, Quantum Answers* that the book explored important age-old questions about the meaning of life. It's what I believed. After I posted it, I heard nothing from my father, who up until that time had been calling multiple times a week. Sensing that he might be disappointed that my review had not uniformly colored him or his opus as brilliantly omniscient, I called him. "Hi Dad," I said. "I haven't heard from you for weeks. Is everything OK?" Icy silence followed. "Everything's fine," he finally spit back. I tried to remain calm but could feel his fury with me. Trying a different subject, I asked, "So, how's Gina [his wife], I hope she's feeling better and able to get out to do some gardening." "She's fine too," he responded, his tone seeping with rebuke. I was instantly reminded of the father from my childhood. "Dad, what's wrong? You seem pretty angry with me." I knew the reason but wanted to see if he would cop to being angry about my review. Clipping his words, he said, "I'm not angry." Silence again. "Well, it seems like this call isn't going too well," I said, "so I am going to get off. Talk to you later. Bye." I hung up. Not only did I not have any reserve of good feeling for my father as a parent—he had coldly disposed of us as children—no one I was close to spoke to me the way he did.

A week later he called me back, pretending that he had never spoken rudely to me. I seized my opportunity and told him that if he were upset with me we should talk about it, but I would not tolerate his treating me rudely. He promised it would never happen again. His pledge didn't last long. Soon after that incident, my father took another U-turn, this time over a contract. In need of some help on a new business venture, he called to ask if Morgan would urgently review a contract for him. Although not a contracts attorney, Morgan agreed to look it over, and instructed my father to e-mail it to him. Two weeks later my father sent the contract and then called me, demanding that Morgan review it immediately. It was late at night and we were heading to bed, so I told him Morgan would review it the next day. An explosion cracked the line. In an ear-puncturing angry voice my father yelled, "I need him to look at it now!" This time I didn't wait for a follow-up debriefing call. I told him he was out of line, and I hung up.

Time-outs didn't seem to have any effect on my father and I was growing impatient with him, a mood that was probably encouraged by the fact that I was finally free of the gummy residue that coated me after each interaction with my mother. Unable to control himself, my father behaved brutishly toward me for a third and last time. The denouement occurred when I called him to discuss my coming to Arizona, where he was living at the time, to celebrate his eightieth birthday. His wife, Gina, who was

310

open to organizing a small get-together, picked up the phone. She and I chatted for a while about the party and then she passed the phone to my father, who had just walked through the door.

The minute I heard his strained hello, I could tell his agitation was on the way to full throttle. To bring his tension down a notch, I hastily told him how excited I was to celebrate his birthday. He responded that he didn't care. To soothe him, I told him how much I cared about him and how fun his party would be. He bitterly shot back, "I'm just trying to get off this fucking phone!" Incredulous, I hung up. Angry tears welled up in my eyes. Fifteen minutes went by. Then I sat down at my desk and wrote him a brief e-mail. I asked that he never contact me again.

For a long time, my father tried to reconnect with me. First he sent articles on peace and forgiveness. When I didn't respond, he left numerous voice messages, some pleading and angry, some not. The most disturbing was a denunciation of me as psychotic. His definition of psychotic seemed much broader the definition of schizophrenia and other psychotic disorders listed in the Diagnostic and Statistical Manual of Mental Disorders. In addition to hallucinations, delusions, and disorganized speech and behavior, and other negative symptoms, by my father's account, it now appeared to include individuals who refused to speak to people they find abusive. In his world, I rejected him, ergo I was psychotic. Toward the end of his voice mail rant on my psychotic behavior, my father squeezed in the comment that most people on the planet are psychotic—a change apparently from his earlier assessment that everyone is borderline. It seemed a last-minute attempt to soften the effect of my new diagnosis. I guess he wanted me to know I had lots of company.

A few years later he updated my diagnosis. In another voice message he said, "Well let's say this, you have decided not to speak to certain people and I am in total support of that. I have down-regulated your psychosis to neurosis, which everybody is. Anyway, if that makes you happy just go with that . . . I am in full support of this." I did go with that. But he never quite caught on that not only did I go with that, but that I was gone . . . long gone.

Chapter Nine

Curtain Call

Scars can be big, small, hard, or soft. They can be visible or hidden. They can pulsate with pain or be pain free. Regardless of their form, all scars represent a literal or figurative mark of trauma to the body, the mind, or the spirit. Knowing a scar is different from owning it. To know a scar is to recognize it exists. To own a scar is to stop defining it as ugly, a mark of disfigurement, and to see and cherish the beauty of what it really represents: the strength of survival and courage. To own a scar sometimes requires a journey.

After I disconnected from my mother, it took many months before I felt emotionally ready to address the thick braided scar of her that coiled in and around me, a scar I did not yet own. With the help of a deeply kind and skillful therapist, I started to realize that I had minimized most of my feelings and responses to the hurt, fear, rejection, and confusion I experienced as a child. Dismantling the fairy tale that was my mother was my first step to reconnecting with those emotions. I had lived a long time believing in the legend of her. Even after I became a practicing social worker and had greater consciousness about my upbringing, I continued making excuses for her, asserting to myself and others that she had done the best she could. After all, she had been a single parent of six children and my childhood wasn't that bad. I hadn't been locked in a closet or beaten daily. It was time for me to see and hold the painful truth of how my mother did treat me.

As far back as I can remember, my mother defined herself as *the* ultimate victim. To know if this was the reason she treated us the way she did, examining this claim up close seemed an important first step in my healing process. Stripping away confabulation and embellishment, I had empathy for my mother. She was indeed the victim of many painful circumstances and experiences: depression and mental illness, hoarding, a difficult childhood that included the death of her mother, a strained marriage, and Parkinson's disease. But questions remained unanswered. Did she suffer more than anyone else? Did she mistreat us, intentionally or unintentionally, because of her extreme suffering? I will never know how much she suffered, but I felt I could determine the cause of her mistreatment if I knew two things. Did her treatment of us meet the definition of child abuse? If so, were her actions the result of mental illness or the conscious choice of a person with capacity to distinguish right from wrong? Divining the truth of each seemed crucial.

On the question of child abuse, my mother's treatment of us appears to meet the definition of child neglect and emotional abuse. Whether she abused us because of mental illness and an inability to differentiate between right and wrong, however, was murkier. No question my mother struggled with mental illness, but she was not completely disabled. She held down a job for most of her adult life and could engage with people for short periods of time, despite substantial impairment in empathy and intimacy. The more I looked for a straight line to a conclusion, the wigglier her line became. When I tried to discern if she could differentiate between right and wrong, the line went haywire. Then I found a pattern. My mother consistently voiced and sometimes actively advocated for right over wrong but, I discovered, only when the issue, person, or situation didn't involve her decisions or actions.

A particularly poignant example was when she was teaching in LA and helped a young female student in her class. The student confided in my mother that she was being sexually abused at home, a confidence that catalyzed my mother. After reporting the information to the school, my mother made sure the student received outside help and support. Whether my mother was uniquely motivated by the child's plight or inspired to help because it gave her the opportunity to play the heroine, I will never know. Similarly, I will never know what internally drove my mother's behavior: whether she cherry-picked her ethics and morality, and we were just never the cherries, or that she was so compromised she couldn't do the right thing when it came to us.

The emotional walkabout that I took in therapy to find my mother's truth led me back to where I started . . . a place with no definitive answers. It was time to let the jigsaw puzzle of my mother be, minus a few pieces. The moment I made that decision, I felt free to focus on the impact of her indifference and cruelty toward me, on my thoughts and feelings. That's when I admitted thoughts in my head that I dared not tell anyone: *I can't make a mistake or I won't be loved; I should only give, never take;* and *I shouldn't enjoy myself too much, because I don't deserve happiness.* They were thought beasts so powerful I needed no hair shirt to do penance.

Guided by my therapist, I learned how to challenge these negative thoughts that seemed to have taken root when I was a young child. They didn't go away easily. Each time they popped up, I would identify the various distortions within them, before replacing them with positive thoughts that I knew to be more realistic. It was a hard-fought battle, but I eventually extinguished a good chunk of the mutinous anger I routinely directed toward myself for simply being human.

Yet, there was one feeling I couldn't easily disarm. My anxiety. Excavating the roots of this powerful emotional response to perceptions of threats coming from everywhere proved difficult. Determined to tackle my angst, I focused on the one trigger of my anxiety that I was conscious of, my belief that if I were perfect I could control what came next. It was faulty reasoning with a price. Each mistake I made, or thought I made, in my relationships, work, or school would trigger an emotional embolism from my childhood, and an *I'm not good enough* feeling would come over me. Debilitating anxiety followed. As consciousness regarding this chain reaction increased, my anxiety lessened, but I had a long way to go. Desperate to manage my anxiety, to feel better, I knew I had to go deeper to see what was buried below. Following various cognitive behavioral exercises, I discovered that I harbored a substratum fear of abandonment, and then below that a single bedrock belief that held up all my distorted thoughts, the belief that *I am unworthy and unlovable.*

Disarming my fear of abandonment and my belief that I was unworthy and unlovable was intensely difficult. Together, they had wreaked the most damage in my intimate relationships. In response to them, I unwittingly interpreted every marital argument, disappointment, or hurt as intentional abandonment or evidence that I was fundamentally undesirable. Catching myself periodically sinking into a quagmire of anger and doubt because of these beliefs, and then pulling myself out, took work. As I gained confidence in my ability to challenge and defeat my negative thoughts when they surfaced in my marriage, I turned to my other most important relationships—my three children. By the time I was ready to assess how my childhood wounds had affected them and my parenting, they were all young adults.

When my children were born, I welcomed them to the world with a flood of positive emotion. I loved them from the moment I knew of their existence and was determined to communicate in every way I could that they mattered. I touched, held, and rocked them. I celebrated the big moments that thrilled and the small moments that fit in a pocket. I did what I said I would do, and was where I said I would be. I made sure they had lots of food for their bodies and nurturing for their souls. When Morgan and I were raising them, we sat down to dinner as a family, and we listened to them. Consciously, I tried to be everything my mother was not. What I didn't realize was that I unconsciously brought baggage from my childhood into my parenting, behaviors that had consequences for them as they got older.

The day my children entered elementary school, I was afraid for them. I began worrying that if they made a "bad" decision or a "mistake" with their classwork, choice of friends, or in sports, they would go spiraling into some void. My caution and constant surveillance had kept me alive; I was sure they needed to do the same. I counseled, cajoled, and urged them toward greater hyper-vigilance, sometimes to such an extent that my husband had to intervene to calm my fears. I never realized that my worrying didn't make them safer or that communicating excessive angst was harmful. When my children got older and repeatedly told me that my out-of-control anxiety was unwarranted, I often felt frustrated, overwhelmed, and, at times, angry. My anxiety made sense to me. Why, I wondered, didn't it to them?

It was not until our youngest child left home for college that I understood that my children were never at risk of tumbling into a black hole. The anxiety I expressed about them and to them was my own, born of my deprivation and despair. Understanding that motivated me to start repairing the parts of my relationship with each that had been damaged by my worry. With extraordinary grace and compassion, my children have been loving and patient with me, as I work hard to reduce my anxiety and become more the mother they need and deserve.

My journey toward owning my scar has not been fast or easy. It has been messy and sometimes emotionally painful. What made the scar was ugly, but because of it, I understand suffering a bit more, my suffering and the suffering of others. Looking at it, I no longer just see my flaws and insecurities. My battle-worn mark tells me I survived. Equally important, it confirms that a tiny corner of me has always stubbornly insisted that I matter. That corner gave me the courage to tell my brother he could not continue to molest me, and demand that my mother make him stop. It gave me the strength to challenge my parents' lack of empathy and finally separate from them. That scrappy little corner of me, I see now, is what gave me hope.

My healing journey will likely continue for the rest of my life, but I now own my beautiful scar.

Acknowledgments

Without the important mentors that I describe in my story, I would not be the person I am today. Each embraced and nurtured me at a critical moment in my life. I am profoundly grateful to them all.

Cynthia Leslie-Bole, my writing coach, deserves special thanks. Cynthia worked patiently with me, while I brought my story to life. Her unwavering support and zeal for the artistry of writing are only matched by her exquisite ability to bring out the best in writers.

I would also like to thank Allison Landa for generously sharing her keen edits and collegial support, and Ann Bundy, Rhonda Barovsky, Shari Nagy, and Bob Edwards for reading various drafts of the manuscript. Their spot-on feedback and encouragement were inspirational and truly appreciated.

Dr. Valerie Hone was the north star of my journey. From beginning to end, she deeply believed in me and the importance of telling my story. My publisher, Karen Mireau, Azalea Art Press, is simply amazing. Her indefatigable creativity and positivity enabled me to complete my book, so I could share it with others.

Last, I would like to thank my children and my husband, Morgan—my heart. Their love, laughter, and light made this book possible.

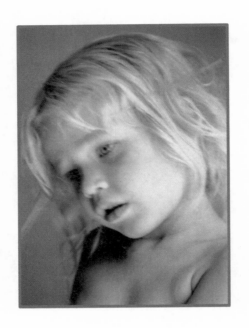

About the Author

Writing has always been Monique Parrish's passion. She became fascinated with poetry and prose in high school and began keeping journals and writing poetry in college. She continued both while serving as a Peace Corps community development and health volunteer in the Central African Republic.

She received her Master of Public Health and Master of Science in Social Work from Columbia University and her Doctorate in Public Health from the University of California, Berkeley. For over 25 years, Monique has been helping others find their emotional balance—something that was entirely absent in her own childhood.

Monique is the founder and director of *LifeCourse Strategies*, a health care consulting firm addressing the needs of underserved and disadvantaged communities. She is the author of numerous studies on the health and social service needs of older and disabled adults, and frequently presents on health care issues. Monique has three adult children and lives with her husband in the San Francisco Bay Area, where she is a volunteer counselor at a drop-in center for homeless women.

To order more copies of this book:
please visit www.lulu.com

To contact the Author:
please email monique.parrish@mac.com